Praise for *Creating a Missional Culture*

"JR Woodward reads widely, writes deftly and lives deeply. *Creating a Missional Culture* reflects all of that. Read it and explore what leading can be in the strange new worlds of mission in North America."

DAVID FITCH, B.R. Lindner Chair of Evangelical Theology, Northern Seminary, and author of *The End of Evangelicalism?*

"I have been craving a book that would facilitate the reimagination of church culture, and it is finally here. This is a book I hope many will devour."

DWIGHT J. FRIESEN, associate professor of practical theology, The Seattle School of Theology & Psychology, and author of *Thy Kingdom Connected*

"A relevant and important book for every congregation. The chapters on polycentric leadership alone are worth the price of the book."

MARYKATE MORSE, professor of leadership and spiritual formation, George Fox Evangelical Seminary, and author of *Making Room for Leadership*

"While some erroneously insist on dichotomizing between missional and spiritual formation, JR makes a solid case for the necessary integration of the two. Indeed, authentic spirituality is missional through and through. JR's work accentuates this holistic approach to our distinct yet integrated calling as equippers: as an apostle, prophet, evangelist, pastor or teacher."

WIL HERNANDEZ, director of the Master of Arts in Spiritual Formation and Leadership, Spring Arbor University, and author of *Henri Nouwen and Spiritual Polarities*

"JR Woodward blends head, heart and hands to reinvigorate the church. I highly recommend this book for those studying missiology, ministry and ecclesiology."

AMOS YONG, J. Rodman Williams Professor of Theology, Regent University School of Divinity, and author of *The Bible, Disability, and the Church*

Forge Books from InterVarsity Press

How can God's people give witness to his kingdom in an increasingly post-Christian culture? How can the church recover its true mission in the face of a world in need? Books published by InterVarsity Press that bear the Forge imprint help birth and nurture the missional church in America and beyond. For more information on Forge America, visit www.forgeamerica.com.

PRAXIS

EQUIPPING LEADERS FOR MINISTRY.

"...TO EQUIP HIS PEOPLE FOR WORKS OF SERVICE,

SO THAT THE BODY OF CHRIST MAY BE BUILT UP."

EPHESIANS 4:12

God has called us to ministry. But it's not enough to have a vision for ministry if you don't have the practical skills for it. Nor is it enough to do the work of ministry if what you do is headed in the wrong direction. We need both vision *and* expertise for effective ministry. We need *praxis*.

Praxis puts theory into practice. It brings cutting-edge ministry expertise from visionary practitioners. You'll find sound biblical and theological foundations for ministry in the real world, with concrete examples for effective action and pastoral ministry. Praxis books are more than the "how to" – they're also the "why to." And because *being* is every bit as important as *doing*, Praxis attends to the inner life of the leader as well as the outer work of ministry. Feed your soul, and feed your ministry.

If you are called to ministry, you know you can't do it on your own. Let Praxis provide the companions you need to equip God's people for life in the kingdom.

www.ivpress.com/praxis

CREATING
A MISSIONAL
CULTURE

EQUIPPING THE CHURCH
for the
SAKE OF THE WORLD

JR WOODWARD

foreword by ALAN HIRSCH

IVP Books
An imprint of InterVarsity Press
Downers Grove, Illinois

InterVarsity Press
P.O. Box 1400, Downers Grove, IL 60515-1426
World Wide Web: www.ivpress.com
E-mail: email@ivpress.com

InterVarsity Press® is the book-publishing division of InterVarsity Christian Fellowship/USA®, a movement of
students and faculty active on campus at hundreds of universities, colleges and schools of nursing in the United States
of America, and a member movement of the International Fellowship of Evangelical Students. For information
about local and regional activities, write Public Relations Dept., InterVarsity Christian Fellowship/USA, 6400
Schroeder Rd., P.O. Box 7895, Madison, WI 53707-7895, or visit the IVCF website at <www.intervarsity.org>.

All Scripture quotations, unless otherwise indicated, are taken from the Holy Bible, Today's New International
Version®, NIV® Copyright © 1973, 1978, 1984, 2010 by Biblica, Inc.™ Used by permission. All rights reserved
worldwide.

Table 5.2 on page 71 is reprinted from Memories, Hopes, and Conversations: Appreciative Inquiry and
Congregational Change by Mark Lau Branson, with permission from the Alban Institute. Copyright © 2004 by
The Alban Institute, Inc. Herndon, VA. All rights reserved.

While all stories in this book are true, some names and identifying information in this book have been changed to
protect the privacy of the individuals involved.

Cover design and illustrations: Oliver Munday
Interior design: Beth Hagenberg

ISBN 978-0-8308-3653-6

Printed in the United States of America ∞

Library of Congress Cataloging-in-Publication Data has been requested.

P	20	19	18	17	16	15	14	13	12	11	10	9	8	7	6	5	4	3	2	1
Y	29	28	27	26	25	24	23	22	21	20	19	18	17	16	15	14	13	12

Dedication

To the missional leaders in the Ecclesia Network—

your faith, hope and love inspire me. Your willingness to explore

new ways to be the church with a focus on making disciples of Jesus,

through the power of the Spirit to the glory of God and for the good

of the world, brings great encouragement to my heart.

Contents

PART 1: THE POWER OF CULTURE

PART 2: A LEADERSHIP IMAGINATION THAT SHAPES MISSIONAL CULTURE

PART 3: THE FIVE CULTURE CREATORS

FIGURES

TABLES

Foreword

As our best leaders know, in just about every Western cultural setting that the church finds itself, we are facing something of a crisis. The somewhat gloomy situation brought about by long-term institutional and spiritual decline has been forcing church leaders to ask some pretty probing questions about the church's identity, purpose and practices. It's fair to say that there has been some panic, as well as a fair bit of denial. But a crisis there is anyway.

This is not all bad. While the theological, spiritual, organizational and missiological malaise poses a direct threat to Christendom church-as-usual, at the same time it presents us with an opportunity to clean out, to do some necessary pruning. Any decent crisis does this: when it is well-faced, it facilitates for the movement or organization a radical recovery of its defining ideas.

This is perhaps truer of the church than it is of other organizations. As people who believe in the authority of Scripture and the unique role of our Founder, we must constantly return to the selfsame energies that initiated the early church if we are to truly rediscover a sense of who we are, why we are here and how we must go about being the church that Jesus intended in the first place.

Learning systems theory asserts that all learning takes place when programming is subjected to questioning (L=P+Q). An organization begins to (re)learn when it applies honest, exploratory questioning to all key aspects of the organization/system. This questioning in turn initiates a search for better answers than the ones currently on offer. Applying the lessons of learning systems theory, then, what are the purposes of the church? What is the nature of our core message, and how do we actually embody and extend it? Is the gospel really capable of renewing the world and transforming the hearts of all human beings? Did God really mean for the ecclesia to be the focal point for the wholesale renewal of society? Are we really called to be a colony of a much-disputed kingdom, or did Jesus actually intend that we become the chaplains of a so-called Christian civilization in the West? Why do we do things the way we do? These are questions that take us to the roots of the church.

Undergoing such radical questioning initiates a serious pursuit for the rediscovery of our most basic scripts—or, to use another metaphor, our orienting maps—in an attempt to reorient or resituate ourselves in the world. In many ways it can be said this is exactly what constitutes the heart of *re-newal*. And if we do it well, with all the intellectual integrity and spiritual passion that we can muster, we will recover a much more authentic understanding (and experience) of ourselves *as ecclesia* than the one we now possess.

Having spent much of my adult years grappling with the factors that together form a dynamic, distinctly *missional* ecclesiology, I also fully believe that the ecclesia (church) that Jesus intended was specifically designed with built-in, self-generative capacities, and was made for nothing less than world-transforming, lasting, revolutionary impact (see, for example, Mt 16:18). We were almost certainly not meant to become a domesticated civil religion! As far as I can tell, Jesus intended us to be something of a *permanent revolution*—no less than an expansive outpost of the kingdom of God. When we are not actually being *that*, then we have got to take stock in a big way.

We get glimpses into the design and purposes that Jesus intended for his ecclesia in various texts scattered throughout the New Testament. But few are as clear, authoritative, and significant for the church as those found in the book of Ephesians. Ephesians is rightfully considered the constitutional document of the church. Everything about it has the ring of constitutionality. To use another metaphor, it has long been considered as containing the basic genetic codes of the church—

particularly in its Pauline expression. Therefore the images of both constitution and DNA grant us direct clues to the defining nature of the text. This can be no less true for Ephesians 4:1-16 as it is of the rest of the book. I am on record as being utterly convinced of the sheer power of the typologies of ministry (what JR Woodward here calls "the five equippers"—apostles, prophets, evangelists, shepherds and teachers, or "APEST") laid out in this passage to bring renewal to the life of the church.

Not only does Ephesians 4:1-16 point us to a dynamic manifestation of ecclesia, but it implies that there can be no lasting effectiveness to the church's mission without the fully functioning ministry that Jesus has once-and-for-all "given" (v. 7) to his people. We are called to be the fullness of Jesus in the world, and according to Paul's logic in Ephesians 4:1-16 we achieve this not through the twofold shepherd-teacher model of ministry and leadership that we have become so used to, but through this fivefold, equipping approach.

For reasons I (and my co-author Tim Catchim) have tried to explain in *The Permanent Revolution*, by effectively exiling the apostolic, prophetic and evangelistic (APE) functions from the life and structures of the church, we have done terrible damage to the church's capacity to mature. In order to respond to the missional challenges that we now face, we have to learn again what it means to operate with *all five equippers*. In particular, we must work doubly hard to integrate the exiled ministries of apostle, prophet, and evangelist back into the functioning imagination, language, leadership and ministry structures of the church. In the end I do believe that without these more generative and adaptive ministries, we will neither advance the cause of the church in our time nor achieve any significant and lasting missional impact.

JR knows this from deep personal reflection on the Scriptures, as well as from being involved in leading-edge church planting in difficult circumstances. As a result, you are holding a hard-won treasure. This is not some fluffy, shallow, exploration of the topic—those caricatures abound already. This book is well written, theologically well considered, and peppered with the kind of missiological insights that only an apostolically inclined leader can bring. As a long-time practitioner of these ideas, JR brings a distinctly practical edge to the equation, and so the reader is given real, live possibilities to implement locally. But by uniquely combining missional theology with the concept that each equipper creates a certain culture, which in turn shapes meaning and practices in the community, JR has developed an excellent heuristic for leaders to actually make Ephesians 4 a living reality in the local churches. By actively enhancing each distinct equipper-culture, and by developing what he calls polycentric leadership, he provides churches with a direct pathway to activating the dormant energies contained in Jesus' ecclesia.

The sociologist Alvin Toffler once rightly observed that the illiterate of the future will not be those that cannot read or write. Rather, they will be those that cannot learn, unlearn and relearn. If you are indeed willing to unlearn the cloying, missionally impotent ecclesiology of the traditionalist paradigms, and subsequently relearn what the Bible itself (and the history of missions) directly says in this matter, then there will be much hope.

ALAN HIRSCH

Acknowledgments

Mom and Dad
I'm thankful for your love, your provision, your encouragement and the example you have been for me through the years. It has been more than I could have imagined.

My Brothers and Extended Family
Joe, Suzanne, Luke and Kara Woodward, I always enjoy hanging with you. Allen, Elaine, Kurt and Wil, you guys bring a lot to my life. I'm also thankful for the rest of our large tribe, my many aunts, uncles, nephews and nieces.

Pavi Thomas
This book would not have been written if it were not for all the conversations that we have had over the years. Thanks for your friendship and support.

Kairos Los Angeles
I'm grateful for your courage and willingness to experiment with new ways of approaching leadership and being the church. A special thanks to all of you who have served as equippers at the various congregations—Greg Larson, Audrey Blumber, Dave Kludt, Don Chesworth, Andy Bleyer, Joe Racek, Debbie Kim, Daniel Cunningham, Dustin James, Jeremiah Caleb, Matt Mabrey and Maria Drews (honorary equipper).

Forge America and Alan Hirsch
It's an honor to serve God's kingdom with you. Alan, I appreciate the many conversations that we have had, and your down-to-earth way of life. Kim Hammond, thanks for welcoming me so warmly into the Forge Tribe.

Rick Mysse and RCA

This book became a reality because you commissioned me to write on the five equippers for the Classis of SoCal. Thanks, Rick, for your consistent encouragement.

The Turkana Tribe in Kenya

It has been a real privilege to walk beside you for nearly a decade. I look forward to what God has in store for us in the future. I'm especially thankful for Bishop Kaaleng, Joshua Lemuya, Moses Lorukudi, Michael Lojao as well as Mike and Jessica Thomas.

Some of My Life-Giving Friendships

Dustin James, Rudy Hermanto, Joe and Lisa Racek, Chris, Rachel and Elliana (godchild) Backert, Joshua and Rachael Swanson, Jim and Tracy Pace, Michael Chen, Will Andrian—I deeply appreciate each of you.

My Ministry Partner Team and GCM

Without you I wouldn't be able to live out my calling in life. Thanks to my fellow GCM board members and all who work at the office. A special thanks to Tom Mauriello, KZ and Dave Meldrum-Green.

Hope International Bible Fellowship

I'm inspired by your example. Thanks for serving the neighborhood and us. I want to give a special thanks to Pastor Ed, Lenny and Richard.

[nlcf] in Blacksburg, VA

I'm thankful for all of you (1200+) whom I've had to opportunity to connect with in my time in Blacksburg. You helped me become a better person.

Ecclesia Network

I've thoroughly enjoyed the journey of planting more missional churches with you and experiencing your faith, hope and love along the way. You're the best. Now help me sell this book. lol.

My Fellow MAGL'ers

I'm grateful to all my fellow classmates and professors in the Master of Arts in Global Leadership (MAGL) program at Fuller Theological Seminary. You guys are the real deal. I want to give a special thanks to

Bob Freeman, who had the faith to start this program, to Eddie Gibbs, who made himself available for independent studies, and to Shelley Trebesch for just being you.

East Hollywood Neighborhood Council

I'm honored to have had the opportunity to serve with you in seeing our neighborhood become more of what it could be.

Those Who Gave Me Helpful Feedback

David Fitch, John Chandler, Jonathan Williams, Kurt Fredrickson, Chad Smith, Noel Hiekkenen, James Paul, J. R. Briggs, Greg Larson, Chris Backert, Heidi Simanjuntak, Jason Malec and Audrey Blumber. Thanks for taking the time out of your busy schedule to give me valuable feedback.

Those Who Went Above and Beyond Expectations

Maria Drews, Scott Boren, David Kludt, Samuel Smith, Scott Nelson, Keas Keasler, Nathan Elmore, Jason Lee, Joey Tomassoni, Wil Hernandez, Dustin James and Jen Collins. Your feedback was valuable beyond estimation.

InterVarsity Press

I'm deeply thankful for all those who supported me at IVP, especially my editor Dave Zimmerman, who gave me suggestions that made this book much better than it was. And thanks to Andrew Bronson and team—Adrianna Wright, Nathan Baker-Lutz, Leah Kiple and Suanne Camfield—for your warm welcome and for all you are doing to help me get the word out about this book.

Triune God

Father, thank you for your undying love. Jesus, thank you for your limitless grace. Holy Spirit, thank you for your comfort, direction and power. I am blessed, and my prayer is that this book might be a blessing to many for your glory and the good of the world.

Introduction

How would you characterize the typical person in the congregation you serve? A mature follower of Christ? A consumer of religious goods and services? Or something in-between?

In your attempt to make disciples, do you ever feel as if you are swimming against the current? Do you have a desire to see the congregation be a greater blessing to the neighborhood and to those far from Christ?

When you consider the congregation you serve, would you say the community is full of love, joy and peace? Do you ever feel overwhelmed when it comes to equipping the church to live *in* the world *for* the sake of the world, without being *of* the world?

As a church planter, I have been haunted by these questions. I've started churches that continue to thrive, multiplying disciples and churches around the country. I've also started churches that have been slow to get off the ground. I've celebrated with church planters whose churches have thrived and are a great blessing to their neighborhood. I have also walked with church planters through the agony of having to close church doors. Through much reflection, reading and many sleepless nights, I've discovered that effective church planting requires thinking about *the culture of the congregation.*

More than a strategy, vision or plan, the unseen culture of a church powerfully shapes her ability to grow, mature and live missionally. Successes and failures alike in church planting confirm the role that the culture of a congregation plays. The unstated assumptions embedded in a congregation's culture either aids or hinders it in its mission.

Culture is like gravity. We never talk about it, except in physics classes. We don't include gravity in our weekly planning processes. No one gets up thinking about how gravity will affect their day. However, gravity impacts us in everything we do, every day. Like gravity, the culture of a congregation can either pull people down to their base instincts or lift people up to their sacred potential. We create culture, and culture re-creates us.

If we want to create a *missional* culture in the congregations we serve, we need to understand how the different elements of culture work. The *language* we live in, the *artifacts* that we make use of, the *rituals* we engage in, our approach to *ethics*, the *institutions* we are a part of and the *narratives* we inhabit have the power to shape our lives profoundly. In addition, we need to cultivate *learning*, *healing*, *welcoming*, *liberating* and *thriving* environments. We do this by yielding to the work of the Spirit in our lives by developing communal rhythms of life—grace-filled spiritual practices which engage our senses, grab our hearts, form our identities and reshape our desires toward God and his kingdom.[1]

It's not enough to simply *manage* the culture we operate within. For while management acts *within* culture, leadership *creates* culture. In fact, our very *approach to leadership* shapes culture in profound ways. Hierarchical leadership tends to breed an individualistic approach to spiritual formation, while polycentric leadership lends itself to a more communal approach. If we desire to connect with the digital generation, we need to learn to live as a community of leaders within the community.

Back in 1998 my friend Pavi Thomas and I started meditating and thinking deeply about the book of Ephesians, in particular the first half of Ephesians 4. When planting our churches in LA, we sought to experiment in how to inhabit this text, because in this passage the apostle Paul makes a direct link between the spiritual maturity of the church and the five kinds of equippers operating in the church: apostles (what I nickname dream awakeners), prophets (heart revealers), evangelists (story tellers), pastors (soul healers) and teachers (light givers). As the equippers incarnate their lives and ministries within the body, the whole body will be aroused and awakened to live in the world, for the sake of the world, in the way of Christ.

MY HOPES FOR THIS BOOK

In this book you will

- understand what missional culture is and why it is important

- discover the five environments that unleash the missional imagination of God's people

- learn how to assess the culture of the congregation you serve through the cultural web

- understand how the culture of the congregation you serve will help or hinder the maturity of the church

- learn how to identify, cultivate and multiply the five equippers in the congregation you serve

- learn why polycentric leadership makes more sense than hierarchical leadership or flat leadership

- discover the power of stories, liturgies, rituals and rhythms in developing a discipleship culture that reshapes peoples desire for God and his kingdom

- get practical tools that will enhance your ability to lead as a team of cultural architects, cultivating environments where good things run wild

I hope to add to the rich conversation about the missional church. While some think it is just another fad or strategy, people like Craig Van Gelder have helped us to understand that the missional church has a rich history and has been in the making over the last century.[2] One important development has been the refusion of church and mission, ecclesiology and missiology.

As a person who seeks to love the church (warts and all) as Christ does, and understanding that "he gave himself up for her" (Eph 5:25), I try to refer to the church throughout the book as "she" or "her" instead of "it." Not only is the church referred to as the bride of Christ throughout the New Testament (e.g., Jn 3:29; 2 Cor 11:2; Eph 5:27; Rev 18:23; 19:7; 21:9; 22:17), but by using a personal pronoun we are likely to hold the church more dear. This metaphor for the church lends itself to a stronger ecclesiolgy in a day when, in some people's writings, the church seems to have vanished. On top of that, I've always been fond of St. Cyprian's saying, "You cannot have God for your Father unless you have the church for your Mother."[3]

My hope and prayer is that this book will help the church to be a faithful sign, foretaste and instrument of God kingdom, that is here and coming. As Lesslie Newbigin has said,

> The question which has to be put to every local congregation is the question whether it is a credible sign of God's reign in justice and mercy over the whole of life, whether it is an open fellowship whose concerns are as wide as the concerns of humanity, whether it cares for its neighbors in a way which reflect and springs out of God's care for them, whether its common life is recognizable as a foretaste of the blessing which God intends for the whole human family.[4]

As you read this book, ask God to show you what is helpful that you should apply, what is unhelpful that you should disregard, and for the wisdom to know the difference.

Shalom.

JR WOODWARD
Hollywood, California

PART ONE

The Power of Culture

1

What Is Missional Culture and
Why Does It Matter?

*The Church is called to be a provisional demonstration of God's will
for all people.*

PRESBYTERIAN BOOK OF ORDER

*Don't become so well-adjusted to your culture that you fit into it
without even thinking. Instead, fix your attention on God. You'll be
changed from the inside out. Readily recognize what he wants from
you, and quickly respond to it. Unlike the culture around you, always
dragging you down to its level of immaturity, God brings the best out
of you, develops well-formed maturity in you.*

THE APOSTLE PAUL, ROMANS 12:2 *THE MESSAGE*

I was driving in Columbus, Ohio, when I came upon a hitchhiker who
alternated between holding his thumb out and clasping his hands together as if he were praying. I picked him up.

His name was Mike, and I soon discovered he was a hardcore Aryan
(white supremacist), pointing to a passage in Scripture about being "a
chosen people" as the reason for his convictions. I asked if he would be
willing to reread the passage in context. He agreed. As I reached in the

back seat to grab my Bible, he pulled a gun and pointed it at my head. I assured him I was just getting my Bible, so he put his gun away, and my heart started to beat again.

I realized Mike had no place to stay that night, so I invited him to stay with me.

"You mean you would trust me to stay with you after pulling a gun on you?" he asked.

"Yes," I said, "because God has given me a love for you that I can't explain, and he loves you." As I was saying this, I was saying to myself, *Yeah, what am I thinking?*

Tears welled in Mike's eyes.

We got back to the hotel where my roommate Tom and I were staying. I woke up my roommate to ask him if Mike could stay with us, mentioning that he had a gun. He wasn't favorably disposed to the idea, so I ended up getting Mike another room. Mike didn't want me to, but I insisted. It gave me the chance to share more of the gospel with him.

We talked until 4 a.m., and I told him about the Jesus the apostles wrote about, this Jesus who had become my hero, my Savior and my example. I told him how Jesus was the liberator of those oppressed, the lover of those rejected and the deliverer of those seduced by consumerism, and Mike responded with tears of surrender.

Later that week he took me to a Chinese restaurant and continued to inquire about Jesus. I told him how Jesus lived his life for the sake of others, how he died so we could live, and how he rose again to show what God was going to do for the world.

Something in Mike changed that evening; he understood in a profound way who Jesus was and what he had done for him and the world. When I left Columbus, Mike had a heart to share with his Aryan friends what he had learned, hoping they would let go of their racism and be part of a community that included people from every race, tongue, tribe and nation.

As I reflect on my encounter with Mike, it reminds me of two realities: we live in a messed-up world filled with violence, prejudice, racism, poverty, greed, pride, envy, lust and gluttony; and Jesus has invited messed-up people like us to partner with God in the redemption of the world.

The Federal Aviation Administration once developed a cannon-like device to test the strength of windshields of airplanes. They actually shot a dead chicken (I'm serious) into the windshield at the approximate speed of a flying plane to simulate a bird hitting a plane while in flight. Well, a British locomotive company heard about this test. So they asked the FAA if they could borrow the device. They had just developed a high-speed train and they wanted to likewise test their windshield.

They loaded the bird up and shot it at the locomotive at its approximate running speed. The bird went through the windshield, knocked over the engineer's chair and put a dent in the cab of the locomotive. They couldn't understand what had happened. So they asked if the FAA would please review all the things that the locomotive company had done. The FAA's final report said, "You might want to try the test with thawed chicken."

Why did everyone in the locomotive company conclude that a frozen chicken was used in this experiment? There wasn't even a debate about whether this should be a frozen chicken or a thawed chicken—regular or crispy? No one asked this most basic question.[1]

We often jump to conclusions about how to make the church work better or how to develop a missional strategy—without asking some of the most basic questions. Questions like What does it mean to be the church today? What does it mean to create a missional culture and why does it matter?

Creating a missional culture is more than just adding some outward programs to the church structure. Creating a missional culture goes to the heart and identity of God, to who we are and who we are becoming.

MISSIO DEI

One of the most influential theologians of the last century, Karl Barth, was instrumental in the reintroduction of the classic doctrine of *missio Dei*.[2] We find *missio Dei* in Scripture: God the Father sends the Son and the Spirit into the world, and the Father, Son and Spirit send the church into the world *for* the sake *of* the world. In other words, mission does not originate with the church but is derived from the very nature of God. As Jürgen Moltmann has said, "It is not the church that has a mission of salvation to fulfill in the world; it is the mission of the Son and the Spirit through the Father that includes the church."[3]

When we read the Scriptures, we learn that it is God's mission to set things right in a broken and messed-up world. God's mission is to redeem the world and restore it to its intended purpose. The church exists to fulfill God's mission, and when we participate in God's mission we become living signs of God's intended future for the world, bringing glory to God. In other words, mission exists because God is a missionary God. And "a church which is not on mission is either not yet or no longer the church, or only a dead church—itself in need of renewal."[4]

If we seek to create a missional culture, it is imperative that we understand that God created the church as a sign, foretaste and instrument by which more of his kingdom would be realized here on earth.[5]

CHURCH AS SIGN, FORETASTE AND INSTRUMENT

Sign. The church is to be a sign of God's coming kingdom, pointing people to a reality that is right around the corner. Jesus said, "You are the light of the world." We are called to be lights that point others toward God, his Son and his future. So what kind of sign are we? What kind of sign do we want to become?

Foretaste. The church is called to be a foretaste of God's kingdom, a place where people can get a taste of the future in the present. When the church is a foretaste, it demonstrates what life is like when men and women live under the rule and reign of God, when the people of God love one another, exhort one another, encourage one another, forgive one another and live in harmony with one another. In this way the church becomes a concrete, tangible, though not perfect, foretaste of the kingdom that is to come.

Instrument. Creating a missional culture requires not only understanding that the church is called to be a sign and foretaste of God's kingdom, but also an instrument. When writing to the church in Ephesus the apostle Paul talks about how the church is God's chosen instrument to show the manifold wisdom and grace of God to both the visible and invisible world. He says, "His intent was that now, through the church, the manifold wisdom of God should be made known to the rulers and authorities in the heavenly realms, according to his eternal purpose that he accomplished in Christ Jesus our Lord" (Eph 3:10-11). We see throughout the letter to the Ephesians that the church is to be like a preview or movie trailer of what is to come. The church is an instrument through which God's will for justice, peace and freedom is done in the world.

Creating a missional culture helps the church live out her calling to be a sign of the kingdom, pointing people to the reality beyond what we can see, a foretaste of the kingdom where we grow to love one another as Christ loves us, and an instrument in the hands of God to bring more of heaven to earth in concrete ways. For the church is to be a credible sign, foretaste and instrument, it needs to be a community rich with the fruit of the spirit.

THE PROBLEM

Yet in our most honest moments we recognize that we aren't the kind of people that God wants us to be. We aren't even the kind of people that we hope to be. To be honest, *sometimes* when I look at the worldwide and local church, including churches I have pastored, I think, *God, this is just one big mess!* And apparently, I'm not the only one who thinks this.

In March 2009 we received the results from the widest religious survey conducted in the United States, the ARIS (American Religious Identification Survey) study. There is much to gain from this report, which is based on over 54,000 interviews conducted from February to November 2008. This survey was a continuation of the ARIS surveys in 1990 and 2001, which are part of the landmark series by the Program of Public Affairs at Trinity College in Hartford, Connecticut.

The report indicates major shifts in the American landscape in the past eighteen years, including the fact that the percentage of people who call themselves some type of Christian has dropped more than 11 percent in a generation. One of the most widely cited results from this survey is the significant rise in the number of those who claim no religious identification or faith. This group has grown from 8.2 percent in 1990 to 15 percent in 2008. Ariela Keysar, the associate director of the study, says that the none's (nonreligious) are the only group to have grown in every state of the union.

So why are more and more people in the United States no longer identifying themselves as Christians? What is turning people off to the church, or at least some forms of the church? And why is the digital generation the least involved?

While there is no simple answer to these questions, I want to suggest that at the heart of the matter is the lack of mature missional disciples, not just as individuals but as communities of God's people. We need to be more like Jesus.

Neil Cole makes a good point when he says,

> Ultimately, each church will be evaluated by only one thing—its disciples. Your church is only as good as her disciples. It does not matter how good your praise, preaching, programs or property are; if your disciples are passive, needy, consumeristic, and not [moving in the direction of radical obedience,] your church is not good.[6]

Stanley Hauerwas says the same thing in another way, "[The most important social task of Christians] is nothing less than to be a community capable of forming people with virtues sufficient to witness to God's truth in the world. . . . [T]he task of the Church . . . is to become a polity that has the character necessary to survive as a truthful society."[7]

So why do we lack mature disciples and mature communities of faith? One reason is that we fail to understand the hidden power of culture in life transformation.

Individualism saturates American culture to the point that we no longer notice it. Individualism tells us we can become more like Jesus by ourselves, through a self-help program or more effort. But the gospel tells us transformation happens as we embrace the work of the Spirit in *our* lives together. Becoming more like Jesus is not a matter of trying but yielding, setting the sails of *our* lives to catch the wind of the Spirit. It happens when we develop a communal rhythm of life—a collection of thick, bodily practices (liturgies) that engage our senses, grab our hearts, form our identities and reshape our desires toward God and his kingdom. As we collectively engage in grace-filled spiritual practices, we cultivate particular environments that help to create a missional culture, which in turn reshapes us. As coworkers with God, we create culture and culture reshapes us. Understanding the transformative power of culture is vital if we want to have mature communities of faith.

Phillip Kenneson, in his book *Life on the Vine*, gives a vivid picture of what it means to be a mature community of faith. Using the fruit of the Spirit listed in Galatians, he offers a picture of what Christ is seeking to do in and through us. A mature community cultivates a lifestyle of love in the midst of market-style exchanges: a lifestyle of joy in the midst of manufactured desire, peace in the midst of fragmentation, patience in the midst of productivity, kindness in the midst of self-sufficiency, goodness in the midst of self-help, faithfulness in the midst of impermanence, gentleness in the midst of aggression, and self-control in the midst of addiction.

THE POWER OF CULTURE

In *Theories of Culture*, Kathryn Tanner makes this remarkable statement,

> Although less than one hundred years old, the modern anthropological meaning of "culture" now enjoys a remarkable influence within humanistic disciplines of the academy and within commonsense discussions of daily life. "In explanatory importance and in generality of application it is comparable to such categories as gravity in physics, disease in medicine, evolution in biology."[8]

In other words, the idea of "culture" shapes everything we do as humans, from our thoughts while alone to how we develop family systems, to our interactions at the workplace, to the ways a specific country does its politics.

Kenneson understands the power of culture in the development of character. Culture has particular *narratives*, *institutions*, *rituals* and *ethics* that shape us as people. The dominant culture seeks to squeeze us (the church) into its mold of market-style exchanges, manufactured desire, self-sufficiency and addiction. The apostle Paul puts it this way,

> Don't become so well-adjusted *to your culture* that you fit into it without even thinking. Instead, fix your attention on God. You'll be changed from the inside out. Readily recognize what he wants from you, and quickly respond to it. *Unlike the culture* around you, always dragging you

down to its level of immaturity, God brings the best out of you, develops well-formed maturity in you. (Rom 12:2 *The Message*)

Paul tells us that the dominant culture shapes who we become. According to cultural theory, culture is largely made up of artifacts, language, rituals, ethics, institutions and narratives. In other words, the *language* we live in, the *artifacts* that we use, the *rituals* we engage in, our approach to *ethics*, the *institutions* we are a part of and the *narratives* that we listen to have the power to shape our lives profoundly.

As we look at the culture around us, here are some questions to help us understand how we are being shaped:

- What is the guiding *narrative* of our host culture?
- Which *institutions* most shape our lives?
- What *ethics* are we developing in light of the stories and narratives that bombard us from every side?
- What *rituals, practices* and *liturgies* are we engaging in that shape our desires, our idea of the "good life" and the kind of people we are becoming?

If we take a quick look at American culture, we can see that an individualistic and consumer *narrative* shapes much of our culture and thereby socialized us. We are all socialized beings.

Socialization—the process of growing up within a culture—involves internalizing our culture's way of seeing things. . . . The result is that we do not simply "see" life, but we see it in enculturated ways. . . . We are likely to feel good or not good about ourselves on the basis of how well we live up to the messages and standards of culture internalized within us.[9]

Our *narrative* of growth and success includes the ability to purchase comfort, security and stability. We are socialized from a young age to believe that fulfillment comes through products. Research indicates that children can identify a brand as young as eighteen months, and youth influence about $600 billion of adult spending.[10] Some of our strongest *institutions* are chain stores. We create *rituals* around product consumption and hold closely to our brand-name *artifacts*.

If we hope to experience transformation, we need to develop a culture in the congregation that encourages people to live *in* the world for the *sake of* the world, without being *of* the world. Gerhard Lohfink, in *Jesus and Community*, makes a strong case that it has always been God's intention to work through a visible, tangible concrete community that lives as a contrast society *in* the world *for* the sake of the world.[11] Tim Keller concurs when he says, "Christians are truly residents of the city, yet not seeking power over or the approval of the dominant culture. Rather, they show the world an alternative way of living and of being a human community."[12] When we grasp the power of culture, it gives both perspective and fresh hope for transformation.

LEADERSHIP AND CULTURE

Leaders of God's people uniquely contribute to the cultivation of a culture distinct and different from the dominant culture. For it is the role of Spirit-filled leaders to create a missional culture within the congregation. If we hope to create a missional culture, we must understand the power of culture in shaping the life of the congregation, and learn the basic elements of culture.

In addition, we must examine our very *approach* to leadership. For an individualistic approach to leadership often leads to an individualistic approach to discipleship, while a shared approach to leadership often leads to a communal approach to discipleship with an appreciation of the life-shaping power of culture. To change the *ethos* of the church we also need to change *our approach* to leadership. I will address this later. But first we need to understand the nature of culture and how it works.

2

How Culture Works

The idea that one can or could at any time separate out by some process of distillation a pure gospel unadulterated by any cultural accretions is an illusion. It is, in fact, an abandonment of the gospel, for the gospel is about the word made flesh. . . . There can never be a culture-free gospel. Yet the gospel, which is from the beginning to the end embodied in culturally conditioned forms, calls into question all cultures, including the one in which it was originally embodied.

LESSLIE NEWBIGIN

So here's what I want you to do, God helping you: Take your everyday, ordinary life—your sleeping, eating, going-to-work, and walking-around life—and place it before God as an offering. Embracing what God does for you is the best thing you can do for him. Don't become so well-adjusted to your culture that you fit into it without even thinking. Instead, fix your attention on God. You'll be changed from the inside out. Readily recognize what he wants from you, and quickly respond to it. Unlike the culture around you, always dragging you down to its level of immaturity, God brings the best out of you, develops well-formed maturity in you.

THE APOSTLE PAUL, ROMANS 12:1-2 *THE MESSAGE*

Culture **is considered one of the two or three** most complicated words in the English language.[1] We talk about pop culture, high culture and folk culture. Different people groups (*ethnos*) have different cultures (*ethos*). But what does the word mean? Simply put, culture is what humans make of creation.[2] In *Culture Making*, Andy Crouch makes the case that being culture makers is at the heart of what it means to be made in the image of God. For Crouch, we become culture makers when we create cultural goods (artifacts) to be shared with the public— from omelets to poems, from building bridges to making laws. Cultural influence is related to the degree to which the specific cultural goods that we create shape and affect specific groups of people.[3] While there is a place for condemning, critiquing, consuming and copying culture, the primary posture Christ followers are to have in the world is as culture makers.

In regard to history, the word *culture* is Middle French and comes from the Latin *cultura*, which is borrowed from the Latin word *colere* meaning to till, cultivate or tend.[4] Thus you have hort*iculture*, the science and art of cultivating plants, agr*iculture*, the science and art of cultivating land and livestock, and in regard to anthropology (study of humans), culture is about *cultivating* or developing a way of being in the world. The anthropological sense of the word only developed within the last century, primarily in America, and refers to the idea that different people groups have particular ways of life.[5]

ELEMENTS OF CULTURE

Anthropologists and theologians with an informed philosophical anthropology give more detailed definitions of culture, sharing the various elements that make up culture. William Romanowski defines culture as "a collection of ideals and beliefs, values and assumptions, that makes up a kind of master plan for living and interpreting life."[6] Philip Kenneson, while conceding that there are numerous strengths and weaknesses to varying definitions, says, "cultures are distinguished from one another by those shared *practices, convictions, institutions* and *narratives* that order and give shape to the lives of a particular group of people."[7]

As I've read on this topic I've noticed that some authors make it very simple while others make it so complex that the average person has difficulty understanding what they are saying. Choosing to live between complexity and simplicity, my approach to understanding culture involves six elements—*language, artifacts, narratives, rituals, institutions* and *ethics*. These elements interrelate to create culture and make up what I call the "cultural web."[8]

THE CULTURAL WEB

Language. We are born into a world filled with words. The world was created with words. Words create worlds. Words bring life and death. Words shape us and form us.

When someone says, "Let's go to church," it reveals ignorance of the nature of the church. The people of God are the church. Church is not something we go to, it is something *we are*. We *go to* a weekly gathering, we *attend* a worship service, but we *are* the church. The language we speak, and the language that is used in the congregations we serve, reveals how missional the culture of the church is. With our tongues we can build a missional culture, and with our words we can destroy it. Language is central to any culture. It is through language that we have a narrative to inhabit.

So, what does the language of the congregation you serve reveal? Do the words people speak reveal an understanding that God is missional in his essence, and that we, like him, are a sent people, and that we are to live in the world for the sake of the world?

Artifacts. In addition to *language*, the use of and creation of *artifacts* (cultural goods) are central to creating culture. An essential *artifact* for Christ followers is the Holy Scriptures. Within this divine-human *artifact* is the narrative that shapes the missional congregation. As we read the history, poems, proverbs, psalms, prophetic utterances, Gospels, letters and apocalyptic literature, we discover that God is on mission in the world. We learn from Scripture that the Holy Spirit is breathing on people to write the *artifacts* (scriptural books) as they are on mission, so that we gain an understanding of how the good news incarnates itself into various cultures through the passage of time.

How do the members of the church you serve approach Scripture? Do they seek a theology of mission in the Scripture, or do they recognize that Scripture is a byproduct of mission, revealing a missional theology, which is forming them to join God in his mission? Do they look to the Scripture to inform or transform them? Do they spend more time critiquing the Scriptures or allowing God to critique them through Scripture? Does the community understand the Scriptures as static or dynamic?

The bread and wine are primary *artifacts* as well. They are earthy *and* divine. Jesus takes these elements of the Passover meal, by which the Hebrews remember how God rescued them from the Pharaoh, and transforms them into his body and blood.

When people come to the Table in the congregation you serve, do they remember that Jesus' body was broken for all and that his blood was spilled for the whole world, and thus seek to be bearers of God's saving purpose for his whole world (see Col 1:20; 1 Jn 2:2)? Or do they view themselves as exclusive beneficiaries of God's grace? Jesus takes the table of fellowship and extends it to include the tax collectors, prostitutes and those left out by the religious system. How well does the congregation you serve do this?

The rich hymns and the liturgy that the church has inherited are *artifacts* that have shaped the culture of the church through the centuries. Examining the songs we sing and our approach to liturgy are important if we want to develop a missional culture. In fact, congregations with missional cultures take their cue from former generations and seek to write new songs for new times and new places, and thus become culture makers.

Narratives. The dominant story of a particular culture gives meaning to the *language* and *artifacts* of a culture, and the *narrative* shapes and forms a community in powerful ways. The *narrative* of Scripture provides the church for "a sufficiently truthful account of our existence" by which the community of faith can navigate the ambiguities of our lives.[9] The presuppositions that we hold, knowingly or unknowingly, as a community, are based on the primary narrative we live by. The narrative is the guiding story that helps the community answer the question *What is God's calling for our church?*

Stanley Hauerwas writes, "Just as scientific theories are partially judged by the fruitfulness of the activities they generate, so narratives can and should be judged by the richness of moral character and activity they generate."[10] As you consider the congregation you serve, is the narrative of the community shaping people to love Christ more, be more like him and deeply engage the world in order to see God's kingdom become a greater reality?

Elements strongly related to the narrative include *theology*, *stories* and *doctrine*. *Theology* is a systematic approach to understanding the story, taking into account various theological disciplines, such as biblical, historical, contextual, practical and philosophical. If we want to develop a missional culture, we need to move from a theology of mission to a missional theology, understanding that Scripture is created by people on mission, for people on mission.

When I say *stories*, I mean the primary stories that are shaping the community. What are the Scripture stories that the group focuses on, and how do these stories help them love God, their neighbors and their enemies more? What stories or testimonies are discussed within the community? What stories from the church's history are rehearsed? What current missional stories are being retold? These stories convey what is valued in the community. Developing a missional culture requires sent people to share how God's mission is shaping their story in everyday life.

Finally *doctrine*s start to form within a community as they develop areas of conviction in regard to the substance of their faith. The primary authoritative teachings of the community, both formal and informal, are the doctrines of the community. Do they reflect a missional theology?[11] In his letter to Timothy Paul says, "Watch your life and doctrine closely. Persevere in them, because if you do, you will save both yourself and your hearers" (1 Tim 4:16). Notice that for Paul, doctrine is a practiced theology and a lived spirituality—which reminds us of the interrelatedness of each of the elements of culture.

Rituals. Rituals are procedures or routines that are fused with meaning. Ritual actions include various rites of passage (birth, marriage, death) or calendrical rites (religious holy days, national holidays), and are characteristically formal and traditional, engage the attention of an audience, and are marked by precise repetition with an appeal to supernatural beings.[12]

> A ritual never exists alone. It is usually one ceremony among many in the larger ritual of life of a person or community, one gesture among a multitude of gestures both sacred and profane, one embodiment among others of traditions of behavior down from one generation to another. In other words, for each and every ritual, there is a thick context of social customs, historical practices, and day-to-day routines that, in addition to the unique factors at work in any given moment in time and space, influence whether and how a ritual action is performed.[13]

Rituals answer the question *What are our core practices?* When talking about rituals, we will look at *rites, practices* and *liturgies.* As we do, continue to assess the congregation you serve in these areas.

Some ritual actions include *rites* of passage, ceremonies that accompany and dramatize major events as birth, graduation, marriage and death. When the early church started to connect with non-Jews, it was common to bring new Christians through an intense catechism, which had four phases of formation and growth marked by three rites of passage: welcome into the church, enrollment of names, and baptism. This is documented in *The Apostolic Tradition*, written by Hippolytus around A.D. 215. Developing a missional catechism with various rites of passage is a way to instill a missional DNA in the congregation. Does the congregation you serve have a missional catechism with rites of passage?

Calendrical rites, which "give socially meaningful definitions to the passage of time," is another way to create a missional culture in the congregation.[14] The Christian calendar is a great example of this. By observing the Christian calendar we concretely and creatively remember what is central to our faith—the birth, life, death, resurrection and second coming of Christ, along with the birth of the church at Pentecost. The season of Advent helps us prepare for Christ's second coming, and reminds us to live incarnational lives. In observing Epiphany, we are reminded of Jesus' desire to redeem the whole world and are freshly motivated to join him on this mission. Ash Wednesday prepares us for the season of Lent, where we travel with Christ on the way to the cross, in deep self-examination, prayer, repentance and fasting. We consider the ways we have failed to join God in his mission to redeem the world. Maundy Thursday and Good Friday prepare us for Easter and the following Easter season, the fifty days where we celebrate the victory that Jesus won at the cross. During the Easter season we remember how Jesus conquered death and celebrate the evidence and first fruits of the new creation. Pentecost is a reminder of the gift of the Holy Spirit and how we can taste the future in the present as we live in Spirit-transforming communities.

In what way does the congregation you serve use calendrical rites to bring a missional meaning to time in a habitual way?

Practices or spiritual disciplines reshape our desires and point our hearts in particular directions. Embedded in practices is the *telos* to which we are being oriented.[15] Practices help us to grow to become mature human beings. Dallas Willard defines spiritual disciplines as "activities in our power that we engage in to enable us to do what we cannot do by direct effort alone."[16] People through the ages have engaged in the spiritual disciplines hoping that these practices become habits that reshape them into the image of Christ. What practices is the congregation you serve engaging in, in order to reshape their desire for God and his mission in the world?

Liturgies are a certain kind of practice. They are *thick* practices. James K. A. Smith, in his book *Desiring the Kingdom,* makes a good distinction between thin and thick practices. Some practices or habits we engage in are *thin*, like exercising or brushing our teeth. We do these habits toward a particular end, to be in shape and have clean teeth. Thin practices don't touch on our identity. "It would be an odd thing, for instance, for me to think of myself first and foremost as a 'tooth brusher.' These practices or habits don't touch our *love* or fundamental *desire*."[17] Thick practices or (liturgies) are rituals of ultimate concern, rituals that are identity-forming and *telos*-laden, that embed particular visions of the good life, and do so in a way that seeks to trump other ritual formations.[18] So what kind of liturgies do the people in the congregation you serve in embody? How do they increase people's honesty and love for God? How do they help shape people for God's purposes in the world?

Institutions. Some may consider that thinking about the church as an institution runs contrary to creating a missional culture, but the fact is that institutions shape and mold us in substantive ways and represent an element of stability. Institutions can be an ally to movements. The issue is not institutions; they will be with us forever. The problem is institutional*ism*, when the institution takes on a life of its own and starts rewriting the story that gave it birth, or when an institution oversteps its bounds and becomes so bureaucratic that death is inevitable. Families, church and government are good; the wrong use of them is what is bad. Institutions answer the question *How will we fulfill God's calling together?*

The church is a living organism as well as an institution. Institutions are necessary for life. Miroslav Volf, with the help of Peter Berger and Thomas Luckman, defines an institution as "the stable structures of social interaction" that develops when at least two people do the same thing together repeatedly.[19] With this definition it is clear the church is an institution. According to Volf, two primary factors shape the life of an institution: the pattern of power distribution and internal cohesion and unity. Understanding how a congregation handles power distribution and how they maintain unity when it comes to their vision, strategy and marks of faithfulness helps discern the culture of the church. If the church as an institution is going to be missional, I believe the church needs a *polycentric approach to leadership*, where the equippers enable their *fellow priests* to live to their sacred potential. Thus the entire body is activated for God's mission in the world. We have all been sent; all of us are to teach one another, share our faith, live in the Spirit and administer healing to one another. How many people in the congregation you serve understand that they are "a chosen people, a royal priesthood, a holy nation, God's special possession" (1 Pet 2:9)?

Structures, *symbols* and *systems* are closely related to the institution. *Structures* deal with the various ministries of the church. They deal with the following questions: How is power distributed? Who makes what kind of decisions? What is the strategy of the group, and how is the group organized to fulfill that strategy?

As you assess the congregation you serve, ask yourself these questions: Does the congregation take a hierarchical or grass-roots approach? Does one person wield authority, or is authority revolving and dispersed (a polycentric approach)? Is there a bottleneck in the structure, or does the church take a more open-source approach? Is cohesion maintained by rigid authority or through relationships and collaboration?

Our lives are surrounded by *symbols*—a wedding band, golden arches, a Nike swoosh—artifacts that at a glance bring a rush of thoughts and emotions. Symbols have been a long part of what it means to be human, from the Egyptian hieroglyphics to the drawings found on the walls of catacombs. The architecture of the building we meet in and even how it's set up and organized symbolize different things. In developing a missional culture the leaders ask questions like: What does the physical environment signal to people? What does our logo or church name signify to our community? What are the symbols of success in the community? Do they help move people toward God and his mission for the world?

Systems work alongside structures to help a congregation to move forward in their sacred calling. Our bodies have a number of systems that work together to keep us healthy, the gastrointestinal tract, bones and nervous system carry out their various functions. Every congregation has ways (systems) in which they monitor the health of the church and encourage people to grow as a community. Systems ask the questions: Do the structures we have bring synergy and energy to our vision? What are the written and unwritten rules that shape our culture? What behaviors are considered faithful to the church's sense of calling and thus celebrated? What behaviors are considered disloyal to the vision and thus frowned upon or punished? Examining these questions will help you discern how missional the culture might be.

Ethics. Every community has moral convictions that inform how the community lives, which are the *ethics* of the group. Equippers remind people that ethics aren't limited to outward compliance, for God is concerned about the *heart* of the community. Missional ethics is relational in nature, for we live in a covenant relationship with a holy and missional God who calls us to live in healthy relationship with each other and all of creation. Equippers encourage a missional ethic by encouraging the community to do good in the world for the sake of the world, as well as to avoid doing evil. The equippers seek to help the community walk in the Spirit, for "as God's image-bearers we are to reflect God's character to each other and to all creation by aligning ourselves with the divine cause in the world."[20] Ethics answers the question *What does it mean for us to be faithful and fruitful in God's mission?*

As you consider the congregation you serve, is there a clear understanding of what it means to be faithful and fruitful, and does it reflect something more substantial than how many people come to a service and how large the budget and building are?

When talking about ethics, I'm talking about *being, doing* and *reflecting* in a cyclical nature. Because missional leaders understand that *doing* proceeds from *being,* they help people understand *who* they are in Christ prior to *what* he has called them to do. In Christ we have a new identity and a new *telos* (end or goal), a new aim for our lives—joining God in the renewal of all things, which brings glory to God. *Being* involves abiding in Christ. Jesus said, "Remain in me, as I also remain in you. No branch can bear fruit by itself; it must remain in the vine. Neither can you bear fruit unless you remain in me" (Jn 15:4). We can't bear fruit on our own—the fruit of the Spirit is reflected in our lives as we learn to abide in Christ. Abiding in Christ means inviting Jesus to walk with us at every moment of our lives. It is a way of staying connected to God, being nourished by the Spirit. In what ways does the congregation you serve equip members to abide in Christ, to get into rhythms of life that reshape their desires?

Because of *who* we are, we *live* differently. When we realize we are sent people, when we understand we are ambassadors of Christ, it shapes us for mission. *Doing* is about bearing the fruit of the Spirit, making the choice to walk in the Spirit instead of walking in the flesh. As we learn to abide in Christ through thick practices of the heart (liturgies), we will develop a connection with God, a flow of life between God and us—like a branch to the vine. God's life will flow into ours as we take time to engage in a rhythm of life, in spiritual disciplines. Over time it will change the way we act, see and speak. In what ways is the congregation you serve concretely blessing the neighborhood, living as sent people and ambassadors of Christ?

When being and doing are combined with *reflecting*, we engage in praxis, where the process of action and reflection, practice and thought is repeated cyclically, each informing the other. Maybe that is why Paul says to "practice hospitality" (Rom 12:13). Being able to think about, assess and examine our lives belongs to the essence of what it means to be human, and it is indispensable for our growth and development. If we don't reflect on our life, it eventually loses its meaning. In what concrete ways does the congregation you serve engage in reflection?

OVERVIEW OF ELEMENTS

So the cultural web involves *language* and *artifacts* as well as *narrative, rituals, institution* and *ethics*. Seek to stash these six elements in your mind. As you reflect on *narrative*, remember it involves *theology, stories and doctrines*. As you reflect on *rituals*, call to mind *rites, practices* and *liturgies*. As you think about *institution*, let it trigger the memory of *structures, symbols* and *systems*. And as you dwell on *ethics*, let it bring to mind *being, doing* and *reflecting*. Each of the elements interrelates and gives us an understanding of culture as a whole. Take some time to familiarize yourself with these elements, because these ideas are woven throughout the book, sometimes in more focused ways.

Having grown in our understanding of culture, let's now take a look at the five environments needed to create a missional culture. As we do, as yourself, *How strong are these environments in the church that I serve?*

3

What's Going On in the Culture
of the Church You Serve?

*Missional leadership is about cultivating an environment that innovates
and releases the missional imagination present in God's people.*

ALAN ROXBURGH

*Christ himself gave the apostles, the prophets, the evangelists, the
pastors and teachers, to equip his people for works of service, so that
the body of Christ may be built up until we all reach unity in the faith
and in the knowledge of the Son of God and become mature, attaining
to the whole measure of the fullness of Christ.*

THE APOSTLE PAUL, EPHESIANS 4:10-13

Helen Keller, the blind-and-deaf woman who made history by learning
to overcome her disabilities, was once asked if there was anything worse
than being blind. She answered, "Oh yes! There is something worse
than being blind. It is being able to see and not having any vision."[1]

While most leaders have vision statements, how many would you say
have clarity in regard to the kind of culture they desire to cultivate in
the congregations they serve? As leaders recognize the power of culture,
it becomes imperative to clarify the kinds of environments that will

need to be developed. I suggest that there are five kinds of environments we need to cultivate if we are to create a missional culture. As we look at these five environments, take some time to assess the congregation you serve. In chapter seventeen we will talk about specific ways to cultivate these five environments. At this point, ask the Spirit to give you a sense of the strengths and weaknesses in the church you serve.

LEARNING ENVIRONMENT

Cultivating a learning environment is essential to creating a missional culture. A learning environment helps the congregation to *inhabit the sacred text* in such a way that Scripture is understood as not simply a book to be read but a voice to be heard. Through Scripture we encounter the voice of God and meaningfully connect with him in such a way that we experience transformation and hear his call to join in his mission to transform our neighborhoods, cities and world.

While learning environments might include weekly gatherings, midweek studies and Bible studies, it goes beyond these meetings. Real knowledge is knowledge that is practiced in everyday life. *Praxis* characterizes a learning environment. It takes place when people engage in a learning activity based on a new understanding, attitude or concept, and then immediately reflect on what they just did. This process of action and reflection, practice and thought, is repeated in a cyclical process, each informing the other.

A learning environment involves dialogue, not just monologue. Learning environments invite people to immediately use knowledge and experience its benefit, thus increasing the motivation to learn more. A learning environment requires active learning, where people are given learning objectives that help them to think, feel and do.

Cultivating a learning environment enables people to live *in* the Word, and as they live in the Word—and have the Word live in them—they become instruments of love, joy, justice and peace in the world. Historically, when the people of God have dwelt in the sacred text, they have left the comforts of home to go to the four corners of the earth to share the good news of Jesus through their actions and words. They have built hospitals and schools. They have given sacrificially to help alleviate suffering in the world. They have promoted peacemaking, by overcoming evil with good. They have crossed social, economic and racial barriers, recognizing that every person is made in God's image. They have appreciated beauty by creating art like Handel's *Messiah* and Bach's epic *Mass in B Minor* and the great churches of Byzantium, the Gothic cathedrals and Renaissance basilicas. Even more impressive, "they've done their work as teachers, farmers, bricklayers, nurses, scholars, mechanics, sellers, public servants, scientist, homemakers, cab drivers, and cooks with a special sense of purpose, love and joy."[2] They lived their everyday lives for God, turning their jobs into sacred callings, by which they glorified God.

Jesus said, "If you remain in me [the living Word] and my words remain in you, ask whatever you wish, and it will be done for you. This is to my Father's glory, that you bear much fruit, showing you to be my disciples" (Jn 15:7-8).

Learning Environment

As you think about the congregation you serve, how you would rate it in regard to cultivating a learning environment? Here are some questions to guide your reflection:

- In what ways does Scripture shape the community you serve?
- Is the community listening to God through the Scriptures and practicing in their everyday lives what they are learning? How?
- In what ways are people actively reflecting on what they are practicing?
- What percentage of the congregation is immersed in God's story and teaching the Scripture to others?
- How many are actively interacting with the God's story as it relates to their local context and mission?

HEALING ENVIRONMENT

If a congregation desires to become more whole and holy, they need to cultivate a healing environment as well, where people can take off their masks and live into their true selves in God. Too often churches are over-programmed and leave too little time for people to relax, play and enjoy one another. Frantic ministry and busyness sometimes are ways to avoid facing our true selves. A congregation that both works and plays becomes family. A healing environment creates space for people to pursue living out a life-giving spirituality within community and engage in habits that refresh them physically, recharge them emotionally and renew them spiritually.

A healing environment helps the congregation *seek wholeness and holiness*. This comes first through understanding God's unending love for us: "Most of us were taught that God would love us *if* and *when* we change. In fact, God loves you so that you *can* change. What empowers change, what makes you desirous of change is the experience of love. It is that inherent experience of love that becomes the engine of change."[3] As John has said, "We love because he first loved us" (1 Jn 4:19). So for deep healing to take place in our lives, there needs to be an atmosphere of acceptance. As Paul has said, "Accept one another, then, just as Christ accepted you, in order to bring praise to God" (Rom 15:7). What does it mean to accept someone?

Healing Environment

How would you rate the healing environment in the church you serve? Think about these questions:

- Do the rhythms of the church make space for people to have down time and just hang with each other?
- Are their regular times for people to be genuine with one another—with no masks?
- How well do people know each other and share life with each another?
- What percentage of the congregation considers the church as family?
- How many are experiencing healing from past hurts and moving toward wholeness spiritually, physically, mentally and emotionally?

It is a remarkable action, difficult to define, yet unmistakable when we experience it. To accept people is to be *for* them. It is to recognize that it is a very good thing that these people are alive, and to long for the best for them. It does not, of course, mean to approve of everything they do. It means to continue to want what is best for their souls no matter *what* they do.[4]

Not only does an atmosphere of acceptance help cultivate a healing environment, but it is important for the congregation to have a realistic picture of community and understand that community-building is a process filled with both pain and joy. If people come into community expecting utopia, they will likely leave hurt and disappointed. Paul's letters clearly reveal the messiness of community. Community is messy because it is a collection of imperfect people, seeking to be transformed by God together.[5]

WELCOMING ENVIRONMENT

Cultivating a welcoming environment means helping the community practice hospitality as a way of life. We have all felt the pain of exclusion, of feeling unloved, unwelcomed or unappreciated. We can all recall wounds we have received. And we have all felt the longing to be a part of some exclusive group. While the narrative of our world encourages us to be exclusive, the narrative of God encourages something quite different.

Our God is a welcoming God. From the call of Abraham—where God said he would bless him and all the nations of the earth through him—to John's vision of people from every tongue, tribe and nation gathered around the throne of Christ, we see that God is welcoming. Jesus exemplified this, consistently extending the table to those who were marginalized by the people of God and society. Jesus constantly crossed boundaries to demonstrate that God welcomes all, and as Christ's disciples we should seek to do the same.

A number of women at Kairos Los Angeles have at times assisted a local ministry that helps women who are in transition. They provide housing and often help these women find jobs. Some of these women started to get involved with our congregation in Hollywood. A number of years ago, one lady by the name of Latifah came up to me, and as she was introducing herself, she said, "And by the way, I am a Muslim." Latifah was welcomed into our congregation, and later she told me, "You know JR, I have visited a number of churches, and most of the time when I tell them that I am a Muslim, people start to exclude me. It's like a wall goes up. But as I have come here to Kairos, people have welcomed me. I wanted to thank you for that."

Latifah continued to come to our weekly gathering, Sunday after Sunday. I started a seven-week series on the life, death and resurrection of Jesus, and she came faithfully each week to listen. By the time we finished the last talk, Latifah, who happened to be sitting in the center of the room, jumped out of her seat, put her hands in the air and shouted, "Jesus is Lord, Jesus is Lord, Jesus is Lord!" She then fell down to her knees, bowed her head and cried. Latifah felt welcomed and accepted. As a result she desired to hear more about Jesus and ultimately recognized him as her Lord.

Welcoming Environment

Is your church cultivating a welcoming environment? Use these questions to attain a new vision for the culture of the church you serve:

- How many people genuinely welcome others into their tight community?
- How well does the faith community reflect the diversity of the neighborhood?
- What ministries are in place to help orient people into the life of the congregation?
- What percentage of people meaningfully connect with others in the neighborhood, at work or in other missional spaces?
- How well does the community incarnate the good news within the various missional spaces?
- How willing are people to sacrifice their own cultural comfort to meet people where they are?
- How many people willingly initiate with people who are different than them?

Cultivating a welcoming environment, where we practice hospitality as a lifestyle, helps the congregation to *incarnate the good news.* It goes beyond how the church receives people. It means we take the initiative to live out our mission incarnationally, but this comes at a price. The price is that the church "must always be willing to die to its own cultural comfort in order to live where God intends it to be."[6] We must cultivate a community of faith *for* them, *among* them and *with* them, under the spirit of God. We need to have a listening and learning posture as we live with them. Jesus said, "I tell you the truth, unless a kernel of wheat is planted in the soil and dies, it remains alone. But its death will produce many new kernels—a plentiful harvest of new lives" (Jn 12:24 NLT). If we are willing to die to our comfort and personal preferences and faithfully plant ourselves incarnationally among the people groups and neighborhoods God sends us to, fruit will abound. Living incarnationally is "entering their world. Taking it as seriously as they do and helping them find Christ there."[7]

LIBERATING ENVIRONMENT

Cultivating a liberating environment encourages people to embody a holistic gospel, helping people experience liberation from personal and social sins by forming Spirit-transforming communities. A liberating environment encourages people to overcome addictions, grow in personal holiness and live in the power of the Spirit.

Ultimately a liberating environment helps the congregation *pursue God's shalom*—"the way things ought to be."[8] It is about seeing the reality of God's kingdom brought to bear on the earth. It's when enemies are reconciled, injustices are made right, hurts are healed, anxieties are soothed and cities flourish.

A liberating environment cultivates shalom makers: people who see what could be, pray that God's will be done on earth as it is in heaven, and then join God in the renewal of all things. Shalom makers seek to restore all that was lost at the fall—our relationship with God, with each other, with creation and within ourselves. They care about all of creation and seek to be good stewards for the sake of the whole. A liberating environment encourages us to speak truth to the powers that be and root out oppression in the church and in the world.

We have all heard the story of the good Samaritan. A guy is traveling on the road between Jericho and Jerusalem, and falls among robbers. He is stripped and beaten and left for dead, and the good Samaritan comes and picks him up, cleans his wounds, takes him to a hotel and cares for him until he recovers. The good Samaritan did the right thing. "But if every day two or three people get mugged on the road between Jerusalem and Jericho, there comes a point at which we must realize that being Good Samaritans is not enough. At some point, if such crimes abound, we have to figure out how to put up a better lighting system on the road and perhaps have it patrolled by police, and put an end to people being mugged on that dangerous highway. In short, it's one thing to care for the casualties from the system, but sooner or later we have to change the system so as to not have so many casualties in the first place."[9]

Liberating Environment

How much of a liberating environment has been cultivated in the congregation you serve? Pray through these questions:

- What percentage of the congregation is pursuing God's shalom in the power of the Holy Spirit?
- How many people are actively using their spiritual gifts to build the body and serve the neighborhood?
- Is the congregation walking alongside the poor and oppressed? In what ways?
- How is the congregation speaking to the powers and subverting systems that perpetuate injustice?
- How much of the congregation seeks to be good stewards of all creation for the sake of the whole world?

One of the passions we have had at Kairos Los Angeles is helping the poor and the hurting. For a few years we partnered with Central City Mission, a ministry located in the heart of skid row. Out of the

80,000 homeless that live in Los Angeles county, 20,000 live on skid row. The fastest growing segment of the homeless population is children, and 600 to 800 kids live on skid row. We have helped out with an after-school program designed to help kids develop physically, spiritually, intellectually and socially. In this way we seek to subvert the current system, joining others to create an environment whereby these children might reach their sacred potential.

But a liberating environment is not just about helping the poor and oppressed, it is learning to walk with them, calling the church to God's new social order where the rich and poor live in community together. It would be like the Bloods and the Crips (gangs in LA) finding themselves sitting next to each other worshiping God. It would be like a homeless person teaching someone from Beverly Hills about God. Where else can we find mortal enemies enjoying fellowship? Yet this is what God is doing by creating one new humanity.

THRIVING ENVIRONMENT

Creating a missional culture also involves cultivating a thriving environment where a strong discipleship ethos is developed and the multiplication of disciples, ministries and churches takes place. In a thriving environment people are getting in touch with their primal passions by discovering how God has made them and are learning to match their passion with the needs around them. Mentoring and coaching is taking place at every level. People are being encouraged by word and example to find experienced mentors and peer mentors, and are starting to mentor others.

A thriving environment helps the congregation to *live out her calling* in the world for the sake of the world. People begin to link Sunday with Monday, and their work transforms from a job to a sacred vocation. They learn to bring God's power to bear on human need. The banker or person in finance looks for ways to live out jubilee; judges help the court system move toward conflict resolution instead of ever increasing litigation. Realtors try to house people according to their need instead of their greed. Engineers and architects look to bring a sense of order and beauty to cities. Artists seek to disturb, awaken and enlighten us in hopes that we might be more present to ourselves, our world and to the One who is behind all of creation. People learn to live out their calling in their vocation in a way that blesses others and brings glory to God.

Thriving Environment

So how is the congregation you serve doing in cultivating a thriving environment? Take some time to respond to these questions:

- How many people are discovering their calling and living it out with great passion?
- To what degree is the multiplication of disciples taking place?
- What percentage of people are being mentored and are mentoring others?
- Are there apprentices for each ministry?
- What percentage of people has a sense of ownership in the congregation?
- Are there ministries in the congregation that intentionally help match people's passions with the needs of the church, the neighborhood, the missional spaces and social justice issues?
- How many people see their work as a sacred vocation by which they are able to serve their neighbor and bring glory to God?

CULTIVATING A MISSIONAL CULTURE

Since we need to cultivate a *learning, healing, welcoming, liberating* and *thriving* environment to create a missional culture, we need to think about the kinds of leaders needed to cultivate these environments. No one leader can do this, hence the reason we need polycentric leadership—the subject of chapter four.

4

Polycentric Leadership and Missional Culture

*If one wishes to distinguish leadership from management or adminis-
tration, one can argue that leaders create and change culture, while
management and administration act within culture.*

EDGAR H. SCHEIN

*We are God's masterpiece. He has created us anew in Christ Jesus,
so that we can do the good things he planned for us long ago.*

THE APOSTLE PAUL, EPHESIANS 2:10 NLT

What if you had the opportunity to go back to A.D. 60 and ask the
apostle Paul's advice about the church you serve? What do you think he
might say?

Paul was a wise builder of the church.[1] He was an incredibly humble,
gifted and devoted man. God used him to pen many of the letters of the
New Testament. Most were situational, written to address particular
problems within a church in a particular location. Certainly, we can
understand that! We all have problems in our churches. Some of Paul's
letters were pastoral, written to other church leaders. And others were
general letters. In these letters, Paul answers general questions and
paints with broad strokes.

Besides the pastoral letters, the book of Ephesians is one of the very
last general letters that Paul wrote, and it is all about how the church

can be a sign, foretaste and instrument of God's kingdom. Catholics call it the hallmark book on ecclesiology (the study of the church). The book of Ephesians was likely written near the end of Paul's life and contains some of his most mature reflections on how to *be* the church. In this letter Paul encourages us to embody the good news in a way where power is distributed rather than centralized, and truth is embodied instead of debated, thereby speaking to a host culture that is skeptical of power and truth.

GOD'S CULTURAL MASTERPIECE

Watchmen Nee, a Chinese missionary, summed up the book of Ephesians in just three words—*sit, walk, stand*. That is the flow of the letter to the Ephesians.

Sit. The first thing Paul tells us is that God chose us to be with him, to be his adopted sons and daughters, and to be a part of this new humanity he has created. He says that we have been seated with Christ. We have a place at his table.

Walk. After three chapters of sitting with God, seeking to understand his plan and purpose for the world from the foundation of the world, Paul tells us to get up and walk. He urges us to walk with God in light of all that God has done for us.

Stand. As we begin to live in the world for the sake of the world, when we start to make right what is wrong, we will encounter the onslaught of the forces of darkness and the enemy of all that is good. It is at those times, we need to learn to rely on God's power to stand.

With this in mind, let's take a closer look at how Paul describes the path to maturity *in* Christ, so that we may be *like* Christ. After three chapters of sitting with Christ and understanding his plan and purpose from the foundation of the world, Paul instructs us how to walk as a community. This is where we see how God has designed his masterpiece. Paul mentions earlier in this book, "We are God's masterpiece. He has created us anew in Christ Jesus, so that we can do the good things he planned for us long ago" (Eph 2:10 NLT). When Paul says that we are God's masterpiece, he is talking about the church. He refers to the collective whole, not just to individuals. This is why he uses *we* instead of *you*.

So *we*, the church, are a work of art in progress. We are a painting on a canvas. The canvas is the collection of our souls in community—we are the material that God works on. He picks up his brush and, with all of the energy and depth that he possesses, begins to paint. At the end of his creative work, there is a masterpiece.

When I think of masterpieces, I think of art. But what is art? I like the way that Thomas Hoving, who was the director of the Metropolitan Museum of Art in New York, put it: "Art happens when anyone in the world takes any kind of material and fashions it into a deliberate statement."[2] I like that because, as I reflect on my life, the life of the prophets, the life of a church, and the life of the people of God throughout time, I see how God does that with people and communities of people. He crafts us to make a statement in, to and for the world.

It is important to have churches that cross ethnic, class and age barriers because one of the statements our world needs to see is that there can be unity in diversity when Jesus is king of that community.

But how can we tell if a work of art is good? Hoving has some great ideas about this as well. There are six good questions to consider when understanding the value of art:

- Does it express successfully what it's intending to express?
- Does it amaze you in a different way each time you look at it?
- Does it grow in stature?
- Does it continually mature?
- Does its visual impact of mysterious, pure power increase every day?
- Is it unforgettable?[3]

Those are helpful questions to think about when it comes to what God is doing in our lives and our communities. Jesus talked about being a light to the world and living in a way that brings our Father great honor.

Hoving also gives us this incredible definition of great art:

As you climb the stairs of quality, you'll meet individual works that you'll need for the rest of your life, works that will thrill you, energize you, lift your soul, soothe you, make you smile, make you think about the fate of mankind and the universe, make you have to see them again and again for the good of your psyche, state of mind, and strength of heart.[4]

Wouldn't that description be great to hear from someone who has come to visit our communities of faith? "Man, I had the most amazing time tonight. I sensed a great power in the room. It was an experience I won't soon forget!" As I look through the book of Acts, those are the kinds of comments that people made w en they connected to God's community. Shouldn't that be the case for us today as well, since we have God as our ultimate Artist? So how is God creating his masterpiece?

The apostle Paul begins Ephesians 4 by addressing our *attitudes*. Then he talks about our *common creed*, reminding us, though we are all different, we are all made from the same cloth, the same DNA. The chapter contains a hymn, an early Christian confession: "There is one body and one Spirit, just as you were called to one hope when you were called; one Lord, one faith, one baptism; one God and Father of all, who is over all and through all and in all" (Eph 4:4-6). Finally, Paul speaks of *the diverse gifts* that God gives the church so that it might grow into maturity and be like Christ himself. He describes how Christ has given the church five different equippers—apostles, prophets, evangelists, pastors and teachers—who embody their gifts in such a way that the entire body is awakened and moves toward the full stature of Christ in both character and mission (Eph 4:7-16).

If we want to become God's masterpiece, we need to take the apostle's teaching seriously. First, we see that the exalted Christ establishes this design and gives the church a particular structure. God appoints Christ to be head over the church and the universe, and Christ then gives certain gifts to the church. Notice that the gifts Christ gives are not personal services but particular servants—apostles, prophets, evangelists, pastors and teachers. An interesting thing to remember is that each of these titles, except for prophets describes a secular occupation in the first century.[5] Paul bypasses impressive Old Testament titles such as king, priest, scribe or Levite.

As I understand this passage, Paul sees each of these five equippers and the ministries they represent as the "very mechanism for achieving mission and ministry effectiveness as well as Christian maturity."[6] Paul seems to say that without a fivefold ministry pattern, we cannot mature and become the masterpiece that God intended. Commenting about this passage, Frost and Hirsch say, "If this is true, it is impossible to estimate what terrible damage the church has done through the loss, even active suppression, of this crucial dimension of New Testament ministry and leadership."[7]

Perhaps one of the reasons for the immaturity that we find in the Western church, and for the church being tossed here and there by every wind of doctrine, is because these five different equippers have not been appreciated, understood or nurtured.[8] To grow up and become like Christ we need each equipper, and we must have a clear understanding what each of them bring to the body.

LEADERS, CULTURE AND MATURITY

In Paul's letters, including the letter to the Ephesians, we learn how our *environment* powerfully shapes who we become. We also see how *our approach* to leadership is vital if we are to help the church grow to the maturity of Christ. The beauty of the vision that Paul is laying out for us is that as we learn to develop *a diverse team of leaders* who together can cultivate communities to be more like Christ. As Markus Barth points out in his commentary on Ephesians, "The whole church is the clergy appointed by God for a ministry to and for the world."[9] Paul tells us that when each of the equippers are equipping well, the whole body will grow up to the full stature of Christ. This implies that the five equippers together represent the full ministry of Jesus. And while there are many other gifts that the Holy Spirit gives for the building up of the body (see Rom 12; 1 Cor 12; 1 Pet 4:7-11), each of these gifts are activated and flow in the ministry path of each of the equippers.

A POLYCENTRIC APPROACH TO LEADERSHIP HELPS CREATE A MISSIONAL CULTURE

In the United States it is common for churches to have a hierarchical leadership structure, with a senior or lead pastor, then associate pastors, other staff and finally those who give of their time freely. Yet how does this structure speak to people skeptical of power? And how does this kind of structure take seriously what we are learning in the sciences?

One of the reasons the church is losing the digital generation is we have failed to incarnate *an approach* to leadership which takes seriously the major shifts our culture is experiencing. If we are going to be a sign, foretaste and instrument of God's kingdom and incarnate the good news in our context, we must learn to navigate the megashifts I will be addressing in chapter five: the *media shift* from print and broadcast to the digital age, the *philosophical shift* from modernity to postmodernity, the *science shift* from classic science to emergent science, the *spatial shift* from rural to urban, and the *religion shift* from Christendom to post-Christendom. These cultural shifts highlight the vulnerabilities of a centralized leadership structure, which I contend never should have characterized the church in the first place. If we are to meaningfully connect with the digital generation and live more faithfully to the narrative of Scripture, we need to shift from a hierarchical to a polycentric approach to leadership, where equippers live as cultural architects cultivating a fruitful missional ethos that fully activates the priesthood of all believers.

While the term *polycentric* may seem a bit eccentric, the richness of its meaning is important. As Suzanne Morse writes in *The Community of the Future*,

> Successful communities, even those with long traditions of organized community leadership, will continue to broaden the circles of leadership to create a system for the community that is neither centralized nor decentralized, but rather polycentric. The polycentric view of community leadership assumes that there are many centers of leadership that interrelate.[10]

The apostle Paul was ahead of his time, for he does not propose a centralized leadership structure or a flat leadership structure. Rather he reveals to us a polycentric structure, where leaders interrelate and incarnate the various purposes of Christ in such a way that the entire body is activated to service and matures in love. The five equippers are gifted by God to help the congregation move toward maturity in Christ and see the reality of God's kingdom, which is both here and coming.

If we are to cultivate mature communities of faith, we need missional equippers who live as cultural architects, with a heightened sense of contextual awareness and the ability to shape and cultivate *culture* within the congregation.

EQUIPPERS AS CULTURAL ARCHITECTS

As we have learned already, all organizations have a *culture*, including churches. And the *culture* shapes the community in profound ways. Understanding, analyzing and creating culture is the work of a cultural architect.

By definition a leader, an equipper, is a cultural architect. As Edgar Schein, a specialist in organizational culture and former professor at MIT Sloan School of Management, says, "If one wishes to distinguish leadership from management or administration, one can argue that leaders creates and changes culture, while management and administration act within culture."[11] Equippers should have a growing awareness of what *culture* is and how it is shaped, because the *culture* of a group can either help or hinder the community from fulfilling her mission in God's world.

When it comes to equippers living as cultural architects, it is important to remember that both God and we have a part in cultivating the culture of a congregation. Paul said, "By the grace God has given me, I laid a foundation as an expert builder" (1 Cor 3:10). He became skilled worker, by God's grace, in building the church, recognizing that the foundation of the church is Jesus Christ. Paul understood that he planted seeds, Apollos watered them, but God causes the growth. In other words, when it comes to being cultural architects, there are some things that we cannot do, only God can. There are other things that God will *not* do, because he has called us to do them. When it comes to creating a missional culture in the congregation, God has his part and we have ours.

In addition, if equippers are going to be wise culture makers, we need to keep in mind that there is more to the church than meets the eye. The church is not just another social organization or human institution. While it has organizational and institutional dimensions, it is more than just the sum of these. The church is the creation of the Spirit. God's divine power and presence indwell the people of God. This makes the church a spiritual community as well as a human community. The church is both a spiritual reality and a sociological entity. It has divine roots in the eternal purposes of God, yet exists as a historically conditioned organization. It is both holy and human, both spiritual and social.[12]

Now let's take a deeper look at how this polycentric leadership works by thinking through the leadership imagination we need in order to lead in this way.

PART TWO

A Leadership Imagination
That Shapes Missional Culture

5

Facing Today's Challenges

Every generation in every culture must take up the hard work of discerning the opportunities for and the obstacles to embodying the gospel faithfully in that place and time.

PHILLIP KENNESON

From the tribe of Issachar, there were 200 leaders of the tribe with their relatives. All these men understood the signs of the times and knew the best course for Israel to take.

1 CHRONICLES 12:32 NLT

Change in culture requires a different approach to leadership. As Eddie Gibbs says,

> Yesterday's solutions and procedures may not provide an adequate or appropriate response to the present challenges. Hence, the biggest hurdles facing long-time leaders may not be in learning new insights and skills, but in unlearning what they consider to be tried and true and what thus provides them with a false sense of security.[1]

Why is the church having a difficult time connecting with people today, especially the digital generation?

I am convinced that shifts in media, philosophy, science and religion in our world provoke a shift from the traditional hierarchal approach to leadership to a communal polycentric approach.

MEDIA SHIFT

A YouTube video from the *Today Show* in 1994 shows Bryant Gumbel and Katie Couric asking each other "What is the Internet?" and debating if the "@" symbol means "at" or "about."[2] The world is very different today.

Culture is shaped by the primary medium of an era. Marshall McLuhan is widely known as the father of media studies. He coined the famous phrase "the medium is the message" in 1965. And while some today believe that the medium or method of communication is neutral and that only the content of the message is vital, those like Marshall McLuhan who have spent a lifetime studying the effects of media would say otherwise. He writes, "societies have always been shaped more by the nature of media by which men communicate than by the content of the communication."[3] McLuhan made the case that we are often blind to the way that the medium shapes us, and that "any understanding of social and cultural change is impossible without a knowledge of the way media work as environments."[4] A number of Christians who have thoughtfully engaged in the study of technology agree.[5]

Technology and media are extensions of humans. The phone is an extension of the ear and the mouth. The car is an extension of the foot. We create our tools and then our tools recreate us.

The medium of the day shapes us surreptitiously. For example, the medium of the car has profoundly shaped the way cities operate. Cites in the United States that developed before the car, like New York, Boston and San Francisco, tend to be centralized and cover small areas of land. Cities like Los Angeles, whose boom years happened to coincide with the invention of the car, tend to be polycentric and cover much more geographical space. For instance, you can fit the land areas of San Francisco, Manhattan, Boston, Minneapolis, Cleveland, Pittsburgh, St. Louis and Milwaukee within the city limits of Los Angeles, with space to spare. When we contrast the way life takes place in a centralized city like New York or San Francisco, and the way it takes place in Los Angeles, we soon recognize that the creation of cars has drastically reshaped urban life, especially in those cities that experienced their growth after the invention of the car.

New media creates new kinds of people. Print media causes humans to become more detached and logical, while the Internet causes people to become more involved and participatory.

After twenty-five years of researching social change throughout history, Rex Miller found that the best way to organize the major societal shifts over time was by considering the dominant medium of the age. He states,

> The Millennium Matrix builds on the premise that when the primary means of storing and distributing information changes, our worldview changes. Here's how this works. When our means of storing and distributing information change, our perceptions change. Changed perceptions create changed understandings and even changed psychology. Changed identity affects relationships. Changed relationships affect the traditions and institutions that support those relationships.

These changes eventually reach a cultural critical mass, igniting a battle between old and new worldviews. Communication is the medium for relationship, community, and culture; so a more efficient or powerful tool of communication results in their restructuring.[6]

The middle of Miller's book presents a twenty-three-page chart that indicates changes in how we believe, how we know, how we live together, how we see beauty and how we work and trade. He contends that there have been four different eras defined by the media of the day. These are the Oral Age (? B.C.–A.D. 1500), the Print Age (1500-1950), the Broadcast Age (1950-2010) and the Digital Age (2010-). What is fascinating is that for the first time in the history of the world, we have people living who have been predominantly shaped by three different forms of media. Table 6.1 summarizes my understanding of Miller's thoughts in regard to how the different eras approach leadership.[7]

How are we to understand *our approach to leadership* as we begin to immerse ourselves in the digital age? Miller says, "An impartational style of leadership based on mutual trust will replace today's top-down, hierarchical leadership styles," which is why he devoted an entire chapter in his book to the topic of leadership.[8]

Table 5.1. Leadership Viewed Through the Millenium Matrix

	Print Age 1500–1950	Broadcast Age 1950–2010	Digital Age 2010–
Kind of Leaders	Intellectual Leaders	Motivational Leaders	Impartational Leaders
Kind of Structures	Functional units, division of labor, a hierarchical chain of command; view organization as a living machine; maintain cohesion through structure and inertia	Purpose driven, empowerment, information driven, buildings and programs; maintain cohesion through psychological stimulation and sense of mission	Collaborative, grass roots oriented, roving leadership, open-source approach, dispersed authority; maintain cohesion through relationships and collaboration
Focus of Leadership	Like field generals, they seek achievement and efficiency, using tried and true methods; they teach by instruction	Like motivational speakers, they seek to harness the potential of the organization around the mission; they teach by exhortation	Like gardeners they cultivate a collaborative approach to current conditions, opportunities and challenges; they teach by example
Nature of Relationships with others	Hierarchical	Appointment oriented; relationships often become a functional way to complete objectives	Unscripted, personal, familial; people use organizations to fulfill their missions for mutual benefit
Approach to Discipleship	Takes place in the classroom; logical presentations	Takes place in the sanctuary; programmatic, seminar oriented	Takes place in the living room and streets; relational, interactive, mentorship
Qualities and Skills Needed	Intellectual expertise, maintaining predictability, achieving stability	Communication, persuasive, high profile image, innovative, interpersonal skills, novelty, ability to think on one's feet and utilize the big event	Approachable, agile, networker, touchable, accessible, missional, transparent, advocate, sustainability, resilient, collective achievement, storytelling

PHILOSOPHICAL SHIFT

In addition to the media shift there has been a *philosophical shift* from modernity to late modernity/postmodernity. James K. A. Smith's book *Who's Afraid of Postmodernism?* examines the work of the philosophers Jacques Derrida, Jean-François Lyotard and Michel Foucault, helping us to understand how to live in this culture without marrying the spirit of the age. He suggests that these postmodern philosophers "might in fact push us to recapture some truths about the nature of the church that have been overshadowed by modernity and especially by Christian appropriations of modernism."[9]

Derrida and Foucault changed how we understand power, knowledge and truth. "In 1966 Derrida was invited to present a paper at a Johns Hopkins University conference and ended up calling the entire history of philosophy in the West into doubt."[10] Derrida, standing on the shoulders of Friedrich Nietzsche, Sigmund Freud, Martin Heidegger and Ferdinand de Saussure, authored more than twenty books and spawned the *deconstruction* movement, which is still reverberating throughout our culture.

Deconstructionism has created a culture that is *skeptical* of truth and *cynical* toward those in power. Derrida suggested that the entire world is a text that needs to be interpreted.[11] None of us have pure, unmediated access to reality or truth. We all see through a mirror dimly. As Smith notes, "To assert that our interpretation is not an interpretation but objectively true often translates into the worse kinds of imperial and colonial agendas, even within a pluralistic culture."[12] Yet simply because everything is interpreted doesn't mean there is no truth. Some interpretations of reality are better than others, yet, because there is no uninterrupted reality, all of us come to the world with our set of presuppositions, which shape our interpretation. As Christians, it is our aim to see the world and reality through the lens of Scripture rather than through the propaganda and ideologies of the world.

Postmodernism helped the church reiterate the importance of community. Derrida argued that "we can't interpret a text, thing, or event without the conventions and rules of an interpretive community; indeed language itself is inherently communal and inter-subjective."[13] Thus we need to approach our understanding of the Scripture with the help of the entire church, including the marginalized, global and historical church.

Michel Foucault, the late philosophy chair at the prestigious College in Paris and a visiting professor at UC Berkeley, famously reversed the adage "knowledge is power" to "power is knowledge."[14] Through his case studies of the history of prisons and hospitals, Foucault focused on the relationship between knowledge and power. In Foucault's study of institutions he demonstrated that institutions use their power, through positive and negative disciplines (practices and rituals), in order to make people "normal." For Foucault, those in power determine knowledge, which in turn determines what is considered normal and abnormal, and who should be included and excluded. Because Foucault revealed how "the powers that be" determine knowledge and seek to push for their agenda, those who swim in the postmodern current are more apt to operate with a *hermeneutic of suspicion*, especially in regard to those in power.[15]

The church needs to embody an approach to leadership that can reach those skeptical of truth and cynical of power without embracing the idea that "freedom" means being an autonomous individual, unanswerable to anyone or any institution.

As previously mentioned, the founder and director of Yale Center for Faith and Culture, Miroslav Volf, defines an institution as "the stable structures of social interaction" that develops when at least two people repeat the same thing together.[16] Theologians like Volf recognize at least two primary factors that shape the life of an institution—the pattern of power distribution and internal cohesion and unity. Volf says, "With regard to the distribution of power, one can distinguish between symmetrical-polycentric and asymmetrical-monocentric models; with regard to cohesion, one can distinguish between coerced and freely affirmed integration."[17] Which of these approaches to leadership demonstrates a healthier approach to power? Which approach models for the community what it means to submit to one another under the headship of Christ, in order to be conformed to his image?

SCIENTIFIC SHIFT

Science has shifted from a mechanical to an organic approach. Kurt Fredrickson states, "This new way of viewing and structuring the world offers a non-mechanistic, more fluid understanding of structures. This new understanding of structures permeates culture and philosophy, organizational theory, natural and social sciences."[18]

Mark Lau Branson compares and contrasts the older scientific paradigm with the emerging new scientific paradigm, which is summarized in table 5.2.[19]

Table 5.2. Classical Sciences Versus New Systems Sciences

Classical Sciences	New Systems Sciences
Newtonian mechanics—discover the parts, their differences, and their interactions	Quantum theory—discover the connectedness in the invisible whole
Accurate descriptions and predictability as we understand enough of the parts	Chaos theory—discontinuity, randomness, unpredictability
Parts are connected through sequences of distinct causes and distinct effects	Simultaneity—the invisible whole features interdependence and instantaneous multiple effects
Change through hierarchy	Self-organizing systems—order arises out of intricate parts
Seek order and continuity through control	Complexity theory—discerns and affirms "order at the edge of chaos" where new images and forces are discovered

Kester Brewin's book *Signs of Emergence: A Vision for Church That Is Organic/Networked/Decentralized/Bottom-up/Communal/Flexible {Always Evolving}* contends that the current demise of the church in the West stems from living in the past instead of progressing into the current context. He calls for the "need to become 'wombs of the divine' and completely rebirth the church into a host culture."[20]

Studies of self-organizing, emergent systems, in areas such as computing, biology and economics, demonstrate the necessity for organization to move from the top-down institutional approach to a bottom-up, adaptable network approach that can meet the challenges of our fast-changing culture. Brewin mentions six characteristics of emergent systems we discover in new science:

1. Emergent systems are open systems.

2. Emergent systems are adaptable systems.

3. Emergent systems are learning systems.

4. Emergent systems have distributed knowledge.

5. Emergent systems model servant leadership.

6. Emergent systems only evolve in places between anarchy and rigidity.[21]

In light of this new environment Brewin proposes the church today must exist at the edge of chaos, between anarchy and rigidity. For in cities or communities where there is overregulation life is stifled or people revolt, and where there is underregulation "the society degenerates into lawlessness."[22] So while a rigid church would have dictatorial, hierarchical leadership, and the anarchic church would have no leadership, the church at the edge of chaos would be more decentralized and have polycentric, servant-hearted leadership.[23]

SPATIALITY SHIFT

The *spatiality shift* from rural living to urban living has created complexities that demand a team of leaders instead of solo leaders. According to the Population Reference Bureau, as recently as 1800 only 3 percent of the world's population lived in urban areas. By 1900 almost 14 percent were urbanites. But it is within this past decade that the world reached a symbolic point, where more than half the world's population now live in urban areas. According to the United Nations, by 2025, 61 percent of the people will live in urban areas.[24] "The world is now an urban place. The resources and concerns of the church need to acknowledge this. This new situation means that, more than ever, theological reflection is needed on cities and the future of urban life."[25]

The shift from rural to urban raises all kinds of issues, from social justice within and outside of the city, to the issue of globalization. Globalization is an amalgamation of new technology; new transportation and new communication networks that have created a global village where time and space have been redefined and old boundaries like nation-state have been blurred. This new world has given rise to new international and transnational entities that are shaping the future with increasing pervasiveness, based in significant cities in the world. The accumulative forces of globalization continue to widen the resource gap and create new questions in regard to social justice, identity and a sense of belonging. If the church is going to live her faith well in the city, she will need a community of leaders who learn to specialize in various ways in order to be a blessing to the neighborhood and world.

RELIGIOUS SHIFT

Finally, there is a *religious shift* taking place in a number of cities in North America, from the Christendom era to the post-Christendom context. A small movement in Jerusalem eventually expanded throughout Judea, Samaria and the rest of the world. The initial ragtag group, many of whom were poor, tended to operate on the margins of society. For the first 250 years they were often misunderstood, maligned and sometimes persecuted. But as they lived as a contrast society in the midst of the Roman Empire, more and more people were attracted to their way of life and to their Lord. They didn't own church buildings or train leaders through formal institutions, and yet their influence expanded into the Roman Empire. By the early fourth century, the Roman emperor Constantine decided to join their ranks, which made way for Theodosius the Great, the last emperor to rule both halves of the Roman Empire, to declare Christianity as the only legitimate imperial religion. These events eventually gave birth to the era called Christendom.

In *The Origins of Christendom in the West*, Alan Kreider identifies three common characteristics of Christendom: common belonging, common belief and common behavior. All the people were a part of both civil society *and* the church (*common belonging*). Infant baptism was the means of initiating children into Christian society. The clergy were professionalized, which exaggerated the difference between clergy and laity. The state and the church were in bed together; the church legitimized the state, and state authorities provided resources and enforcement of religion. Mission was deemphasized while pastoral care and maintenance of structures became central. Religious and civil leaders affirmed orthodox Christianity (*common belief*). Religious education informed the society of its beliefs, and heresy was not tolerated. Christian behavior was based on custom, Scripture and the Ten Commandments (*common behavior*). The church and civil courts persuaded people to keep these behaviors.

When we travel to many of the old cities in Europe, we can see the cultural artifacts of Christendom. Cathedrals are often located in the center of the city and are often the tallest standing structures. People congregated here. To be a part of the church was a privileged position.

Craig Van Gelder argues that in the United States the separation between church and state caused a functional Christendom, without a state church.[26] Functional Christendom refers to the fact that that the church operated as the center of society. But one doesn't have to be a strong cultural observer to recognize that the church no longer has the most favored status in North America. Functional Christendom has given way to a "spiritual," secular and pluralist society where a growing number view at the church with suspicion and some with downright disdain.

As I've already noted, recent studies such as the American Religious Identification Survey in the United States showed a 11 percent drop within a generation in those who self-identify as Christians.[27] Those who claim no identification with religion or faith has grown from 8.2 percent in 1990 to 15 percent in 2008. The nonreligious were the only group to have grown in every state during that period.[28]

Gerard Kelly reveals an important reason for the decline of the church as some parts of North American are experiencing a shift to a post-Christendom context. He reports, "Of all the charges laid at the door of the church by many disaffected young people . . . the most frequent and damning is the charge of *controlling leadership* . . . stifling creativity, stunting innovation and imagination, forcing uniformity, silencing dissent."[29]

Stuart Murray, the British Anabaptist leader, believes that controlling leadership is not only a symptom of fallen humanity but is likely a byproduct of Christendom, when professional clergy had "enhanced status, power and wealth." The church began modeling herself after the Roman systems, perverting the Jesus way of leadership.[30]

Leaders with a Christendom mindset expect to be treated as VIPs within the culture, a dangerous attitude for those who follow the Lord and Savior who "made himself nothing by taking the very nature of a servant" (Phil 2:6-8). To check your leadership attitude, consider how you react when someone treats you as a servant. At that moment leaders discover whether our attitude is more in line with Christ or if we have fallen to a Christendom mindset, expecting to live in a state of privilege.

So how are we to approach leadership in an increasing post-Christendom context? When Stuart Murray pictures the church in the post-Christendom context, he sees a harmonious church. "The image of harmony evokes the Ephesians 4 vision of a multi-gifted, interactive, reciprocal, multi-voiced community."[31] He calls for empowering leadership rather than disempowering clericalism, warning against a Christendom reading of the Ephesians 4, which might lead to leadership dependency. Reading Ephesians 4 with a missional hermeneutic, leaders learn to lead from the margins as priests ministering to fellow priests, with Christ drawing all of us toward himself at the center.

Blogger and author Len Hjalmarson writes, "As ministry decentralizes . . . and as we learn to move away from positions and roles and titles to functional leadership, we are learning to lead from the margins."[32]

- Instead of leading from over, we lead from among.

- Instead of leading from certainty, we lead by exploration, cooperation and faith.

- Instead of leading from power, we lead in emptiness, depending on Jesus.

- Instead of leading from a plan, we lead with attention.

- Instead of leading as managers, we lead as mystics and poets, "speaking poetry in a prose flattened world" and articulating a common future.

- Instead of leading compulsively, we lead with inner freedom.

- Instead of leading from the center, we lead from the margins.[33]

As we consider the *media shift* from the print and broadcast age to the digital age where we live in a more collaborative, open source environment, shared leadership makes more sense than top-down styles.

When considering the *philosophical shift* from modernity to postmodernity, shared leadership engenders greater trust in those who are cynical to truth and power. The *science shift* from classic science to new systems science is demonstrating quite clearly that organic, decentralized structures are to be preferred over mechanistic centralized structures. The *spatiality shift* from rural living to urban living has created complexities that demand a team of leaders instead of solo leaders, and the *religious shift* from Christendom to our post-Christendom context demonstrates the need for apostles, prophets and evangelist in the local congregation, in addition to pastors and teachers.

Living contextually is not optional, for "if we take the incarnation seriously, the Word has to become flesh in every new context."[34] Spirit-shaped leaders create missional culture, and *our approach* to leadership and structure is not neutral. The cultural shifts we are undergoing have highlighted the vulnerabilities of a hierarchical leadership structure, which I will contend in the next few chapters should have never characterized the church in the first place.

6

Hearing the Story

There is no such thing as the New Testament Church order. Even in New Testament times circumstances were very varied, and it may be vital for the ecumenical dialogue that we should admit this. . . . This does not mean, however, that Church order is a matter of indifference, or is to be dictated simply by the existing practical, political, or economic conditions. The New Testament's pronouncements on Church order are to be read as a gospel—that is, Church order is to be regarded as part of the proclamation in which the Church's witness is expressed, as it is in its preaching.

EDUARD SCHWEIZER

I will pour out my Spirit upon all people.
Your sons and daughters will prophesy,
your old men will dream dreams,
your young men will see visions.
Even on my servants, both men and women,
I will pour out my Spirit in those days.

JOEL 2:28-29

I stepped inside a church in the Chicago suburbs and sat down in anticipation of the worship service. As a first-timer and one who loves to observe, my eyes wandered all around, looking at people and my surroundings, taking in as much as I possibly could.

The first thing I noticed was the way the room was organized. This church met in the round. It looked like it seated a couple hundred people. I've seen a number of churches that meet in the round, and typically when it is time for the pastor to preach, where do you suspect he or she stands when preaching? You guessed it. The center. This way the pastor can make good eye contact with each person while sharing the Word of God with the congregation.

But this church was different. When one of the pastors stood to give the word of the Lord, he didn't do it from the center but at the edge of the circle. Instead of chairs being lined up toward a stage, where I saw the back of people's heads and passively took in the message, I was sitting in a circle, looking at the faces of people ready to engage. When the worship began, I noticed how the band was a part of the circle, leading us in worship from the margins of the church.

Then it came time for the reading of Scripture. The four different passages were read from the four corners of the room. The readers read from the edge of the circle. It felt as if the word of the Lord was spreading throughout the earth, from north to south and from east to west. And when it was time for someone to deliver the word, they spoke at the very edge of the circle on the east side. Not the middle. What was in the center of the circle? I think you might be able to guess: a table, the Table with the bread and wine, the Lord's body and blood.

This church understood that the medium is the message. What we do often speaks louder than what we say. In *A Theology of the Built Environment*, T. J. Gorringe argues that theology ought to be concerned about space, architecture, design, public policy, ecological sustainability and city planning, because *all of life expresses our theology*, and even buildings "make moral statements."[1] So what message does *our approach to leadership* proclaim?

LEADERSHIP IN REVELATION

If godly leadership is ultimately about influencing others to pay attention to and follow God with their entire lives so that they might offer themselves as a living sacrifice to God for the sake of the world, then John the Seer gives us a peek at what leadership looks like when God reigns fully.

> Whenever the living creatures give glory, honor and thanks to him who sits on the throne and who lives forever and ever, the twenty-four elders fall down before him who sits on the throne, and worship him who lives for ever and ever. They lay their crowns before the throne and say:
>
> You are worthy, our Lord and God,
>   to receive glory and honor and power,
> for you created all things,
>   and by your will they were created
>   and have their being. (Rev 4:9-11)

We are told earlier in the chapter that God is on his throne, at the center. And around the throne were four living creatures, and beyond them are the twenty-four elders. Eugene Peterson says that the twenty-four elders are a double twelve, "the twelve Hebrew tribes and the twelve Christian apostles, the old Israel and the new Church."[2] If missional leadership is about joining with God and helping people and communities to live up to their sacred potential—living lives of daily worship to God, bringing the reality of his kingdom to bear at home, at work, in the neighborhood and within the congregation—then leading *in* community, in the round, with God at the center might be a good way to approach our leadership. Peterson warns us that failure to worship God together removes our center and "consigns us to a life of spasms and jerks, at the mercy of every advertisement, every seduction, every siren. . . . People who do not worship are swept into a vast restlessness, epidemic in the world, with no steady direction and so sustaining purpose."[3]

With God at the center, the leaders of the church are at the periphery. Part of our job as leaders is to consistently help people remember that we are under-shepherds who, like them, are seeking to follow the Shepherd of our souls, who is the Head of the church. Our approach to leadership should reflect this approach. We should mirror on earth what is in heaven.

LEADERSHIP IN THE HEBREW SCRIPTURE

Polycentric leadership seems like a good idea in our context, but don't we need leaders like Moses and David and Deborah in our day? Don't they exemplify what we need in godly leaders? Despite their faults, these leaders are among the great leaders in the Hebrew Scripture, from whom we can learn much. When we talk about leadership in general, there are various *kinds* of leadership that God uses at various *times* to accomplish his purposes, which is why we must be like the leaders of Issachar, *understanding our times* so that we know what course we should take (1 Chron 12:32).

When God wanted to call a people out of four hundred years of slavery, he used a humble leader like Moses to help deliver his people from the oppressive regime of Pharaoh so that God might bless his people and that they in turn might be a blessing to all nations. It seems that God uses situational leadership. In other words, differing *situations* require different approaches to leadership at different times, even when aiming for an ideal. This is why structure ought to submit to Spirit, and as we pursue an approach to leadership that reflects heaven on earth, we must approach it dynamically instead of with rigidity.

Those who study the topic of leadership typically ask three questions: What type of person makes a good leader? What does a good leader do? What kind of leadership does our current situation demand? So you have various kinds of leaders with varying styles. Discernment requires knowing what the situation demands.

Unique to the Old Testament is the depiction of God forming a people, a nation, to be a light to the other nations, using various forms of leadership within Israel at different stages. Israel, being a nation, not only had religious leaders but political authorities as well. There were judges and eventually kings who were often critiqued and balanced by the prophets. Each tribe had elders. And there were priests as well as those who studied, transcribed and taught the Torah, the scribes, the sages and the rabbis.[4]

The following are a couple of things worth pointing out relating to the Old Testament. First, reading through the Hebrew Scripture, we get the sense that God desires to rule his people directly and personally. At the same time, his people desire a tangible mediator between them and God.

As God was working through Moses' leadership, he desired to speak to Moses in a way that *all* could hear God's voice. So Moses had the people consecrate themselves, and he instructed them to stand at the foot of the mountain to meet with God. Then God spoke the Ten Commandments, but "When the people saw the thunder and lightning and heard the trumpet and saw the mountain in smoke, they trembled with fear. They stayed at a distance, and said to Moses, 'Speak to us yourself and we will listen. But do not have God speak to us or we will die'" (Ex 20:18-19). They were more comfortable with Moses mediating God's presence to them.

We see the idea of the people wanting a mediator a second time. The elders of Israel came to Samuel to let him know they wanted a king like other nations since Samuel was growing old and his sons had become corrupt. So Samuel went to the Lord about the matter. How did God respond? "It is not you they have rejected, but they have rejected me as their king. . . . Now listen to them; but warn them solemnly and let them know what the king who will reign over them will claim as his rights" (1 Sam 8:7, 9). Samuel warned them that the king would create a powerful centralize government, send their sons to war and take the best of what they created for himself. He warned them that as this happens, they would come running back to God, but God would not answer them.

In spite of this warning, the people insisted on a king, and so God allowed it. Sure enough, as we read through the Scriptures, we discover that there weren't many good kings. They were never meant to wear "the ring." Only a holy God can handle that kind of power. We aren't designed to sit on God's throne; we were designed to be God's vice-regents, acting together as his stewards, and reflecting this in our approach to leadership.

The third and final development in regard to the Hebrew Scriptures is how the prophets painted a trajectory for the fuller participation of the people of God in responsibility and leadership. Isaiah paints the picture of the new heavens and new earth. Joel speaks of the day when God's Spirit would be poured out in such a way that both men and women, old and young, servants and maid servants will experience new empowerment from God. Interestingly enough, Joel also talks about blood, fire and smoke, reminding us of the same elements present at the foot of the mountain, when God wanted to speak to his people directly and personally at Mt. Sinai.

God allowed Israel to have a king, but the visions of John the Seer, Isaiah and Joel show us that God's ideal may be quiet different. In the Hebrew Scriptures we see that God is at work among his people, so that the elders or leaders are leading as a community, as a circle in the round, with the chief Shepherd at the center. God uses prophets, priests, rabbis, scribes, elders and even kings to pull people toward God's future.

LEADERSHIP IN THE GOSPELS

By the time we get to the Gospels, the chief Shepherd has come; the one who sits at the right hand of the Father has arrived. The King is now living in flesh and blood among the people of God. What does this human who was God and this God who was human have to teach us about leadership?

First, notice that Jesus didn't call one person to be a senior shepherd and others to be assistants. Why? Maybe the best way we act as image bearers is to lead as under-shepherds as opposed to senior shepherds. Calling the Twelve obviously evokes a connection to the twelve tribes of Israel and gives us a clue to Jesus' mission. And while three disciples were part of Jesus inner circle, he didn't promote solo leadership, and typically warned against people desiring the greater role.

So, how can our leadership best mirror what has been delivered to us from heaven? Leadership in the round, in community, with God at the center, offers a tangible picture of the kind of leadership that moves others to pay attention to and follow God with their entire lives, using their gifts and passions to build the body of Christ and bless the world.

But doesn't the church require a flesh and blood quarterback to call the plays and give the instructions so that the team can reach goal line? This is a fair and practical question. It moves the conversation from theory to practice in important ways. It may be one of the reasons the disciples continually argued about who among them was the greatest. After all, someone needs to lead, right? Someone needs to push things forward, right?

Let's look a little deeper at the disciples' argument. John 13 helps set the stage. Let me walk you through a summary of how Gayle Erwin thinks the Last Supper went down, because I find it compelling.[5] It is Passover. Jesus knew that his time had come. He is getting ready to show the full extent of his love. Then we are told that "Jesus knew that the Father had put all things under his power, and that he had come from God and was returning to God" (Jn 13:3).

So Jesus has all power, and he knows who he is and whose he is. There is something freeing about knowing who we are in God, for when we know who we are, there is no need to prove ourselves to others. Jesus has all power, but what is he going to do with it? What would you do if you had *all* power?

Before looking at what he does, let's place the story in its historical context. The Roman triclinium (Latin for "three couches") was the most common table of the day, primarily found in the finer homes, which is where Jesus and the disciple met for the Last Supper. It was a low table that looked like a squared off horseshoe. The way the seating was arranged, according to archaeologist and theologian James Fleming, is that the table at the left was the head table, with the host, guest of honor and the right-hand man (or assistant).[6] And then the rest of the guests would sit from left to right in decreasing order of rank.

Jesus asked, when you go to a banquet, which seat should you take? The lowest, right? If you sat yourself at a higher seat and the host came and asked you to move, that would be quite embarrassing. With this historical backdrop, we can see now why this was one of the most common apostolic arguments. Every time they sat down to eat, the issue of rank arose. With this in mind, let's see if we can figure where some of the disciples may have been sitting. We know that Jesus was the host, and we also have a suspicion of who may have been sitting in the right-hand man's position: John said of himself that he was the disciple that Jesus loved, who leaned against his breast.[7]

We can also place the guest of honor, because the custom in that day echoes ours. Having a meal with others carried a significant social meaning for the people of God. To eat with someone was to literally become a part of them. Thus the Pharisees consistently critiqued Jesus for eating with the "tax collectors and sinners." In that day, the host and the guest of honor would typically dip from the same bowl. The host would often start the banquet by taking the first bit and putting it into the mouth of the guest of honor, saying, "You do me honor." Who dipped into the bowl with Jesus? Judas.

While we know *who* the rest were at the table, we don't know *where* they sat, until we get to the person at the lowest seat. For at one point Jesus said, "One of you will betray me" (Mt 26:21). They all asked, "Is it I?" Then Peter signaled across the table to John and said, "Ask him which one he means" (Jn 13:24-25). What is Peter doing in the seat reserved for the least? This is no place for a pope, is it?

Some suggest that Peter lost the argument. Maybe Peter argued for a high seat and lost the argument. Peter says, "Hey guys, I was with him on the Mount of Transfiguration." And they might have replied, "Yeah, and who got it wrong and wanted to build three tabernacles?" Peter comes back, "But who had the great revelation that Jesus is the Messiah?" And they say, "Yeah, to whom did he say, 'Get behind me Satan'?"

What was Peter doing in the last seat? Some people think that as they were arguing about who was the greatest, Peter finally started to remember Jesus' teaching about how the rulers of this world lord it over people and flaunt their authority, but whoever wants to become great in the kingdom becomes a servant, and the greatest a slave. So Peter decided to sit in the last seat.

But here is the thing, even if you choose the lowest seat in a moment of humility, it is difficult not to get a bit uncomfortable and feel the need to prove to the rest that you do not actually belong there. Peter's discomfort in the lowest seat probably brought tension to the table.

Finally, the supper is being served and nobody's feet had been washed. To welcome a guest in Jesus' day, the host would wash the guests feet. The job went to the one of lowest rank in the household, normally a servant. I can imagine the guys thinking, *Why isn't Peter washing our feet?* And Peter thinking, *I'm not going to wash anyone's feet. If I do, they will think that I belong here.* So things were uncomfortable because everyone's feet were dirty.

Remember, in this tense situation, Jesus holds all the power—the power that flung the galaxies into being, the power to raise the dead—and his disciples get into another argument of who is the greatest. So Jesus gets up from the table and straightened out his guests. Is that what happened? No, it says he got up and started washing their feet.

Oh, so this is what you do when you want to show the full extent of your love. This is what you do when you have all power but aren't corrupted by it. This is what you do when you are confidant of who you truly are.

What form of leadership best demonstrates what Jesus consistently tried to teach the disciples? A symmetrical monocentric approach to leadership, which the apostles argued over, or an asymmetrical polycentric approach to leadership, which Jesus seemed to encourage?

LEADERSHIP IN ACTS AND THE EPISTLES

It's Pentecost. The Holy Spirit falls on the church and the people speak in tongues, and everyone hears the good news in their own language. As this is happening Peter recognizes that the prophecy of Joel was coming to light. The Holy Spirit fell upon people regardless of their sex, age or social status. In the New Testament we see women as apostles, teachers, evangelists and prophets. We see the poor empowered by the Spirit just as much as the rich. God's favor fell upon all without discrimination.

The church in Jerusalem was led by a plurality of leaders, James, Peter and John being among them (Gal 2:9). At the church in Antioch we see a variously gifted multiethnic leadership team worshiping, fasting and looking to the Holy Spirit for direction. And as they were in community and communion, Barnabus and Saul were "sent on their way by the Holy Spirit" (Acts 13:4).

While the book of Acts is commonly referred to as the Acts of the Apostles, it actually records the acts of the Holy Spirit. The Holy Spirit was guiding people in mission, giving direction, motivating, encouraging and comforting the people throughout the early church.

We learn a lot about early church leadership through the council described in Acts 15. The question they sought to answer is: Does one have to become a Jew in order to become a Christian? A community of leaders took time to debate, share their experiences, examine Scripture and look at how God worked through history. When coming to a conclusion that the Gentiles didn't have to become Jews to be Christian, we see how they were led by the Spirit (Acts 15:28). Whether strategic decision making, like sending Paul and Barnabas, or theological decision making, like the gathering of the first council, decision making was done in the context of a community of gifted leaders who sought to follow Christ under the guidance and direction of the Holy Spirit.

The picture given throughout Acts and the Epistles is that the under-shepherds live together as a communal example, priests ministering to fellow priests, not lording it over others but recognizing the need to care for, encourage and exhort those entrusted to them by the chief Shepherd, Jesus Christ. As they follow Christ and share the Word by the power of the Spirit, the people of God respond to the work of the Holy Spirit in their lives, and more leaders (elders) are raised up to equip others. As this happens the current leaders appoint new leaders (elders) in every church, based on the Spirit's work (character, knowledge and skill development) in their lives, so that they might exercise their gifts for the common good. As a result, the entire people of God contribute to the building up of the body of Christ and expanding the kingdom.

We see in the book of Ephesians that Christ has given the church—apostles, prophets, evangelists, pastors and teachers—to collectively equip the entire body so that it would build itself up in a love. And the church's love spilled into the entire world, from Jerusalem and Judea and Samara to the uttermost parts of the earth.

Throughout the New Testament letters, we are reminded that Christ is at the center. He is the quarterback. He is on the throne, not the pastors and teachers. We see that the apostles, prophets, evangelists, pastors and teachers live in communion with God, and in community with each other and under the guidance and power of the Holy Spirit they are pulled toward the John the Seer's vision in Revelation.

Recognizing God is at the center, the elders lead in the round, serving at the periphery to activate the entire people of God to use their gifts in bringing the blessing of Christ to their cities and world.

Sitting in the round, encircling the Table of bread and wine, the church I visited in the suburbs of Chicago reflected the heavenly reality of God at the center.

7

Deepening Theological Roots

*Theological commitment must be applied to life—to the theologian's
own Christian walk and to the life of the church—in order that faith
can issue forth in discipleship.*

STANLEY GRENZ

*For the word of God is alive and active. Sharper than any doubled-
edged sword, it penetrates even to dividing soul and spirit, joints and
marrow; it judges the thoughts and attitudes of the heart.*

HEBREWS 4:12

"In the beginning is communion."[1] Scripture and subsequent creeds
testify that before the foundation of the world, for all eternity, God has
existed in perfect community as Father, Son and Holy Spirit. God is
not the solitary One. He is neither lonely nor alone. From the beginning
the Father, Son and Holy Spirit have been in an unending dance of
mutual enjoyment and love for one another. God abides in rich community. As theologian Leonardo Boff writes, "Community is the
deepest and most foundational reality that exist."[2]

In *After Our Likeness* Miroslav Volf writes that we live in a society
where "faith lived ecclesially is being replaced by a faith lived individualistically."[3] A common saying in our day is, "I like Jesus, but I hate the

church." Why? Volf, along with many others, says that "people in modern societies have little sympathy for top-down organizations, including for churches structured top-down."[4]

THE SOCIAL TRINITY AND LEADERSHIP

How should our understanding of the inner relationship (social aspect) of the Trinity shape our approach to leadership? As we understand and reflect on the social Trinity and allow our understanding of the relational nature of God to shape our approach to leadership, we will become more interdependent, communal, relational, participatory, self-surrendering and self-giving. In the first section of this chapter I will bring Volf's and Boff's thoughts into the conversation. [5]

While the Trinity is the ultimate reality revealed in Scripture, the doctrine of the Trinity is the attempt of the church to give a greater understanding and explanation of the Father, Son and Spirit. Because it is second-order speech, the articulation of the doctrine of the Trinity has continued to evolve through the church's history. Boff makes the case that there are three primary developments of trinitarian thought, each of which arose to address particular errors in a given culture and time.[6] First, in Roman culture, where polytheism was prevalent, the Latin fathers emphasized the oneness of God. When the Greek fathers were battling Arianism or modalism, they focused more on the diversity in God. Ultimately they settled on unity through diversity. Finally, in our context, where individualism reigns, we ought to focus on the social Trinity, looking at the rich, mutually encouraging and mutual dependent relationship between the Father, Son and Spirit.

The social view of the Trinity puts emphasis on this relational nature of God. For Boff, "The trinitarian vision produces a vision of a church that is more communion than hierarchy, more service than power, more circular than pyramidal, more loving embrace then bending the knee before authority."[7] He believes that one of the best ways to help overcome clericalism and authoritarianism in the church is through a radical trinitarian understanding of God.[8]

Volf considers the Trinity to be a loving community of persons, each fully sharing all the divine attributes. He therefore finds it inconceivable to find *eternal* hierarchy and subordination within the perfect community.[9]

Central to Boff's and Volf's understanding of the relational nature of the Trinity is the Eastern Orthodox notion of *perichoresis*, which has no good translation into English. It can be roughly understood as interpenetration, where each divine person permeates and is permeated by the others without confusion. Jesus speaks of this intimate union when he says, "the Father is in me, and I in the Father" (Jn 10:38). This union is dynamic and reciprocal. As Boff says, "Each Person is *for* the others, *with* the others and *in* the others. The everlasting love that pervades them and forms them unites them in a current of life so infinite and complex as to constitute the unity between them."[10] This mutual embodiment means they each share in each other's work. The Son and Spirit join the Father in creation; the Father and Spirit join the Son in redemption; and the Father and Son join the Spirit in sanctification, which doesn't preclude there being primary actions of each person. So how does the inner life of the Trinity speak to our ecclesiology and approach to leadership?

The ontological (nature of being) and relational understanding of the Trinity leads Volf to conclude that the ecclesiastical structure that most corresponds to the social Trinity does not divide the church between the general and particular priesthood, but holds to the equality of the priesthood of all believers. He believes that a polycentric approach to officers in the church best reflects Scripture and the social Trinity. For Volf, ordination is a matter of divine gifting, character and reception by the entire congregation under the guidance of the Spirit.[11] While ordination is not necessarily to be considered an appointment to a lifelong task, he considers gifted leadership to be more lasting than other gifts, for leadership adds to the stability, cohesion and unity of the whole.

For Boff, when the church models itself after the *perichoresis* of the Trinity, there will be an emphasis on interdependency, mutual care, intimate sharing and mutual self-giving. Boff reminds us that all in the church are born from a response of faith, and that all Christians are to be students of Christ, and the entire church is called to make disciples. Learning and teaching (with power) are two functions, not divisions in the church. "They are two adjectives that describe two practices of the whole community. They are not two nouns that split the community."[12] Boff allows hierarchy to develop within the community when it is good for the community and all remember that we are first brothers and sisters. For "before hierarchies and differences, Jesus sought to introduce fellowship, participation, community."[13] Leadership, for Boff, comes *after* community, not before.

Reflection on the social Trinity reminds us of the importance of the priesthood of all believers, and that the five equippers in Ephesians 4 are to be a community of leaders within the community, as priests equipping fellow priests. As we seek to imitate God in our approach to leadership, we ought to remember that "Believing in the Trinity means that truth is on the side of *community* rather than exclusion; *consensus* translates truth better than imposition; the *participation* of the many is better than the dictate of a single one."[14]

COMMUNAL NATURE OF THE CHURCH AND LEADERSHIP

Growing up in a culture where individuality reigns supreme, I can see how it has affected the church's approach to being the church. There are a number of theologians today who properly emphasize community and communion while retaining a sense of personhood. Stanley Grenz's emphasis on the nature of the church as "the eschatological covenant community" is profound and has practical implications for today, especially in the way we approach leadership. Michael Battle puts it brilliantly when he says, "Christian life is not about an aggregate of individuals in pursuit of their experience of God, but a communal way of being in which Christian pilgrims and disciples display relationships and behaviors akin to how Christ displayed relationships and behaviors."[15]

We in the West tend to start with the oneness of God, but John Zizioulas and the church in the East begin with the three-in-one God. Thus God in community is foundational for Eastern Orthodox ecclesiology. And since the church is the icon of the Trinity, true personhood is found in community. Becoming a Christian is moving from "biological individuality" to "ecclesial personhood."[16] When we become members of the church, we take on God's "way of being," and this way of being is in communion with God and community with others. And when we come to the Communion Table, we are reminded that the work of Christ constituted by the Spirit "anticipates the eschatological gathering of the *whole* people of God."[17] While the church in the East emphasizes the communal nature of the church, "every form of communion which denies or suppresses the person is unadmissable."[18]

How does this communal approach shape our approach to leadership? I propose that the church ought to be led by a Spirit-gifted polycentric team of apostles, prophets, evangelists, pastors and teachers who model and equip *their fellow priests* in the communal way of life patterned after our triune God. Then we can more fully follow Christ into the world for the sake of the world, by the power of the Holy Spirit, where we seek to join God in the renewal of all things.

THE POWERS AND LEADERSHIP

The last time I was in Rome I was able to see the pope. I happened to be in St. Peter's square and discovered that Pope John Paul II would be speaking there that afternoon. So my friends and I managed to get tickets and sat among the massive audience and listened to the pope speak in Latin. Of course, I didn't understand a thing he said. But what struck me was the atmosphere. I couldn't help but compare the picture that was in front of me with the picture of Jesus at the Last Supper and his walk toward the cross. Before my eyes was a man dressed in a white robe with a literal crown on his head. To his left and right were men dressed in bright red, the cardinals. People kissed the pope's ring.

Pope John Paul II, in my estimation, did some amazing things in his life. But this picture puzzled me. (It is likely that I am ignorant of the symbolism.) As I was taking in this scene, the picture of Jesus washing his disciples' feet came to mind. I then started to think about how much of Jesus' ministry was involved in subverting the status quo in the religious and political world of his day, and as a result was stripped of his dignity. On his way to the cross, he didn't wear a crown bedecked with jewels but a crown of thorns. They didn't kiss his ring but spat in his face. The contrast remains with me. Sometimes I wonder, *What system is at work here?*

Not long after my trip to Rome, I took a trip to San Diego to meet with some Christian leaders in the city. As I was waiting to meet the senior pastor of a megachurch, this young associate pastor was giving me the rundown on the different churches and pastors in the city. He mentioned how they often argued about prominent seating on the podium during large gatherings. They likewise argued about who would speak at what event.

As he was speaking, I thought, *We Protestants may not wear fancy clothes and crowns; we are a bit more subtle in our approach to power. Yet we seem to be under the spell of the same system.* I've felt myself under this spell. It seems that only a few, people like Mother Teresa, have been able to break this spell.

Why is this the case? Part of the reason is that too many of us believe that structures are neutral. The longer I live, the more I realize that we shape structures and then the structures reshape us. I've known too many godly people who seemed to have unknowingly or unwittingly become more corrupt because of the system and structure of ministry. As I look to Scripture, it's obvious that Jesus wears the ring, not us. We are to live by the power of the Spirit as a community of believers, seeking to wash feet so that power doesn't do its subversive work in us.

When churches mirror the CEO model in American business rather than the polycentric model we see in Scripture, what can we expect? If we baptize a particular model with Christian language, will we somehow be exempt from its ability to squeeze us into its mold? Throughout Scripture we are told about two main strategies that the evil one uses to shape us toward death-oriented behaviors. One is a personal strategy; the other is a corporate strategy, which in the Scripture is described as "the world" or "the systems of this world." This is why John warns us not to love "the world," its cravings and lust (1 Jn 2:15-16). James says, "where you have envy and selfish ambition, there you will find disorder and every evil practice" (Jas 3:16).

Scripture speaks of the world system or the kingdoms of this world. What does this mean? Walter Wink explains,

All of us deal with the Powers That Be. They staff our hospitals, run City Hall, sit around tables in corporate boardrooms, collect our taxes, and head our families. But the Powers That Be are more than just the people who run things. They are the systems themselves, the institutions and structures that weave society into an intricate fabric of power and relationships. These Powers surround us on every side. They are necessary. They are useful. We could do nothing without them. Who wants to do without timely mail delivery or well-maintained roads? But the Powers are also the source of unmitigated evils.[19]

There is much more to say here. The point I want to make is that structures are not neutral. Structures are theological statements. If our structures mirror "the way of the world," they will shape us powerfully and unknowingly. Structures must be developed with the theological intent to be a sign of God's coming kingdom. I'm not saying that we are unable to learn from organizational dynamics and other fields of study. But we must scrutinize our methods, realizing that the means are just as important as the ends, for the means shape us to a particular end. It has been said that Christianity started out in Palestine as a fellowship, moved to Greece and became a philosophy, went to Rome and became an institution, spread to Europe and became a government, and finally crossed the Atlantic to America where it became an enterprise. What will it take for us to return to fellowship?

THE WORD AND THE SPIRIT AND LEADERSHIP

One of the ways to deal with unhealthy structures is by having a balance between Christ and the Spirit in our approach to being the church. Some communities of faith are heavy on the *Logos* or the Word, and light on the Spirit. Others are heavy on the Spirit and light on the Word. But we must remember that the Father sent the Son (Word made flesh) and the Spirit to birth and shape the church. Thus every congregation is a combination of the concrete *and* spiritual, objective *and* subjective.

Because Christ is the Word made flesh, he is a concrete pattern for our lives. Yet we must hold this in tension with the Spirit, who, like the wind, blows where he pleases.

When it comes to Christ, some only focus on his death. While we need to maintain a focus on the cross, we are simultaneously called to imitate Christ's life and believe that through his resurrection we can live Spirit-imbibed lives in hope of our eschatological communal future.

As a community of faith, we need to hold to the most basic beliefs about Christ, which include his identity, mission, priority, grace and example. In regard to his identity, Jesus is God, the Son, Savior and Lord of the universe, who was born of a virgin and coexists eternally with the Father and Spirit. His mission was to inaugurate the kingdom of God on earth, and he calls us to follow him in the renewal of all things. His priority and creed is that we are to love God and people, especially the least of these. His grace is extended to us in many ways. Through his incarnation he is our priest and can identify with our weaknesses. Through his death he makes it possible for us to be reconciled to our triune God, and through his resurrection and ascension he gives us power through the Spirit to live godly lives. Through his return he gives us hope of a new heaven and a new earth. And through his example he demonstrates what it means to be mature human beings, and he calls us through the power of the Spirit to follow him as the liberator of those who have been oppressed by the system, the lover of those who have been rejected by society and the deliverer of those who have been seduced by consumerism.

The Father also sent the Spirit. The Scriptures speak of the Spirit being the life, breath, wind, fire, water, cloud, dove and *paraclete*.[20] When the church is understood as charismatic in essence, it is seen as a charismatic fellowship of equal persons, the priesthood of all believers. This guards against an overinstitutionalization. The work of the Spirit is not just limited to salvation or to the church; the work of the Spirit is unlimited. The Spirit's work is cosmic in nature. Humans are made with an openness and capacity to encounter God. God's Spirit gives light to all people and woos all people to Christ. Yet while God is at work in all people and all of life, from politics to life-giving projects, in creation, redemption and the coming consummation, he is also at work through special revelation, seeking to reveal with greater clarity who he is and the future he is helping to bring about.

The beauty of the church is that it was not only born of the Spirit at Pentecost, but Christ through the Spirit continues to accomplish his works by giving gifts to each person who confesses Christ, for the sake of the building up of the body to accomplish his work in the world. When it comes to power distribution, it is ultimately the role of the Spirit, not any human or humanly made structures. While humans can try to control things and live with a rigid hierarchy, real authority comes from above, and those who live by the Spirit seek to live on the edge of chaos (between rigidity and anarchy). The Spirit freely gifts the entire priesthood of believers with no regard to gender, age or race. He has also given the church through Christ a polycentric leadership community to lead the church, as opposed to a single leader, so that the body and the world would be drawn to the Head of the church—Christ.

Our approach to leadership makes a theological statement to the church and to the world. If we desire to be a church that is a sign and foretaste of God's coming kingdom, we will seek to reflect our triune God and our communal nature in all we do. We will recognize that structure is not neutral; every structure is a theological statement. We will also appreciate both the ministry of the Son and the Spirit as we live as a community of leaders to build the church and bless the world.

8

Embracing Emotional Health

In emotionally healthy churches, people live and lead out of brokenness and vulnerability. They understand that leadership in the kingdom of God is from the bottom up, not a grasping, controlling, or lording over others. It is leading out of failure and pain, questions and struggles—a serving that lets go. It is a noticeably different way of life from what is commonly modeled in the world and, unfortunately, in many churches.

PETER SCAZZERO

God opposes the proud but shows favor to the humble.

JAMES 4:6

I could tell that his story was still recent and raw, for as this church planter shared with me the emotional hurts he had endured in his attempt to plant a church in a large East Coast city I could feel his heart breaking right before me. His core team decided that they no longer wanted to follow his leadership, so they proceeded to carry out a spiritual mutiny, which left my friend emotionally scarred, probably for life. My heart was touched by his story. As he shared, I could relate to the emotional hits he and other leaders have had to endure in ministry. I have had to endure severe emotional blows in my life, sometimes to the point that I have wanted to throw in the towel and quit—not just my ministry but my life.

EMOTIONAL HEALTH AND LEADERSHIP

A few years ago I was taking a course at Fuller Theological Seminary. The primary purpose of the class was to take time to reflect deeply on our entire life from many different angles so that we might finish well. Bobby Clinton and his team, after studying over a thousand biblical, historical and contemporary leader's lives, discovered that 70 percent of those who begin their spiritual journey well end poorly. They also unearthed five practices that were common among the 30 percent of the leaders who finished well. They engaged in experiences that renewed them; they practiced spiritual disciplines; they had a learning posture; they had ten to fifteen significant mentors in life; and they had a broad perspective.

To gain perspective we created a unique time line, breaking our lives into different segments or phases and then looking at each of these phases from different angles. Part of the exercise included assessing the physical, emotional, financial and vocational parts of our lives. We looked at the highs and lows in these areas, our hurts and difficulties as well as our progress and victories. As I engaged in this exercise I recognized that the first five years of my church plant at Virginia Tech and my church plants in Los Angeles, were some of my toughest.

During my first five years in Los Angeles I was fortunate to plant the church with a co-leader, equal in authority and complementary in gifting. We needed encouragement from each other because we both took many difficult hits. In examining how I was doing physically during these years, I realized I had gone through quite a bit. I was involved in a significant car accident. I had my computer stolen while meeting needs in Africa, and another computer ruined by a flood in my apartment. I had an anonymous threatening letter sent to me after an *Los Angeles Times* article was published about our church. This was a greater emotional hit than I thought it would be. In addition, someone smashed my driver's side car window and stole some important items. On top of all that, I had a bout with shingles and found out that I was grinding my teeth due to stress.

Financially, I can see that God provided in many rich ways. But during the last part of these years I still lived under tremendous financial stress. This was due in part to planting another church during this phase and choosing to redirect some of my funding to new leaders.

A surfing analogy applies well to those first five years. We make some progress as we paddle our way into the ocean, but then a wave hits us. We continue to paddle and make more progress, but then another wave hits us and knocks us back. We get farther out, but then a huge wave comes that pulls us under into what surfers call the "washing machine." But we somehow make it out and come up for air, though not without causalities. Some of my teammates became exhausted during this trying time, others were hurt, and some lost hope.

Some got "called" to another city after the first wave. A few more moved to another city after the second wave, and some sought to find another church in the city. This is always difficult. Statistically, you will lose half or more of your church team during the first year or two of your church plant. But losing people, no matter the number, is difficult to take emotionally.

In all the areas that I examined in my life, I've taken the hardest hits in the emotional area. I've known what it feels like to be stabbed in the back. I have at times felt the repercussions of speaking out for peace and working for the poor. I don't have the time or the emotional energy to share the degree and duration of the hurt and pain I experienced during the first five years in LA. But I can identify with the apostle Paul as it relates to some of his emotional hits he incurred in his ministry (2 Cor 11).

Having a co-leader from the beginning of the church plant allowed us to split the pain and multiply the joy. As I listened to the pain shared by the East Coast church planter, I couldn't help but think that if he had started that church with a shared polycentric leadership approach, that church *may* still be alive and bringing more of God's kingdom to that particular city. Polycentric leadership can be good for one's emotional health.

BROKENNESS AND LEADERSHIP

Genuine shared leadership has the potential to help us experience healing and pursue wholeness in our lives as leaders, whereas a senior- or lead-pastor approach to leadership tends to isolate the leader. It doesn't matter whether the person is at the top (like a CEO) or the bottom of the pyramid (servant leadership), by nature of authority, title and function the person is isolated and separated from the rest of the body.

Because no one has equal authority, there are no peer relationships within this approach to leadership. And when we have no peer relationships, it can be difficult to open up our hearts and deal with our emotional pain. Dan Allender and Tremper Longman remind us how important it is for us to listen to our emotions and work through them well:

> Ignoring our emotions is turning our back on reality; listening to our emotions ushers us into reality. And reality is where we meet God. If we want to know God, we must ponder and struggle with our feelings to gain an understanding of the passions that rule us. . . .
>
> Emotions are the language of the soul. They are the cry that gives the heart a voice. To understand our deepest passions and convictions, we must learn to listen to the cry of the soul.
>
> However, we often turn a deaf ear—through emotional denial, distortion, or disengagement. We strain out anything disturbing in order to gain tenuous control of our inner world. . . . In neglecting our intense emotions, we are false to ourselves and lose a wonderful opportunity to know God. We forget that change comes through brutal honesty and vulnerability before God.[1]

I would add, transformation and change takes place when we are brutally honest and vulnerable with one another. In fact, according to James, some healing only comes about through mutual confession (Jas 5:16).

In the polycentric model, people with equal authority and revolving leadership lead as a community and continually pursue wholeness together. Thus they serve as an example for the entire community of faith. Because more is caught than taught, maturity modeled by a team of leaders shapes the community in profound ways. Most of our brokenness comes from dysfunctional experiences in our family or community, and most healing and wholeness will come in the context of Spirit-transforming communities with Christ as the Head. Leaders need community to pursue wholeness. When we lead as an interdependent team of equippers, each of us models various strengths to others and honestly live with our weaknesses. In this way, we preach Christ and not ourselves.

Sure, community has its difficulties. Henri Nouwen explains:

Nothing is sweet or easy about community. Community is a fellowship of people who do not hide their joys and sorrows but make them visible to each other in a gesture of hope. In community we say: "Life is full of gains and losses, joys and sorrows, ups and downs—but we do not have to live it alone. We want to drink our cup together and thus celebrate the truth that the wounds of our individual lives, which seem intolerable when lived alone, become sources of healing when we live them as a part of a fellowship of mutual care"[2]

Jesus gathered a community of disciples (his future leaders) around him; doesn't it make sense for us to lead as a part of a community, from within a community?

POWER AND LEADERSHIP

It was Lord Acton who coined the phrase, "power tends to corrupt, and absolute power corrupts absolutely." Life often bears this out—unless we learn to use power to serve in the way of Jesus. We have all seen the corrupting nature of power on good people, which is why this adage is oft repeated. It has become a modern proverb in our time.

But another proverb from our time is just as vital to understand. It comes from the pen of Rosabeth Moss Kanter at Harvard Business School. "Powerlessness corrupts. Absolute powerlessness corrupts absolutely."[3] When people feel like a cog in the wheel of someone else's vision instead of a person made in the image of God and called to live in community, it leads to a sense of powerlessness.

I'm extremely grateful that after my conversion experience in college, the first group I connected with had adopted a missional perspective of the church. From the outset they helped me realize that God has called me into the priesthood, with its corresponding privileges and responsibilities. They nurtured me in such a way as to remind me of God's work in me and through me. The whole clergy versus laity dichotomy was not in their repertoire, for we are all priests.

I was encouraged to follow Christ in my everyday life, and as I did, I started to learn the different ways that God had gifted me. They never held me back; they simply walked with me, seeking to fan into flame the power of the Spirit at work within me. I was leading a Bible study after a month and a house church within a year. Within four years of running hard with the Lord by engaging in missional praxis (practice in dynamic relation with thought), they felt I was ready to lead the church.

When I look at any Christ follower, I see a priest with a calling. The role of the equippers, especially those gifted as apostles, is to help people discover and live out their calling in a way that builds the community and blesses the world. When gifted equippers see everyone as a priest, they understand that their role is not to empower others but to recognize how the Holy Spirit has empowered these people, and help them release that power within the congregation and the world. For "powerlessness corrupts, and absolute powerlessness corrupts absolutely."

FOLLOWING AND LEADERSHIP

Lead pastors find themselves constantly leading. They are the ultimate point person. The buck stops with them. Always. All the time. Constantly. Without reprieve. With this kind of pressure, is it any wonder why so many have fallen?

Lead pastors tend to forget their fundamental identity as a follower. In essence, to be a Christian is to be a *follower* of Jesus. Yet when all we do is lead, we sometimes forget how to follow. We say that all good leaders know how to follow, but when we put people in positions where they rarely if ever follow anyone, they lose their follower instinct.

Lead pastors constantly lead. Then we wonder why they have problems with pride and feel indispensable to the mission. But we are all dispensable. God doesn't need us. He just chooses to use us, and only temporarily at that. But when we lead within a community of revolving leaders, we engage in the practice of both following and leading, which facilitates growth in both humility and confidence. Geese travel long distances with revolving leadership; so too can church leaders. I trust we are smarter than geese.

An emotional healthy approach to leadership is polycentric. Within such a community we learn to lead *and* follow, to share our brokenness and victories, and to help each other mature in Christ for his honor and glory.

9

Relinquishing the Need to Control

With the disappearance of God the Ego moves forward to become the sole divinity.

DOROTHEE SÖLLE

> *Two are better than one,*
> > *because they have a good return for their labor:*
> *If either of them falls down,*
> > *one can help the other up.*
> *But pity anyone who falls*
> > *and has no one to help them up.*
> *Also, if two lie down together, they will keep warm.*
> > *But how can one keep warm alone?*
> *Though one may be overpowered,*
> > *two can defend themselves.*
> *A cord of three strands is not quickly broken.*

ECCLESIASTES 4:9-12

I've been encouraged that a number of contemporary churches are exploring the polycentric approach to leadership. From church starts like New Denver Church to mid-sized churches like Life on the Vine in the Chicago suburbs, to larger churches like Riverview Church in East

Lansing, Michigan, to movements of churches like the base grass-roots communities in Latin America, the Spirit is at work seeking to restore missional leadership to the church.

Contemporary churches that approach leadership in a polycentric way tend to see Jesus and the Spirit as the center of their community, not a single human leader. As Noel Heikkinen, a co-pastor at Riverview Church, says, "Jesus is our Senior Pastor." Life on the Vine is the church, referenced in chapter six, that meets in the round with the table at the center and the preacher preaching from the circle. Consequently, they not only meet in the round, but they lead in the round as they are guided by the Spirit, with Jesus at the center.

Maybe the most amazing example comes from the base ecclesial communities (*comunidades eclesiales de base*), which have their origins in Latin America but have spread throughout the world. According to Leonardo Boff, these communities of fifteen to twenty families started in the early 1970s and by 1985 grew to 70,000 in Latin America. These base or grass-roots communities are primarily composed of lower-class, people who live at the base of society, as opposed to the pinnacle of power in the social pyramid.[1] In *Ecclesiogenesis: The Base Communities Reinvent the Church*, Boff describes these churches: They challenge the traditional structures of the hierarchical church by prioritizing community over structures. They are declericalizing the church and restoring it to the whole people of God. And they are focusing on a new way of being the church, emphasizing the study of Scripture and orthopraxis (right living) as they seek to be a sign and instrument of liberation. All of this is happening in the hierarchical Roman Catholic Church (though not condoned by the hierarchy), which ought to be a kick in the butt to Protestants who claim to hold to the priesthood of all believers. The ecclesiogenesis communities of faith now number a million.[2] These poor, uneducated disciples who have been with Jesus have much to teach those of us in the West.

POLYCENTRIC LEADERSHIP EXAMPLES IN RECENT RESEARCH

What is the mystery behind the Apaches' ability to fend off the powerful Spanish army for two hundred years? What power lies behind the largest information resource of our time—Wikipedia? How has Alcoholics Anonymous reached untold millions with only a shared ideology and no leader? What is behind the success of Craigslist and Skype? What have neurologists recently discovered about the function of the brain that might inform our thinking about organizational structure?

These are some of the questions that Ori Brafman and Rod Beckstrom address in their fascinating book *The Starfish and the Spider: The Unstoppable Power of Leaderless Organizations*. In this book they claim that organizations fall into two basic categories: traditional top-down organizations (spiders) and decentralized organizations that rely on peer relationships (starfish).

Throughout the book Brafman and Beckstrom encourage us to take a look at the power of decentralization. They discuss how fragile and inefficient centralized organizations can be, and how decentralized organizations—which seem disorganized—are often more adaptable and durable. They provide many examples to support their claim of the power of decentralization like the Apaches, Alcoholics Anonymous, Al Qaida, Burning Man Festival, the brain and the open source revolution (Napster, Skype, Craigslist, Wikipedia, the blogosphere and the Internet). The metaphor is this: though a starfish and a spider appear to be structured similarly, when we cut off the head of a spider, it dies. But when we cut a starfish in half, we get two starfish. The reason is because each of the major organs of starfish are replicated throughout each arm. And for the starfish to move, "one of the arms must convince the other arms that it's a good idea to do so. The arm starts moving, and then—in a process that no one fully understands—the other arms cooperate and move as well."[3] Brafman and Beckstrom not only give many examples of how decentralized, leaderless movements have taken place in the past and are taking place today, they also show us how it works. The starfish organization does have a weakness. "The moment you introduce property rights into the equation, everything changes, the starfish organization turns into a spider."[4] The authors mention some of the strengths of centralization. And they close the book by introducing the hybrid organization and how to find the sweet spot between centralization and decentralization.

POLYCENTRIC LEADERSHIP EXAMPLES IN POLITICS

After one of my talks at Exponential, an annual church planting conference in Orlando, someone took me aside to explain that although they liked the idea of shared leadership, they thought it would only work with small communities. As I was thinking about this, I was getting ready to meet with some new friends at the conference from Switzerland. N. D. Strupler treated me to a steak dinner along with his team. They were telling me about the missional adventures of helping to start thirty-six churches in Europe. After hearing about their ventures, they asked me about my ministry. As I was sharing about polycentric leadership in the church, they mentioned how their country is led by seven presidents. This has been the case since 1848. The seven members of the Federal Council lead the executive branch equally, with the presidential leadership revolving annually. And while one member takes the role of the first among equals (*primus inter pares*) for a year, and another takes the role of the vice president, the first among equals has no more power than the other sitting presidents. The first among equals is simply the ceremonial head for one year. This ancestral home of democracy deserves more attention and study.

When I asked each of these Swiss citizens if they thought that having seven presidents was a good idea, each of them told me that while there are strengths and weaknesses to this approach, they would not want it any other way. They proudly said that in their 720 years of existence as a country, they had never been to war.

After hearing about this, I went online to conduct a little research of my own. I wanted to see how well this polycentric approach to leadership worked in real life. One of the places I checked out was the Mercer Quality of Living Survey, which ranks cities according to ten different criteria, including the political and social environment, medical and health consideration, public services and transport, consumer goods, economic environment, schools and education, recreation, housing, sociocultural environment and natural environment.[5] I discovered that three of the cities in Switzerland made it into the top ten cities in the world to live: Zurich (2), Geneva (3) and Bern (9). Does polycentric leadership work even when seeking to govern a large group of people? Those who live in Switzerland answer with a resounding yes!

POLYCENTRIC LEADERSHIP EXAMPLES IN ART, BUSINESSES AND NONPROFITS

We have seen how polycentric leadership is working in the contemporary church. We've seen how recent research demonstrates the power behind decentralized organizations. And we've seen how this approach to leadership works in politics. Now let's take a look at how it is at work in the arts, businesses and nonprofits.

What does music have to do with leadership? A lot. The jazz ensemble reveals how to thrive in a chaotic and turbulent environment, where rotating leadership and improvisation are the norm. But what about an orchestra? Doesn't an orchestra require a different kind of leadership? Those who are a part of the Orpheus Chamber Orchestra don't think so.

The Orpheus Chamber Orchestra has no conductor. This orchestra bravely asked themselves, "Rather than relying on a charismatic visionary leader who both calls the shots and engages member's motivation, might it be possible for all members to share responsibility for leadership, and for their differences and disagreements to be sources of creativity rather than something that should be suppressed in the interest of uniformity and social harmony?"[6]

This orchestra was "founded in 1972 by cellist Julian Fifer and a small group of other musicians" who because of the sheer enjoyment of chamber music where "power, responsibility, leadership, and motivation rest entirely in the hands of the people doing the work," they dared to dream to be a orchestra that "was designed to rely on the skills, abilities, and passionate commitment of its members rather than on the monolithic leadership of a conductor."[7]

"For almost 40 years: Orpheus has astounded international audiences and critics alike with its superior artistry, energy, and distinctive approach to music-making."[8] One of the reasons they have been so successful is that each of the performances are infused with passion because each person in the orchestra plays a significant role. They have developed "formal structures to ensure that musicians have real power throughout the organization and participate in all important decisions."[9]

Orchestras are typically in the hands of the conductor, who tends to resist receiving input from the musicians themselves, and sometimes rule with an iron baton. But not Orpheus.

Widely regarded as one of the world's great orchestras, and winner of four Grammy Awards, they "consistently rehearse, perform, and record without a conductor."[10] They are a self-governing organization in which each person is a leader in a revolving way. During the 1999-2000 season, "Orpheus produced a five-concert subscription series at Carnegie Hall; performed more than sixty concerts in cities throughout North America, Europe and Asia; participated in national television and radio broadcasts experienced by more than 8 million people; recorded or released five new CDs, and taught more than twenty-five hundred public school students in New York City." The Orpheus process was founded upon eight principles, which they have taught to businesses like J. P. Morgan Chase, Morgan Stanley, the Ritz-Carlton Hotel and many others, who have been able to discover new ways of doing business.[11] The principles are:

1. Put power in the hands of people doing the work.

2. Encourage individual responsibility.

3. Create clarity of roles.

4. Share and rotate leadership.

5. Foster horizontal teamwork.

6. Learn to listen, learn to talk.

7. Seek consensus (and build creative structures that favor consensus).

8. Dedicate passionately to your mission.[12]

In *Leadership Ensemble*, Harvey Seifter and Peter Economy walk us through each of these principles in very practical ways, showing how the orchestra and various businesses live out these eight principles. Each chapter outlines specifically how to apply these principles to any organization or business. They also explain the potential problems and pitfalls to avoid when seeking to engage in genuine polycentric leadership.

Not only does polycentric leadership work in art and business, but one of the most powerful examples is how it works in one of the most well-known recovery organizations in the world.

Philip Yancey describes this organization:

I once visited a "church" that manages, with no denominational head-quarters or paid staff, to attract millions of devoted members each week. It goes by the name of Alcoholics Anonymous. I went at the invitation of a friend. . . . "Come along," he said, "and I think you'll catch a glimpse of what the early church must have been like."

At twelve o'clock on a Monday night I entered a ramshackle house. . . . Acrid clouds of cigarette smoke hung like tear gas in the air, stinging my eyes. It did not take long, however, to understand what my friend had meant with his comparison to the early church.

A well-know politician and several prominent millionaires were mixing freely with unemployed dropouts and kids with needle marks on their arms. Introductions went like this: "Hi, I'm Tom, and I'm an alcoholic and a drug addict." Instantly everyone shouted out warmly, "Hi Tom!"

The "sharing time" worked like the textbook description of a small group, marked by compassionate listening, warm responses, and many hugs. Each person attended gave a personal progress report of his or her battle with addiction. We laughed a lot, and we cried a lot. Mostly, the members seemed to enjoy being around people who could see right through their facades. There was no reason not to be honest; everyone was in the same boat.

AA owns no property, has no headquarters, no media center, no staff of well-paid consultants and investment counselors who jet across the country. The original founders of AA built in safeguards that would kill off anything that might lead to bureaucracy, believing their program could work only if it stayed at the most basic, intimate level; one alcoholic devoting his or her life to help another."[13]

In 2006 there were a reported 1,867,212 AA members in 106,202 AA groups worldwide.[14] This is an example of the power of a starfish organization. So, does the church you serve operate more like a spider or a starfish? What might the congregation you serve become if you were to awaken the equippers to live as cultural architects who awaken the entire community to join God in the renewal of all things? Let's take a closer look at the five kinds of leaders needed to create a missional culture.

PART THREE

The Five Culture Creators

10

Jesus the Archetypical Culture Creator

Quite simply, a missional church needs missional leadership, and it is going to take more than the traditional pastor-teacher mode of leadership to pull this off.

ALAN HIRSCH

When the Chief Shepherd appears, you will receive the crown of glory that will never fade away.

1 PETER 5:4

Years ago I was trying to fix a drawer and got down to one last screw I had to get loose. The more I worked to loosen the screw, the tighter it seemed to get. I had worked as a carpenter's helper for six months, but our company majored in restoring fire-damaged buildings, which apparently means I got better at demolishing things rather than fixing them. A friend was visiting, and it wasn't too long before he realized I needed some help. Very quickly he said, "Oh, this has a left-handed thread; it's a reverse screw. If you want to loosen it, you need to go in the opposite direction." I'm thinking, "It took me ten years to find out how screws work, and now they change the rules on me?"

Too often we approach leadership and life transformation in pragmatic ways. We uncritically adopt the latest business practices in the church, working hard to tighten the screw, only to find that the tighter the screw gets, the less we become like Jesus. John Howard Yoder paints an inspiring picture of community:

> The political novelty that God brings into the world is a community of those who serve instead of ruling, who suffer instead of inflicting suffering, whose fellowship crosses lines instead of reinforcing them. This new Christian community in which the walls are broken down not by human idealism or democratic legalism but by the work of Christ is not only a vehicle of the gospel or only a fruit of the gospel; it is the good news. It is not merely the agent of mission or the constituency of a mission agency. This is the mission.[1]

If we are going to realize what Yoder extols, we need a reverse screw approach to leadership that releases the polycentric leadership model the apostle Paul wrote about. We need to unleash the gifts Christ has given the church: the apostles, prophets, evangelists, pastors and teachers. As these leaders learn to live *as* a community *within* the community, they can both model and equip the entire body to live *apostolic*, *prophetic*, *evangelistic* and *pastoral* lives, and in turn can *teach* others to do likewise. This reverse approach to leadership was embodied by Jesus the archetypical apostle, prophet, evangelist, pastor and teacher.

MISSION OF JESUS

The central theme of Jesus' life was the kingdom of God. Mark summed up Jesus' mission, saying, "Jesus went into Galilee, proclaiming the good news of God. 'The time has come,' he said. 'The kingdom of God has come near. Repent and believe the good news!'" (Mk 1:14-15).

Throughout his short ministry, Jesus would invite people into the kingdom of God. He told them it's like a mustard seed, or like a person who sold everything to get the field with the treasure. But what *is* the kingdom of God? What is it all about? To understand this, we must understand Jesus' context better.

Recently, there were several people making claims about Jesus' origins. One person said, "I'm going to give you three good reasons why I believe Jesus was Italian. He loved to talk with his hands, he had wine with every meal, and he used olive oil quite a bit." Someone from California said, "I'm going to give you three reasons why I believe Jesus was Californian. He never cut his hair, he walked around barefoot all the time, and he started his own religion." Then a black person declared, "I'm going to give you three reasons why I believe Jesus was black. He called everyone brother, he liked gospel, and he couldn't get a fair trial." After that a woman gave the most compelling evidence of all: three proofs that Jesus was a woman. "He had to feed a crowd at a moment's notice when there was no food, he kept trying to get a message across to a bunch of men who just didn't get it, and even when he was dead he had to get up because there was more work for him to do."[2]

Each of us approaches the Scripture and Jesus with a certain perspective that colors and shapes the way we see him. This is why we must take the pains to look at Jesus from a Jewish perspective. After all, Jesus was a Jew and was fully involved in Jewish culture.

As a first-century Jew, Jesus knew Scripture and the words of the Hebrew prophets that went before him. The central hopes of the prophets pointed to a time when God would intervene and bring restoration to Israel and to all of creation. The word that best captures this idea of complete restoration is *shalom,* a concept we touched on briefly earlier in the book.

For the prophets, shalom epitomized the day when all things are made right again. All things corrupted and polluted will be remade. Through imagery and story, their words paint a picture of how things are supposed to be. People will no longer be regarded as property or tools in the hands of the powerful, but as made in the very image of God. Kingdom building will cease, and all will gladly be a part of the kingdom of God, letting God be God so that peace would prevail in the world. God's good but cursed creation will be freed. The prophets spoke of a time when people will genuinely love each other.

Then Jesus said something that is utterly amazing. When his followers asked him how to pray, he said we should pray that these things would come about. He taught us to pray, "[May] your kingdom come, your will be done, on earth as it is in heaven" (Mt 6:10). He was telling his followers to pray for the coming *shalom,* that the world would be made right again, that peace and beauty would prevail over violence and corruption. If we seek to see this prayer realized as much as we can expect on this side of the new heavens and new earth, we not only need to recover the five equippers but, from the life and ministry of Jesus, we need to understand how he was the archetypical apostle, prophet, evangelist, pastor and teacher.

JESUS AS APOSTLE

After Jesus had risen from the dead, we would expect to find the disciples celebrating. Instead of celebrating, John tells us that on that Sunday evening the disciples were so gripped with fear that they bolted the door. They locked themselves in, keeping the world out. Then, suddenly, Jesus appeared in their midst. The bolted doors weren't enough to keep him out. He stood there facing his closest friends. Although they had pledged their allegiance to him, they had deserted him and were now hiding behind closed doors, living in fear and shame. So how did Jesus repond? Did he accuse them or scorn them? No, he gave them four grace-filled words: "Peace be with you."

In our moments of fear and shame, Jesus kisses us with these words: "Peace be with you." After Jesus' words brought new life into the disicples, he sent them out to breathe new life into the world. After showing them his pierced hands and side, he said, "as the Father has sent me, I am sending you," then he breathed on them and said, "receive the Holy Spirit" (Jn 20:21-22). Upon reflecting on this text, Wesley Allen wisely says, "We cannot keep the Spirit to ourselves. We are gifted with it for the sake of others. God gives the church the spiritual gift of resurrection life so that the church will bring it to bear on the world."[3] Jesus was sent by the Father to bless the world, and we are sent by Jesus to do the same. Apostles understand that they are *sent* people, and in turn they *send* people.

JESUS AS PROPHET

In *Prophets: Words of Fire*, Megan McKenna says, "The prophet interrupts, intervenes, and jolts us into uncertainty or doubt and then turns and points directly at us and says, 'What is wrong with the world is wrong with you!' "[4] Jesus is the archetypical prophet. His anguish over the lives he observed in Jerusalem led him to confront the fraud and hypocrisy that he found in the religious and political institutions of his day. He subverted the status quo and challenged the interpretations and practices of the scribes and Pharisees, especially in regard to the oppressive religious system of privilege and power that had developed. Through symbolic acts and subversive parables he challenged the purity code, which determined who the insiders and outsiders were, and their interpretation of Scriptures.

The poor and marginalized people in Galilee, along with those who heard him from other towns and villages, received Jesus' message gladly. For when they heard the good news, it not only meant forgiveness; it meant new economic, social and political realities. But it was much more difficult for the rich and those in power to receive these words. Jesus the prophet revealed God's heart and exposed the heart of those he touched.

JESUS AS EVANGELIST

The stories of Mark demonstrate how Jesus equipped the disciples to embrace and share his good news, which was personal, social and cosmic in nature. Jesus invited the disciples to dismantle the dominant social order that legitimized oppressive social institutions (Mk 1:1–4:34). Then, at the start of this next section (Mk 4:35–8:9), Jesus began to construct a new social order, helping his disciples understand that a new king and kingdom requires significant change and transition. As we can all attest by our own life experiences, changes in our ultimately loyalties do not come easy.

> That day when evening came, he said to his disciples, "Let us go over *to the other side*." Leaving the crowd behind, they took him along, just as he was, in the boat. There were also other boats with him. A furious squall came up, and the waves broke over the boat, so that it was nearly swamped. Jesus was in the stern, sleeping on a cushion. The disciples woke him and said to him, "Teacher, don't you care if we drown?"
>
> He got up, rebuked the wind and said to the waves, "Quiet! Be still!" Then the wind died down and it was completely calm.
>
> He said to his disciples, "Why are you so afraid? Do you still have no faith?"
>
> They were terrified and asked each other, "Who is this? Even the wind and the waves obey him!" (Mk 4:35-41, emphasis added)

Crossing over to *the other* side means that they were going from the safe land of the privileged Jews and to the shores where the "outsiders," the

Gentiles, resided. Getting from the old world to the new world is very difficult. Metaphorically, it is like getting into a little boat and traveling from Los Angeles to Tokyo, and right in the middle getting caught in a storm. The storm is so furious that wave after wave breaks over the boat, to the point that it is about to go under. And all the while, the One who can do something about the problem seems unaware of the suffering and anxiety experienced.

This story is a direct echo of a story of the Old Testament, one with a journey by boat, a violent storm at sea, a main character asleep through the storm, frightened sailors, miraculous stilling of the waters, a response of marvel by the sailors, and a Jewish evangelist with a message for Gentiles. The story of Jonah resounds through this passage. And the next section of Mark deals with crossing barriers in the reconstruction of a new social order, just as in Jonah. Today it would be like God calling you to go to Afghanistan to share the good news with those who may have been involved in bombing the World Trade Center. However this is exactly what evangelists do, and they call others to cross barriers that the broader culture sets up. Just as the story of Jonah was written to help Israel remember why she was chosen, Jesus the evangelist came to lead Israel to her true calling: to be a blessing to all nations.

JESUS AS PASTOR

When Jesus looked upon the people, he had compassion on them because he saw that they were "harassed and helpless, like sheep without a shepherd" (Mt 9:36). When Jesus came to speak to Israel, many of the leaders who were supposed to be shepherding God's people were oppressing them instead. We see this illustrated in the story of the woman caught in adultery. Jesus was teaching at the temple and a crowd gathered. As he taught, the Pharisees and teachers of the law separated a woman out of the crowd and made her stand in front of everyone. This woman had crossed the line too many times. They said to Jesus, "Teacher, this woman was caught in the act of adultery. In the Law Moses commanded us to stone such women. Now what do you say?" (Jn 8:4-5). Instead of being good shepherds and saving the lost sheep, the religious leaders sought to separate the people from Jesus by using this question as a trap. They didn't bring her to Jesus to be redeemed; they brought her to be killed. To convict someone of adultery, the law required more than just circumstantial evidence. It required at least two witnesses. So what was the good Shepherd going to do? After all, it was many men against one woman. They thought they had Jesus trapped between disregarding the law and condemning her to death.

But Jesus gracefully chose a third way. Jesus stooped down, as if he was hinting to them to be a little more humble, to admit their brokenness. Then he quietly wrote on the ground while they demanded an answer. Finally, he said, "Let any one of you who is without sin be the first to throw a stone at her" (v. 7). Then he stooped back down and continued to write on the ground.

After hearing what Jesus said, and probably looking at what Jesus wrote, one by one, starting with the oldest, they dropped their stones and left, until it was just Jesus and the woman. Jesus asked her if there were any witnesses left to condemn her. She said, "No." Jesus said, "Neither do I. Go and sin no more" (Jn 8:11 NLT). Human sin is stubborn, but the pastoral heart of God is more stubborn. Jesus gave her mercy instead of justice, and after breaking into her world with love and forgiveness, Jesus left her with five last words: "Go and sin no more." These words of challenge are filled with just as much mercy as Jesus had given her moments before. For Jesus, the good Shepherd, desired her holiness and wholeness.

JESUS AS TEACHER

The Jews are known as "People of the Book." Through the centuries Jews have vigorously studied the Scriptures and debated its meaning with one another. As Jesus' ministry as a rabbi grew in influence among the people, he clashed with the teachers of his day and their interpretation of Scripture.

Edwin Broadhead, who explores the literary structures of the Gospel of Mark, points out that the conflict between Jesus and the religious leaders dominates Mark 11:1–13:37, culminating in a death plot against Jesus.[5] Ched Myers labels this section "Jesus' Showdown with the Powers in Jerusalem."[6]

At the grand finale of this showdown we discover Jesus' own herme-neutical lens. In the debate over the greatest commandment, Jesus re-veals his approach to reading and interpreting Scripture:

> One of the teachers of the law came and heard them debating. Noticing that Jesus had given them a good answer, he asked him, "Of all the commandments, which is the most important?"
>
> "The most important one," answered Jesus, "is this: 'Hear, O Israel, the Lord our God, the Lord is one. Love the Lord your God with all your heart and with all your soul and with all your mind and with all your strength.' The second is this: 'Love your neighbor as yourself.' There is no commandment greater than these." (Mk 12:28-31)

Jesus knew the orthodox answer was the *Shema*, "Hear, O Israel: The Lord our God, the Lord is one. Love the Lord your God with all your heart and with all your soul and with all your strength" (Deut 6:4-5). But Jesus does something liberating and life-giving here. He attaches an excerpt from the Levitical code of justice (Lev 19:9-18): "Love your neighbor as yourself" (Lev 19:18), making it clear you cannot love God and exploit your neighbor at the same time. When we read Scripture, we must ask if it increases our love for our neighbor. As Augustine writes in his treatise *On Christian Doctrine*, "So anyone who thinks that he has understood the divine scriptures or any part of them, but cannot by his understanding build up this double love of God and neighbor, has not yet succeeded in understanding them."[7]

THE EQUIPPERS' FOCAL CONCERN AND *TELOS*

The *telos* (end or goal) for Jesus, the archetypal apostle, prophet, evan-gelist, pastor and teacher, was the *shalom* of God on earth, to the glory of his Father. And the *telos* of each equipper is shaped by this vision of shalom. When the apostle Paul was contemplating in Ephesians how the church would grow to the full stature of Christ, he tells us that Christ has given these equippers to the church so that the church might become like Christ, fully mature.

Too many people live less than human lives because we have forgotten what it means to be human. We lack joy and meaning because we have forgotten our calling. Popular ethicist Alasdair MacIntyre[8] reminds us that in the pursuit of the Enlightenment project, our culture has "abandoned most convictions about the *telos* (the 'good,' the created purpose) of human life and human activities. This abandonment of *telos* drains our actions of any real meaning and significance."[9] When we as people forget our *telos*, our sense of calling, our lives lack meaning and motivation. But when we are awakened to our *telos*, our aim in life, we have a new sense of joy, a fresh motivation, a new sense of direction and focus.

In Paul's letter to the church in Ephesus he tells us that we are God's masterpiece. Our *telos* is to become fully mature *in* Christ, becoming *like* Christ, for the good of the world and to the glory of God. Because Christ is the perfect human, the one person who completely fills out the image of God, the more we become like him, the more mature we become, imitating his character and ministry. God made us in his own image, and it is his intent that we become mature human beings. This is the heart of why Christ has given the church apostles, prophets, evangelists, pastors and teachers, so that they might equip the church to be God's masterpiece, his living letter to the world, for the sake of world.

Each equipper helps the congregation move toward God's *telos* in particular ways. Table 10.1 reveals the focal concern of each equipper and the *telos* the equippers are moving the congregation toward. These gifts were incarnated by Jesus, and are evident in Scripture as a whole.

Table 10.1. Equippers, Focal Concerns and *Telos* (Destinations)

Equipper	Focal Concern	*Telos* (Destinations) Marks
Apostle (dream awakener)	Living out our calling	Creating a discipleship ethos and calling people to participate in advancing God's kingdom
Prophet (heart revealer)	Pursuing God's shalom	Calling the church to God's new social order and standing with the poor and oppressed
Evangelist (story teller)	Incarnating the good news	Proclaiming the good news by being witnesses and being redemptive agents
Pastor (soul healer)	Seeking wholeness and holiness	Cultivating life-giving spirituality within community and embodying reconciliation
Teacher (light giver)	Inhabiting the sacred text	Immersing ourselves in Scripture and dwelling faithfully in God's story

As we examine the following portraits of each equipper, please be a Berean. What is a Berean? Luke tells us that the Bereans "were of more noble character than those in Thessalonica, for they received the message with great eagerness and examined the Scriptures every day to see if what Paul said was true" (Acts 17:11). I've developed my understanding of the equippers by not only thinking deeply about the portraits the Scriptures paint, but also through my experience in the crucible of ministry for the last twenty years. So as I describe each of the equippers, examine the Scriptures to discern if the picture that I paint of the various equippers is in line with what you understand of Scripture and of life.

11

Apostles
Dream Awakeners

Calling is where your deep hunger meets the world's deep needs.

FREDRICK BUECHNER

Therefore, holy brothers and sisters, who share in the heavenly calling,
fix your thoughts on Jesus, whom we acknowledge as our apostle and
high priest.

HEBREWS 3:1

After sharing with me the amazing story of his dad, I totally understood why James, my friend from India, wanted me to meet Aby.

Before Aby was born, his dad was a broken man, struggling with alcohol and abusing his wife. They were unable to have children, which was difficult for both of them. Then one day they found out she was pregnant. The doctor told her husband not to do anything that might upset his wife, otherwise she might lose the baby.

An evangelist was coming to town and Aby's mother really wanted her husband to go, hoping that he might meet Christ and discover the transforming power of the Spirit. She made a passionate plea, and because he didn't want to upset her, he relunctantly went to this revival meeting.

Nothing big happened, so she asked him to come back with her the following night. It was at that meeting that this man encountered Christ, found forgiveness and experienced transformation in his life. Soon he received a call from God to start a church among the Untouchables, even though he was Brahmin, the highest caste in India. The church he planted flourished, and so they started another church. In time, a church-planting movement was birthed, and thirty-five years later there are now six thousand churches in northern India and surrounding countries.

God touched someone, transformed his life and then *sent* him to start communities of faith that birthed other communties of faith, cultivating the growth of the kingdom of God here on earth. This man was a "sent one," or what the New Testament calls an *apostolos*.

BEING SENT

I didn't become a Christ follower until the summer of my senior year in college. I didn't grow up in a Christian household, and I was pretty unfamiliar with the Scriptures. I didn't even know the story of David and Goliath. But I did understand that God sent me to be a blessing to people in this world, so I told God that I would try to share my faith with everyone on my hall before the end of the year.

The Resident Assistant (RA) down the hall from me was Tom Hawkes, who grew up near Seattle. We became really good friends, helping each other with hall programs, eating together, talking a lot and enjoying each other's company. I even invited him to some events at the small church I had started to attend.

One day, Tom no longer wanted to talk with me. He never made time to hang out and made it clear he no longer wanted to be my friend. I was deeply hurt and would often be in tears over the loss of our friendship and his coldness toward God. One day I was talking with his roommate about God when Tom came into the room. I continued my conversation, but Tom got so angry that he literally picked me up and threw me out into the hallway.

I went back to my room and talked to God. "Father, I don't understand this. Why doesn't Tom want to be my friend anymore? Please open up his eyes like you did mine. Please! If you do this God, I promise that I will do whatever you want me to do. Just answer me this one prayer, and I'll never doubt you again."

Tom left for New York the next semester, but I continued to pray for him. I would send him letters, and one day I actually got one in return. I was so happy to hear from him again, and even more excited to find out in the letter that he was thinking a lot about some of the spiritual conversations that we had together.

I didn't hear from Tom again for a long time, until one day he showed up on my doorstep and said, "JR, I believe in Jesus—now what do I do?" I was shocked. I didn't know what to tell him, so I said, "Read the Bible and see what God wants you to do." And that is exactly what Tom did. He went home, read night and day, and finished the Bible in a week.

A number of years later Tom felt called to go to Ukraine and Russia to share the good news, and I still remember that awesome day when our community of faith sent him. Tom understood his "sentness" and helped establish communities of faith in Ukraine. He understood what Jesus was talking about when he said, "As the Father has sent me, I am sending you" (Jn 20:21).

You see, we only really have two options: flee from the world behind locked doors, or engage the world with faith, hope and love in the power of the Holy Spirit. If we decide to live as a blessing to the world, like Jesus did, then we shouldn't be surprised if we encounter suffering as we proclaim God's peace. For no disciple is greater than his teacher, and if Jesus suffered for the sake of the world, we will suffer as well. Some might want a safe God, a God made-to-order, but this kind of God never inspires awe, worship or sacrifice. N. T. Wright puts it this way:

> The god I want is a god who will give me what I want. He—or more likely it—will be a projection of my desires. As the grosser level, this will lead me to one of the more obvious pagan gods or goddesses, who offer their devotees money, or sex, or power (as Marx, Freud and Nietzsche pointed out). All idols started out life as the god somebody wanted. . . . [But] nobody falls down on their face before the god they wanted. Nobody trembles at the word of a home-made god. Nobody goes out with fire in their belly to heal the sick, to clothe the naked, to teach the ignorant, to feed the hungry, because of the god they wanted. They are more likely to stay at home with their feet up.[1]

APOSTLES AS DREAM AWAKENERS

I've nicknamed apostles "dream awakeners," because the heart of an apostle is to awaken people and communities to join God in the renewal of all things. Apostles are sent by God to help *create a discipleship ethos* and to *call people to participate in the advancement of God's kingdom*. Apostles seek to help people understand and live out their calling as sent people in the world for the sake of the world. They make disciples, who in turn make other disciples, who multiply ministries that bless the world.

The apostolic gifting carries with it an ability to create culture; therefore, apostles develop a keen awareness of the creation and maintenance of the cultural web of a congregation. Apostles help us remember that the mission of the church is grounded in the mission of God and is to be proclaimed visually and verbally.

Peter and Paul, two gifted apostles, understood what the missional church is all about. They recognized the distinctions between the *nature* of the church (what the church is), the *ministry* of the church (what the church does), and the *structure* of the church (how the church organizes to accomplish the work).[2] Peter and Paul knew that as the people of God grow to understand they are sent people, they are more likely to live out their vocation in a way that joins God in the renewal of all things.

Table 11.1. Apostles

Equipper	Focal Concern	*Telos* (Destinations) Marks
Apostle (dream awakener)	Living out our calling	Creating a discipleship ethos and calling people to participate in advancing God's kingdom

CREATING A DISCIPLESHIP ETHOS

The first *telos* of apostles is to *create a discipleship ethos* in the congregation so that God's people live out their missional nature as followers of Christ. They look at discipleship holistically, beginning with those who have yet to self-identify as Christians and all across the continuum to those who are serving the community from the overflow of their walk with God. They seek to make disciples from the harvest for the harvest, recognizing that some of the most passionate disciples will come from those who have yet to become Christ followers: the people of peace that God connects us with as we live our mission day to day.

In *Journey to Jesus*, Robert Webber explores *The Apostolic Tradition of Hippolytus*, which was penned around A.D. 215, as the church was connecting with a world unfamiliar with the God of Abraham, Isaac and Jacob. From this document we learn the church developed a holistic approach to discipleship at every stage of development. They identified four specific phases of development, from the *seeker* to the *hearer* to the *kneeler* to the *faithful*. Discipleship began with those who had no faith—the *seeker*—and continued toward those who were using their gifts and talents to continue the mission—the *faithful*. When it comes to making disciples of Jesus, I have adapted this premodern paradigm to our current context. Table 11.2 displays the basic discipleship continuum I use.

Table 11.2. Discipleship Continuum

Developmental Phase	Description
Resister	Those who are adversarial toward the church or the Christian faith
Skeptic	Those who are skeptical of the church or the Christian faith
Seeker	Those who are consciously or unconsciously open to God and willing to engage in meaningful discussions of faith
Hearer	Those who self-identify as Christian, the moment of conversion
Kneeler	Young Christians who are growing in their understanding of their new identity in Christ
Faithful	Active members of the congregation who understand and use their gifts and talents to bless others
Worshiper	Those who are learning to worship God with their whole life; servant leaders, core members, often leading or apprenticing a ministry in the church or in their vocations in the world

In making disciples, apostles take an *orient, involve and equip* approach to training. They recognize that making disciples is a process, not a program, and it takes place within the context of engaging in God's mission. Discipleship takes place when we are "with people," like Jesus was with the Twelve, and it becomes personal and powerful in the informal daily rhythms of life. It's about being vulnerable and being open about our brokenness, as Paul was with the Corinthians. Discipleship means inviting people to become whole again, which is partly about overcoming destructive habits, but also about building life-giving habits.

We approach discipleship by learning to call out what the Holy Spirit has put in people. It involves ministering together, praying together and studying Scripture together. Disciples encourage, comfort and challenge one another. Discipleship takes place communally—in smaller groups as well as one-on-one.

Apostles help disciples of Christ to reflect and refocus on their life by asking them meaningful questions and helping them to pay attention to what God is doing in and through them. They walk beside those they are working with, giving them practical assignments (with deadlines) for further growth, based on what God is doing. They recognize that training involves resourcing people theologically and practically so they can embody the good news contextually in every area of their lives.

Dream awakeners understand that discipleship is ultimately about helping people follow Jesus in the concrete realities of life. They recognize the need to be with people in hard times, praying with them and helping them follow Jesus through the valley of the shadow of death. Apostles realize that training takes place more in the living room and the streets than in the classroom and sanctuary. They help people live for the sake of others.

Apostles help people discover and live out their calling and create a discipleship ethos in the congregation.

CALLING PEOPLE TO PARTICIPATE IN GOD'S KINGDOM

Apostles also *call people to participate in advancing God's kingdom* as they multiply disciples, groups, ministries and churches. Apostles are catalysts who get things started. They seek forward movement in mission with the big picture in mind, and they are constantly thinking about how to forge into new missional spaces where others have not yet ventured. They have the heart of C. T. Studd, who is attributed as saying that "some want to live within the sound of the church and chapel bells, but I want to run a rescue mission within a yard of hell." Apostles are the people who live at hell's doorstep, among people on the spiritual frontier. They explore ways to network with other churches and movements to see the transformation of their towns, cities and countries. They have a deep desire to see God's kingdom become more tangible in the world through the church, and they do whatever it takes to see this come about.

As the apostolic gift grows in a person, he or she helps to create the cultural web for the community so the community will thrive and multiply at all levels. Apostles help to create an atmosphere where good things run wild in a synergetic way. They seek to instill faith in people and help them claim God's promises and cling to the vine so they might bear much fruit.

LIVING IT LOCALLY AND TRANSLOCALLY

As the West Coast director for the Ecclesia Network, a relational network of missional churches and leaders, I regularly connect with people who are gifted apostles on both the East and West Coasts. One of the many people that come to my mind is Chris Backert. Chris has multiple roles, local and translocal, which is common for apostolically gifted people. Some of his roles include being the cofounder of Imago Dei, a church in Richmond, Virginia, and the cofounder, director and organizational architect of the Ecclesia Network. Chris has helped start and grow a number of churches, in part because he is a visionary who is good at getting others involved. He excels at helping people find where their passions meet the world's needs. He is a humble, spirit-sensitive leader who is able to hold in mind the big picture and strategically network within and outside of Imago and the Ecclesia Network in order to bring the needed resources to move each of these groups forward in their mission.

Chris has an others-centered approach to life and demonstrates persistence, follow-through, loyalty and faithfulness, which engenders a great sense of trust in the communities he is a part of. Chris is an amazing networker who works part-time with the Baptist General Association of Virginia and participates in advancing the kingdom of God through creating multiple alliances with churches and denominations in his work with Fresh Expressions US and the Missio Alliance.

Chris is the consummate achiever. Yet, like many who are apostolically gifted, he is growing in strengthening the relational end of the relational/task-oriented continuum by making time to live in community in the informal spaces of life. He is also learning the difficult task of how to balance local and translocal ministry through discernment and wisdom from both the local and translocal leaders of the various ministries he serves. In addition to being a gifted apostle, Chris is also a gifted evangelist and teacher. (In my experience in working with and assessing churches, many people are gifted in primary and secondary ways.)

Discerning If You Are an Apostle

- Are you helping to cultivate a discipleship ethos in the congregation you serve?
- Do you demonstrate a passion to multiply disciples?
- Do you help people discover and live out their God-given calling?
- Do you have a history of calling people to participate in advancing God's kingdom by starting new ministries and churches?
- Do you seek to bring the good news of Jesus Christ into places and people groups that have no tangible witness?
- Are you able to equip others to do the same?

12

Prophets
Heart Revealers

We hear the story of the wind at Pentecost,

Holy wind that dismantles what was,

Holy wind that evokes what is to be,

Holy wind that overrides barriers and causes communication,

Holy wind that signals your rule even among us.

WALTER BRUEGGEMANN

"Jesus of Nazareth," they replied. "He was a prophet, powerful in word and deed before God and all the people."

LUKE 24:19

As I was exploring which city in California God was preparing for a new church, I met Pastor Ed. He is what is called a turnaround pastor. He finds dying churches and either gives them a burial or helps bring them back to life, sometimes using shock treatment.

This turnaround pastor told me about a dying church in Hollywood. At one time this church was well known and attended by a few famous people. But just a few years ago it only had thirty members, all of them gray-haired Anglo-Saxons in a long-since diversified neighborhood. "White flight" meant most of the remaining members commuted in from the Valley.

This church was dying. They were self-absorbed and no longer cared for the people in the area. They focused their energy more on their beautifully hand-crafted choir loft, not on the mission of God. Church members were frequently arguing about who had polished the choir loft last week and what color it should be painted next year.

With the church $280,000 in debt, increasing $3,000 each month, the sale of the building loomed on the horizon. My friend, Pastor Ed, was brought in as a last-ditch effort in order to try to turn this church around. After a few weeks of interviewing, the church board decided to accept him as their pastor, but despite looking like the congregation with his pale skin and gray hair, Pastor Ed brought a very different understanding to the congregation.

The morning of Pastor Ed's first sermon started like any other at this church, with fine clothes and singing worship songs. The congregation sat, eager to listen to the message from their newly *acquired* pastor. But then things changed. Pastor Ed pulled out a sledge hammer from behind the podium, and as he preached he dismantled the choir loft, slowly eliminating what they idolized. But he didn't stop there. He invited them to join in the change that was taking place, saying, "If anyone wishes to stay a member of this church, come up here, grab the sledge hammer and give it a swing."

The church shrunk from thirty members to ten that Sunday, but something new was born as well. For new life comes to those who are willing to embrace the reality of death.

Today Hope International Church is still being led by Pastor Ed and continutes to thrive in its neighborhood of East Hollywood. The church is filled with people from many different backgrounds that represent the neighborhood, and what was once a dying church, came to life through the prophetic actions of a daring leader.

PROPHETS AS HEART REVEALERS

I call prophets *heart revealers* because they reveal the heart of God and the hearts of those in the congregation. Prophets *call the church to God's new social order* and help the congregation to *stand with the poor and oppressed*. In the Old Testament, prophets were "God-intoxicated advocates of social justice. . . . Their authority and their social passion came from the immediacy of their experience of God and not from institutional authorization."[1] Prophets have the ability to perceive reality when others are lost in a world of illusion. When prophets come on the scene, reality invades illusion and hearts are laid bare before the living God. Prophets have a way of ripping open our hearts, shattering our illusions and bringing us face to face with our Maker (1 Cor 14:24-25).

Prophets anguish over those who suffer under unjust and oppressive regimes, whether religious or civil. They speak truth to the powers that be, and find creative and subversive ways to liberate the oppressed and include the marginalized. They criticize and dismantle the dominant, oppressive culture, and then envision and energize us with a new view of reality.

Through their example and the fire in their hearts, they have a contagious way of helping people commune with the Holy Spirit and grow in personal holiness. As heart revealers they encourage people to move from a politics of exploitation and oppression to one of justice and compassion. They help the community see how Jesus subverted the world's system and suffered for it, and so, just like their leader, they are willing to suffer.

Table 12.1. Prophets

Equipper	Focal Concern	*Telos* (Destinations) Marks
Prophet (heart revealer)	Pursuing God's shalom	Calling the church to God's new social order and standing with the poor and oppressed

CALLING THE CHURCH TO GOD'S NEW SOCIAL ORDER

The prophet *calls the church to God's new social order.* Through his life, death and resurrection Jesus inaugurated a new world, a new kingdom. The disciples were told to wait for the Holy Spirit. As they were praying in the Upper Room, the Holy Spirit came upon them. Some thought they had too much wine, but Peter reminded them what time it was—both in terms of chronological time, nine in the morning, and *kairos* time, a different sort of time that marks God's appointed hour. For this was what Joel had prophesied about, when God would pour out his Spirit on all people, regardless of gender, age or economic standing.

What we see at Pentecost is the reversal of the Tower of Babel. While God caused confusion by multiplying languages at the Tower of Babel, at Pentecost God enabled those from many nations to hear the good news of the kingdom of God in their own tongue.

From Pentecost onward we see the disciples living in Spirit-transformed communities. Living as a sign, foretaste and instrument of God's coming kingdom, they fleshed out what it meant to love God and one another in real ways. They devoted themselves to the apostles teaching, fellowship, prayer and the breaking of bread. In *Jesus and Community*, Gerhard Lohfink tells us that Jesus gathered the people of God together so that as a divine counter-society we might be a light to all people. He traces this idea from Jesus through the early church, making the case that the good news is not pietistic statements designed for personal contemplation. Rather Jesus' intention is to create new societies that, through their life and practices, demonstrate the arrival of the new world of God in Christ. Here, the Spirit of God "dismantles national and social barriers, group interest, castes systems and domination of one sex over the other."[2] The prophets call the people of God to be the new social order living out the politics of Jesus. Shane Claiborne helps us to see that when we live in the new community in the power of the Spirit, our social order changes:

> When the Bible tells the story of the early church in the book of Acts, it does not say that they were of one heart and mind because they sold everything. Rather, they held all in common precisely because they were of one heart and one mind, as rich and poor found themselves born again into a family in which some had extra and others were desperately in need. Redistribution was not systematically regimented but flowed naturally out of a love for God and neighbor. I am not a communist, nor am I a capitalist. As Will O'Brian . . . says, "When we truly discover love, capitalism will not be possible and Marxism will not be necessary."[3]

People were fascinated with this new community, which is why it says God added to their number daily. They were fleshing out Jesus' teaching in their lives. Even though Jesus had ascended to the right hand of the Father, his body was still on earth through this Spirit-filled community of people, continuing to carry out his purpose in the world. The people of God had become his hands and feet, doing what Jesus had done while he was on earth. They prayed for people's healing, fed the hungry and shared the good news by deed and word, which sometimes got them into trouble with the religious and political leaders.

Prophets equip the people of God to live into God's new social order by helping all the gifts of the Spirit come alive in the congregation. For through the Spirit the community of faith is a sign pointing to God's reality, which is just around the corner, and a foretaste of the kingdom, helping people experience the future in the present.

In cultivating Spirit-transforming communities, prophets help communities of faith to be attentive to the work of the Spirit in their midst, helping people recognize that the Holy Spirit tugs on those who are apart from Christ, assures us when we are doubtful, comforts us when we are down and guides us when we are confused. The Spirit can even warn us of unknown dangers. Paul says, "in every city the Holy Spirit warns me that prison and hardships are facing me" (Acts 20:23).

My friend Scott Davis told me about how the Holy Spirit warned his mother of danger. After falling asleep one evening, she had a nightmare. In her dream she had gotten into this terrible car accident. She was the first car at the stoplight and when it turned green, she did what we all do, she hit the gas. The only problem was that another car decided to race through a red light. She woke up as that car was crashing into hers. That was her dream.

The next day as she was driving, she found herself first at the stoplight, and she remembered her dream. When the light turned green she waited for a moment, and sure enough a car ran the red light. The Holy Spirit warns us of unknown dangers, if we are sensitive to him. Prophets help us to be filled with the Spirit and thus sensitive to the Spirit. They help us recognize the Spirit's work in our lives so we don't miss out on his benefits. The Holy Spirit was given as a foretaste of what is to come. The Spirit allows us to participate in God's new age now.

Living in God's new social order not only requires being sensitive to the Holy Spirit but yielding to the Spirit's inclusive nudge by being a community that welcomes the outcasts and helps them to feel at home. We are all broken and we need each other to become whole. One night a lady in our congregation gave me a call because she had just been in a huge fight with her son. She and her son had been coming to Kairos Hollywood for close to a year. If you met her son, you would not forget him. His face was badly deformed by elephantitis, and he had a hunched back. She told me that her son was building relationships with people who were not a good influence because he was having a hard time making friends at any church, including Kairos. She said he felt welcomed by a number of people at Kairos, but he hadn't made any good friends. When I heard this, it broke my heart and accented our need for more prophets and pastors in our midst who would help create a culture where all were truly included.

STANDING WITH THE POOR AND OPPRESSED

Along with calling the church to God's new social order, prophets help us *stand with the poor and oppressed*. Prophets help the congregation remember that we cannot say we are walking with God on the one hand while sitting in the seat of oppressors on the other. Heart revealers remind God's people that Jesus came to bring the good news to the poor, not just the poor in spirit. They help people recognize that the good news is not just for another time and place, but for the here and now, for the kingdom of God is at hand. They encourage the congregation to pray that God's kingdom would be more fully realized on earth and remind them that action must accompany prayer. They let people know that the good news Jesus came to bring was not just forgiveness of sins but liberation from sin: not just personal sin but social sins—injustices, discrimination and domination. They encourage people to be involved with social justice, reminding them that when we care for the prisoner, the unclothed and the hungry, we care for Jesus. For what we do or don't do for the poor and oppressed will be decisive on judgment day. Prophets proclaim to the congregation that if our gospel isn't good news for the poor, then it is not the same good news that Jesus proclaimed.

In my neighborhood of East Hollywood, we have a number of people who would be considered poor, some who are citizens and others who aren't. Jose is one of many who have made their way to Los Angeles in hopes of opportunity. He wanted to make money in order to support his extended family in his home country.

Jose now waits at a local Home Depot in hopes that someone will drive by and offer him a job for a day, but he will also settle for a half day's work. Sometimes when I drive up to the Home Depot, Jose and his friends run up to the car looking for work. Often I don't need them, leaving Jose and his friends waiting all day in desperation.

Some days Jose waits and waits until the sun sets. Then he returns home, only to return the next day. Repeating this activity daily adds to a deep sense of rejection that penetrates his soul. In a country where people talk about their rights, he tries to imagine that he too is worthy of rights. Low wages begin to take their toll on his psyche. And doing the kind of work that no one wants makes him feel undesirable. Yet Jose continues to wake up and make his way to Home Depot hoping that things might be different for him and his future.

At the heart of poverty is a "web of lies that results in the poor internalizing view of themselves as being without value, and without a contribution to make, believing that they are truly god-forsaken."[4] Heart revealers help communities recognize that "no transformation can be sustainable unless this distorted disempowering sense of identity is replace by the truth" and that the poor are "valuable enough to God to warrant the death of the Son in order to restore that relationship (dignity) and to give gifts that contribute to the well-being of themselves and their community (vocation)."[5]

Prophets equip the community to see that transformation happens through healing the marred identity of the poor and helping them discover their calling in life. At the same time they challenge the nonpoor to relinquish our "god complexes" and employ our gifts for the sake of human beings rather than using our gifts as a source of power and control. The prophets call *all*, rich and poor alike, to step into our new identities and roles in the midst of the in-breaking kingdom of God.

Prophets help the congregation to stand with the poor and oppressed, both in their local community and around the globe. In October 2004 I was in the middle of preparing for a series on the seven deadly sins when I realized that I had never heard a talk on gluttony. During my preparation for this talk, God created a situation in which I met Bishop Kaaleng, who helps to oversee around seventy churches in Kenya.

Twenty of us were sitting in my apartment listening to the bishop tell stories about life in the Turkana region of Kenya. At some point in the evening he shared how some of the people in his tribe were only able to eat one meal every three days because of the famine (which has been ongoing since my first visit in March 2005). A young man asked, "Is there any way we can help out?" When he asked that, the first thought that raced through my mind was, *Don't ask that question. I already have enough on my plate.* Soon, I sensed a rebuke from the Holy Spirit about my lack of love, especially as I began to study the sin of gluttony more thoroughly. In a short time it became extremely difficult for me to live with the reality that thousands of people in the Two-Thirds World are dying *daily* of hunger and preventable diseases, while one of the biggest problems in the West is obesity.

I started asking myself some questions. What do the Scriptures say about this? How is it that I could have been a Christian for over ten years (at that point in my life) and never demonstrated a compassion for the poor and oppressed, other than supporting a kid through Compassion International? Had I adopted a reductionistic version of the good news? Did I have a malnourished understanding of salvation?

The short of the long story is that after my first visit I started what I call a Kenya fast (eating like most of the Kenyan pastors I met eat, one meal a day and meat once a month) until God moved me to join him in walking with the poor. In about a year the Solis Foundation was born. Through the Foundation we give microgrants to help start small businesses in the Turkana region of Kenya.

The more our faith communities in Los Angeles have sought to walk with the poor, the more we realized how the issue of poverty "defies easy solutions and responses," and how complex development can be.[6] But we continue with joy to walk with the poor locally and globally, for when we walk with them we discover our own poverty, the poverty of community. In walking with the poor, they become our family and we become rich.

LIVING IT LOCALLY

I met Maria Drews, a gifted prophetess, as I was a part of a mid-sized community at Kairos Hollywood. Maria's lifestyle often causes me to look more closely at my heart and lifestyle as well as God's heart. Because our group eats together every week, I noticed she (and some others) had different eating habits than I do. I tend to be a carnivore, except when I'm fasting. But Maria doesn't eat meat. In time I came to realize why she became a vegetarian. She decided to give up meat for two primary reasons. First, her understanding of how our global food operations work caused her to become a vegetarian. She came to realize that it takes a lot more grain to produce a pound of meat than a pound of grain. And, living in a world where people are starving, she wanted to give up the privilege of eating meat to stand in solidarity with those who don't have enough to eat. In addition, she felt that the current agricultural system in the United States does a lot of damage to the environment.

Also unlike the typical Angeleno (people who live in LA), Maria chooses not to drive a car. While Maria will get rides from people at times, she has mostly embraced the public transportation system "in all its glory." She also rides her bike to many places, which is really weird for people in Los Angeles, because it is such a car-friendly city and not too nice for cyclists. She does this because she loves the natural environment. She believes that Americans tend to use more than our fair share of the world's resources. So for her, giving up a car helps her to live in a more sustainable relationship with the environment. She values God's creation, and while she understands that we can use it as a resource, she also sees the need to care for creation and be a good steward of what God has given us. Maria engages in a green lifestyle in many other ways.

So not only does Maria's lifestyle and words encourage our congregation to consider how we live in light of our global context, her lifestyle provokes questions from those who don't know Christ and give her opportunities to share how her lifestyle is an outgrowth of her faith. Her lifestyle has given her respect among Angelinos and has allowed her to proclaim the good news with her words as well.

Maria embodies a prophet in other ways as well. Serving as a neighborhood council representative, she has been able to take part in meaningfully meeting the needs of the neighborhood and be an example for the congregation.

While Maria embodies the ministry of a prophet, not everyone in the congregation necessarily sees what I see, which sometimes is the fate of a prophet in the local church. Jesus was not accepted in his hometown (Mk 6:4). Sometimes this is the case for the local prophet as well.

Discerning If You Are a Prophet

- Do you have a passion to see people walk with God?
- Are you sensitive to the Holy Spirit?
- Do you seek to help your community in live in the power of the Spirit and operate in the gifts of the Spirit?
- Do you spontaneously receive a word from the Lord for the sake of your community?
- Does your heart break for the poor and oppressed?
- Do you seek to help people be involved with justice issues either locally or globally?
- Do you seek to call people to live in God's new social order?
- Do you cultivate an environment that includes the outcasts?
- Do you find yourself equipping others to do the same?

13

Evangelists
Story Tellers

Jesus's teaching consistently attracted the irreligious while offending the Bible-believing, religious people of his day.

TIM KELLER

I must proclaim the good news of the kingdom of God to the other towns also, because that is why I was sent.

LUKE 4:43

What does it mean for the body of Christ to "move into" our neighborhoods today. I live in Los Angeles. The Los Angeles Metro Area is home to 17.5 million residents; the county of Los Angeles has close to 10 million people, while the city proper has close to 4 million residents.[1] The city of Los Angeles is divided into seven areas, and Hollywood is located in what is known as the Central Area. Hollywood is divided into roughly three sections. There is West Hollywood (its own city), Hollywood, and East Hollywood. One of the churches I've help to plant is in East Hollywood, were I reside.

With a population of over 52,000, East Hollywood is a 1.8 square-mile area, which is bordered by the famous Hollywood Boulevard to the north, Hoover Street to the East, the 101 Freeway to the south, and

Western Avenue to the West. Our neighborhood is diverse in ethnicity, culture and worldviews. East Hollywood is home to Little Armenia and Thai Town as well as a diverse group of immigrants—including Salvadorans, Mexicans, Filipinos, Koreans, Chinese, Japanese, Russian, Indonesians, Eastern Europeans as well as Middle Easterners.[2]

Each of the various people groups bring their culture and faith to our neighborhood. For instance, in East Hollywood you'll find a Thai Buddhist monastery, a Self-Realization Fellowship (combining Judaism, Christianity, Islam, Buddhism and Hinduism), a Jewish temple, a Japanese Tenrikyo church (a panentheist worldview, some say it is a sect of Shinto), as well as a huge Scientology training center that happens to be across the street from the Fountain Room where we meet. You can find Mormon services in English and Spanish, a Spanish Jehovah Witness center, and at our border the Islamic Center for Southern California.

While various faith traditions are represented in our neighborhood, you can also find churches from each of the three major branches of Christianity—Orthodox, Catholic and Protestant. East Hollywood is a very spiritual place, though according to the percept studies we had done, 49 percent have no faith involvement, as opposed to the 35 percent national average.[3]

It is also a very artistic place. Being in Hollywood, many people are involved in the entertainment industry. There are writers, actors, singers, set designers, radio producers, musicians, costume designers and directors. It is home to Barnsdall Park, which has rotating art exhibitions, as well as the Hollyhock house—the first Los Angeles project designed by Frank Lloyd Wright.

East Hollywood is home to Los Angeles City College (the original UCLA campus) and close by is the University of Southern California. It is also home to Kaiser Permanente Medical Center, Children's Hospital Los Angeles, and Hollywood Presbyterian Medical Center.

Our neighborhood is a transitional place. The cost of living is high, but the median family income is low $24,206, while the estimated median house value is $720,000 for the Hollywood area.[4] The vast majority of people are renters—88 percent, with only 8 percent living in homes they own.[5] It is not uncommon to find a couple of families living in one house or finding more people living in a one-bedroom apartment than is legal. A number of undocumented immigrants live in the area. So do some homeless people.

East Hollywood is a young neighborhood where 46 percent of the population is twenty-nine or younger, and only 10 percent of the population is sixty-five or older. It is also a diverse neighborhood with 55 percent Latino, 22 percent white, 15 percent Asian, 5 percent mixed, 3 percent black.[6]

So this little neighborhood of 52,000, tucked into the huge metropolis of Los Angeles, is diverse, spiritual, artistic, blue collar and transient. It is a place of legal and illegal immigrants, a place well known yet unknown. I share this brief sketch of my neighborhood to reflect on the concrete realities we currently live in, how our neighborhoods are becoming increasingly more complex, pluralistic and global. What does it mean to incarnate the good news into our neighborhoods? This is a focal concern of the evangelist.

EVANGELIST AS STORY TELLER

I've given evangelists the nickname of story tellers, because they help the congregation share God's story in such a way that when those apart from Christ hear the good news and accept it, their life story is transformed for the glory of God and the good of the world. Evangelists equip the church to *proclaim the gospel by being witnesses*, and they help the congregation to *be redemptive agents*, turning their "secular" jobs into sacred vocations. Story tellers remind their communities that God has chosen them to be bearers of the good news. That God chose to bless us, not that we might act as exclusive beneficiaries but that we might bless the nations. Evangelists encourage people to cross to the other side, to engage people on their own turf, and invite others in participate in God's kingdom.

Table 13.1. Evangelists

Equipper	Focal Concern	*Telos* (Destinations) Marks
Evangelist (story teller)	Incarnating the good news	Proclaiming the good news by being witnesses and being redemptive agents

PROCLAIMING THE GOSPEL BY BEING WITNESSES

One *telos* of the evangelist is to equip the church *to proclaim the gospel by being witnesses*. Just before Pentecost Jesus told his disciples that the Holy Spirit would come upon them and give them power to be his witnesses in the Jerusalem and beyond. He said, "you will be my witnesses" (Acts 1:8). Notice he says you will *be* my witnesses. This is because *being* always proceeds *doing* and *saying*. Being witnesses is living out *whom* God has made us in Christ. As recipients of God's grace, we have been given a new identity in Christ; we are children of God, part of the family of God, saints, priests and ambassadors. God has made us new in Christ, and as we are becoming who God has made us together, we begin to live under the reign of God and proclaim the good news by being, doing and saying. This is what it means to be his witnesses.[7]

After studying the New Testament pattern of evangelism, Graham Tomlin makes the case in *The Provocative Church* that evangelism works best in the context where it's an answer to a question. In other words, when we live out our calling as the people of God, under the reign of God—when we become the church where the poor find riches, the lonely find community, the sick find healing, and the broken find wholeness—then our words about the person and work of Christ become meaningful. Thus the evangelist seeks to equip the church to be a sign, foretaste and instrument of God's coming kingdom. People want a sense of purpose, they want something to hope in, they want to love better, live fuller, experience forgiveness and grow in wisdom, for these are some of the essentials to human flourishing. So as the church is equipped to live under the reign of Christ, we have something to offer our neighbors and the world.

One of the questions the evangelist asks the congregation is, *What does it mean to be the church that lives under the reign of God?* Just before Peter talks about giving "an answer to everyone who asks you to give the reason for the hope that you have" (1 Pet 3:15), he calls the community to "be like-minded, be sympathetic, love one another, be compassionate and humble. Do not repay evil with evil or insult with insult. On the contrary, repay evil with blessing, because to this you were called so that you may inherit a blessing. . . . In your hearts revere

Christ as Lord" (1 Pet 3:8-9, 15). Revering Christ as Lord is living under the reign of Christ, the rule of God. As the church does this, we become a light to the world, a sign of the kingdom, pointing others toward God, his Son and his future.

The second question the story teller asks the congregation is, *If God's reign were to be perfectly realized in this neighborhood, what would be different?* This then becomes the mission of how the congregation can practically *serve* the neighborhood. As Dietrich Bonhoeffer reminds us, "The church is only the church when it exists for others."[8] When our church was starting in East Hollywood, I joined the East Hollywood Neighborhood Council in order to listen to the problems and issues that our neighborhood was facing. But there are many ways evangelists can find the heartbeat of the community outside of the church. As the church becomes aware of the needs of the neighborhood, the evangelist seeks to understand how the passions and gifts of the communities might best meet these needs.

One of the needs of our neighborhood was to have more green space and trees. So our community teamed up with the East Hollywood Neighborhood Council, Tree People and others to plant more trees in East Hollywood. After planting the trees our church hosted a lunch for everyone. In this time we got to know our neighbors better as we sought to better the neighborhood with them. We hope our lunch blessed them. In doing this we were able to plant some seeds of a different kind along the way.

The third question the evangelist asks the congregation is, *What are the kinds of idols in our neighborhood that need to be unmasked?* In our neighborhood some people seek identity and worth through the idols of their bodies, cars, houses and fame. People make great sacrifices for these things. Others live vicariously through film and other forms of entertainment. And some are addicted to food and drink.

As we identify some of the idols in the neighborhood, the evangelist asks, *What rhythms of life and what community happenings might challenge these idols and express the kingdom?* We invite various people to be a part of our communities that practice a different way of living, communities that engage in life rhythms which enable us to find our identity and worth in God (see chap. 16). We also host a series of talks on Hollywood and the ancient text. We bring Scripture and the most recent films into conversation with each other. We want people to move past film as escapist entertainment and see how it has the ability to disturb and enlighten us in relation to ourselves and with others, creation and God.

As a way to help people grow in generosity, engage in social justice and appreciate other art forms, my friend Daichi and I started what we call Artist at the Fountain. Every other month we invite various artists to perform or share their art with us. For entry into the event, we ask everyone to give ten dollars to a local or global justice project we are involved in. Thus we blend appreciating good art with raising awareness and resources for local and global needs.

The evangelist asks one other important question: *How do we call others to receive and enter into the kingdom of God so that they might join us in representing God's reign in our neighborhood?* The evangelist needs to help the community to share their faith, to share God's story in a way that meaningful connects with people. James Choung does a great job at helping us share God's story in a meaningful way through his book *True Story: A Christianity Worth Believing In*. He teaches us how to share a summary of the good news in a way that gives a proper focus on transformation and decision, community and the individual, mission life and the afterlife.[9] James also does a great job at helping us share how the good news affects us at three levels: systemic, relational and personal.[10]

Here is an overview of Choung's approach to sharing the gospel. (For greater depth, please read the book.) First, we *ache for a better world*. He starts where people are living. Then, we remind people that we were *designed for good*. God designed us to be in relationship with him, each other and all of creation. But when we took charge, everything became about us; what was designed for good was *damaged by evil*, globally, relationally and personally. But God loves us too much to let things remain a mess. Through Jesus, he *restored all for the better*, systematically, relationally and personally. And now he has *sent us together to heal* our relationship with God, with each other and all of creation.[11] The evangelist needs to help people share the good news in a meaningful way that not only connects with people in today's world but naturally leads people to live as disciples of Christ.

BEING REDEMPTIVE AGENTS

The other *telos* of the evangelist is helping the community *be redemptive agents*. Along with proclaiming the good news by being a witness, the evangelist helps the congregation be salt and light in their vocation, so that the good news might spread to every sphere of the city. This begins by helping people connect Sunday with Monday. For when people embrace their "secular" calling in the world as a disciple of Jesus, it becomes a sacred calling.

When I meet an actor in Hollywood, my first thought is not, *I wonder if they would join our drama team?* The evangelist seeks to help people live out their calling *in* the world *for the sake* of the world. Evangelists help people understand that they are (in the words of Andy Crouch) culture makers. We create culture as we create goods or artifacts, which are in turn shared in public. When someone creates a film (an artifact) and it is shared publicly, he or she creates culture. If someone creates a building, a book, a painting, a film, a gourmet meal, a song, a bridge, software, an app or a legal document and then shares it publicly, the person is creating culture.

Evangelists help people understand that being human means we are culture makers, creating artifacts inside and outside of the church and sharing them with others. "Culture is what human beings make of the world."[12] Culture is created in the *sharing* of artifacts and ideas.

Crouch explains that there are spheres of culture and scales of culture. Different spheres of society have different cultures. The legal world is quite different from the art world. The culture of Wall Street is distinct from a hospital's culture. Each sphere of society, then, has its own subculture. There are also scales of culture: from small independent coffee shops to politics in Washington, D.C.; from small independent films to the large Hollywood blockbuster. In other words, every cultural good we create has a level of influence, large or small.

When evangelists help people understand their calling as culture makers, people rediscover the value of their vocation, and thus a significant portion of their time can be redeemed for the good of God's kingdom. Story tellers seek to cultivate discipleship communities in which members encourage one another in practical ways so that each might fully live his or her vocation for the sake of others. Martin Luther King Jr. put it this way: "If it falls to your lot to be a street sweeper, sweep streets like Michelangelo painted, or Beethoven composed music, or Shakespeare wrote poetry. Sweep streets so well that all the hosts of heaven will have to say, 'Here lies the street sweeper who did his job well.'"[13] The apostle Paul was in agreement: "Whatever your task, work heartedly, as serving the Lord and not men" (Col 3:23 RSV). Evangelists help the congregation to become redemptive agents, seeking to join God in the renewal of all things, while remembering the "now" and "not yet" nature of God's kingdom.

LIVING IT LOCALLY

While his primary gift is apostolic in nature, Aaron Graham's secondary gift is that of an evangelist. Having these two gifts is fairly common for fruitful church planters. As the founding pastor of the newly established District Church in the heart of Washington, D.C., he is doing much to see the church he serves become Christ for the sake of neighborhood and the world, and it has resulted in dozens of people coming to Christ or returning to Christ, and hundreds finding community and living as redemptive agents in the heart of the District.

Aaron and his community demonstrate what it means to be a church *for* the city. The city is one of contradictions. It is one of the most educated cities in the country, yet has the lowest performing public schools. D.C. is one of the wealthiest metropolitan areas, yet it has the highest percentage of people living in extreme poverty. Mistrust between African Americans and the white community runs deep. One of the ways the church is seeking to serve the city is through the Columbia Heights Youth Center, where they are devoting energy to bridging the educational gap to at-risk neighborhood kids. They help with festivals in the city and Aaron wrote an article for the *Washington Post* on the Advent Conspiracy (see www.adventconspiracy.org), seeking to help people spend less, give more and love all. As a newly started congregation they raised over $100,000 for the plight of those living in the Horn of Africa. As they bless their neighborhood through service and incarnate the good news, people join with them and commit their lives to Christ.

It is encouraging to see how Aaron is helping people be redemptive agents. He recently had a three-part series at a weekly gathering in which he handed the pulpit over to six people of the congregation to share how God is using some of their biggest questions and darkest moments to deepen their faith and bless the world. One person who shared in this series was Lindsay, a filmmaker whose work has been featured on CNN many times, who tells the stories of children suffering violence and abuse. She talked about the documentary she is finishing up about two child soldiers she followed in the Congo over the last few years. Five other people shared some amazing ways that God is using them in their vocations, which helps the entire congregation realize how their vocations can be sacred callings lived for the glory of God and the good of the world.

Discerning If You Are an Evangelist

- Do you have a heart for those far from God?
- Do you feel frustrated that the congregation is too inward oriented?
- Are you incarnating the good news in your neighborhood or within a people group?
- Are you helping your community represent God's reign as a sign, foretaste and instrument of the kingdom?
- Do you find yourself helping others in the congregation view their vocation in redemptive ways?
- Do you find yourself equipping others to do the same?

14

Pastors
Soul Healers

My job is not to solve people's problems or make them happy, but to help them see the grace operating in their lives.

EUGENE PETERSON

I am the good shepherd. The good shepherd lays down his life for the sheep.

JOHN 10:11

In his book *Jesus in the Margins,* Rick McKinley shares stories of people who have experienced deep emotional wounds. The book tells the story of Tiffany, a nine-year-old who was molested by a family member. Tiffany stayed silent, fearing the family member and resenting her parents for allowing it to happen. The abuse continued until she was twelve, when she finally told her mother what was happening.

> She [the mother] cried so loud and for so long. I realized then the gravity of what had happened. . . .
>
> I've never been able to scrub the sick feeling off my soul that was put there through the abuse. So I just go through life feeling that if anyone ever knew who I was on the inside, they would simply reject me.[1]

Tiffany was left with deep emotional wounds. She was left with hatred toward men. Her distrust went beyond sexual relationships; she was scared to give herself to them emotionally. She also held anger toward God, questioning his love and willingness to allow this to happen, longing for someone to love her despite her past. But Tiffany eventually found healing.

> I am always amazed at how God has met me in the deepest parts of me. . . . I realize that God has loved me the whole time. The abuse taught me that I was worthless, but Christ has taught me that I am precious to him.
>
> The greatest thing is that in his love I could really forgive the person who hurt me and move on. Moving on is a daily thing for me. I can't say that it's cut-and-dried or that the pain is gone forever, but it is different now.[2]

The abuse Tiffany suffered is too common, but her journey toward healing *is not* common enough. We live in a broken world, a world in which other people have disfigured our souls and we have in turn disfigured others'. We are broken people in need of healing. With the help of God we can move toward wholeness, but it doesn't happen automatically.

PASTORS AS SOUL HEALERS

Pastors, or soul healers, help us work through past hurts and pursue wholeness, not just individually but in the context of community. While most of our brokenness comes from our dysfunctional experiences in family or community, most of our healing and wholeness comes in the context of new community. Soul healers help the community to *cultivate a life-giving spirituality* and *embody reconciliation*.

Pastors have a deep sense of the brokenness with in us and our communities, and they seek to bring healing and wholeness to people and relationships. They recognize the difference between counterfeit community—where people wear masks and try to hide themselves from God and others, creating isolation—and authentic community. Soul healers create a sense of family, where people can learn to live vulnerably.

The pastor helps the community have a realistic picture of community and understand that the community-building process is filled with both pain and joy. If people come into community expecting utopia, they will likely leave hurt, disappointed and possibly never give community another attempt. Paul's letters are filled with the messiness of community. Community is messy because it is a collection of imperfect people seeking to be transformed by God together.[3] Anyone can love the ideal church. The challenge is to love the real church. Soul healers help the congregation do this.

Table 14.1. Pastors

Equipper	Focal Concern	*Telos* (Destinations) Marks
Pastor (soul healer)	Seeking wholeness and holiness	Cultivating life-giving spirituality within community and embodying reconciliation

CULTIVATING A LIFE-GIVING SPIRITUALITY WITHIN COMMUNITY

The first *telos* of a pastor is *cultivating a life-giving spirituality within community*. Soul healers seek to create an environment that facilitates healing, growth and transformation. They seek to create rhythms of life for the community which enables people to be spiritually renewed, emotionally recharged and physically refreshed. A life-giving spirituality is about the formation of the entire person—heart, soul, strength and mind, our "body, emotions, sexuality, consciousness, the unconscious, longings and desires, thoughts, senses and imagination, and much more."[4] Soul healers understand that spiritual formation takes place when people simultaneously grow in self-awareness and God-awareness, self-knowledge and knowledge of God. So they find ways to help the community to engage in practices that increase people's awareness, and help people to be fully present with God and each other.

Because soul healers care about the whole person, they seek to insure that the community is pursuing an inward, outward and upward journey in a life-giving way. They understand that genuine service and mission flow from our communion with God. For "only a deeply rooted communion can enable the growth of our character in Christ and consequently empower our service for him."[5]

Soul healers help us to recognize that intimacy with Christ (the upward journey) and becoming like Christ (the inward journey) come prior to service to and for Christ (the outward journey). They remind us that if we hope to live missional lives that are fruitful and sustainable, then we must stay connected to the vine. For "spiritual formation is the lifelong journey of experiencing the presence of Christ such that we become increasingly formed in his character and are thus enabled to live our lives for his service on behalf of others."[6]

A life-giving spirituality is something that can only happen within community. As Henri Nouwen has said, "Apart from a vital relationship with a caring community a vital relationship with Christ is not possible."[7] If you cut your tongue off from the rest of the body, it dies. We need the body of Christ to become whole and holy. Thus pastors cultivate an environment where people can develop spiritual friends, spiritual guides, spiritual mentors and spiritual directors.[8] We need each other.

> We need someone who encourages us when we are tempted to give it all up, to forget it all, to just walk away in despair. We need someone who discourages us when we move too rashly in unclear directions or hurry proudly to a nebulous goal. We need someone who can suggest to us when to read and when to be silent, which words to reflect upon and what to do when silence creates much fear and little peace.[9]

Soul healers help us to live in reality, reminding us that the "route toward progressive holiness and union with God is paved with struggle and suffering, as an important prelude to glory."[10] Knowing Christ involves sharing in his suffering as well as experiencing his resurrection power. Soul healers help the community to realize that a "truly powerful and fruitful ministry is unlocked through the exercise of powerlessness and weakness."[11] And finally, that the path to wholeness includes brokenness and woundedness.[12] Soul healers help us become "wounded healers," recognizing that "human brokenness is not a fatal condition of which we have become sad victims, but the bitter fruit of the human choice to say 'No' to love."[13] The pastor thus prays that the congregation might experientially know the heights, the depths, the width and the breadth of Christ's love (Eph 3:18).

Soul healers also cultivate a life-giving spirituality by helping people play together. Social scientists have discovered the serious need for play, not just for children but also for adults. We need to rediscover the joy of just having fun with each other. In *Beyond Love and Work: Why Adults Need to Play*, Lenore Terr notes that while what we do for recreation, like working out at the gym or going to the beach, is beneficial and relaxing, they do not encourage the same spirit of release and abandon that play can provide.[14]

Stuart Brown, in *Play: How It Shapes the Brain, Opens the Imagination and Invigorates the Soul*, not only shares the benefits of play but describes play as a biological drive that is as essential to our health as sleep and nutrition. While he is reluctant to define play, because it is like explaining a joke—analyzing it kind of takes the joy away—he does share some properties of play. He tells us that play is simply done for its own sake in that it has no apparent purpose. Play is fun and makes a person feel good. When we engage in play we lose track of time and have a diminished consciousness of self. Play has improvisational potential in that there aren't rigid rules, so there is room for spontaneity. And play is pleasurable in that we desire to keep on playing.[15]

There are likely some people in the congregation you serve that feel as if they have no one to play with, and this simple fact is beating them up emotionally. Loneliness can lead down a dark path. Soul healers understand this, so they seek to bring some healing and wholeness to the community by simply creating time for people to play together. Communities that pray and *play* together, stay together.

EMBODYING RECONCILIATION

The second *telos* of pastors is helping the congregation *embody reconciliation*. Pastors help the community understand that while conflict is natural, unresolved conflict is sinful. Division is one of the central impediments to representing God's reign to the world. While everyone experiences conflict, those who live in Christ are given both the power and instructions on how to resolve conflict. If we want to be those who bring the good news of forgiveness and reconciliation to all people, we must learn the art of forgiveness and begin practicing it within our own congregations.

Jesus taught frequently about our need to forgive one another and embody reconciliation. One of those times when he was with his disciples he said, "If your brother or sister sins against you, rebuke them; and if they repent, forgive them. Even if they sin against you seven times in a day and seven times come back to you saying 'I repent,' you must forgive them" (Lk 17:3-4). As you might imagine, this was a lot for the disciples to take, so their response was, "Increase our faith!" (Lk 17:5). Ever feel like that after someone has wronged you? Jesus replied, "If you have faith as small as a mustard seed, you can say to this mulberry tree, 'be uprooted and planted in the sea,' and it will obey you" (Lk 17:6). Jesus makes it clear that with the smallest amount of faith we can forgive, if we want to forgive. This issue isn't whether we have the capacity to forgive but whether we have the desire to forgive. Forgiven people forgive people.

Paul consistently called people to forgive one another, saying, "Be kind and compassionate to one another, forgiving each other, just as in Christ God forgave you" (Eph 4:32). Another time he said, "Bear with each other and forgive one another if any of you has a grievance against someone. Forgive as the Lord forgave you" (Col 3:13). The topic of forgiveness is one of the most consistent themes in Scripture, which is why soul healers help the congregation to embody forgiveness. Forgiveness is something we need to practice, and it "entails unlearning all those things that divide and destroy communion and learning to see and live as forgiven and forgiving people."[16]

We are called to represent the reality of God's kingdom to this world by living as people reconciled to God, to each other and to all of creation. We are called *to embody the ministry* of reconciliation so the message entrusted to us is faithfully delivered to the world. Pastors help the congregation to do this.

We live in a world where many people opt for hate and revenge instead of love and forgiveness. If we want to follow Jesus, we must follow his calling and learn to be a people who *love our enemies and do good to those hate us, bless those who persecute us, and pray for those who mistreat us* (Lk 6:27-28). We need to learn the art of reconciliation and forgiveness.

Most of the time when we are wronged, we simply want to wrong others as well. Forgiveness doesn't come naturally. It's like the story that I heard. A guy saw a Porsche for sale in a newspaper for $50. He couldn't believe it, but it was true. He went to see the car and discovered that it was a relatively new car in mint condition. He said to the woman at the house, "Is this the Porsche being advertised in the paper for only $50?" She said it was. Amazed, he asked why she was selling it so cheap. She said, "Not too long ago my husband divorced me and ran away with a younger woman. He told me, 'You can have the house and everything, but just sell the Porsche and send me the check for what you were able to get from it.'"[17] Revenge is one of the common ways we respond when people hurt us, but have you noticed that when we seek revenge, it usually hurts us more?

Unfortunately, I've seen how badly some people can hurt themselves. Some who have gone a little further, who I saw while I worked at St. Alban's psychiatric hospital. I happened to be working in the closed unit one particular day, and they called "male alert," which meant all of the available males were to go to one place in the hospital because someone was endangering his or her own life and possibly the lives of others. I know that this individual was on the way to my unit.

He finally got there, and they sat him down in the lounge area. He sat a couple of seats away from me; I tried to engage him in conversation, but he wasn't too congenial at the time. All of the sudden he started swinging his arms around. I ducked so that I wouldn't get hit. He was having hallucinations, seeing big spiders on the wall.

Eventually, for his and others' protection, the staff had to tie the man to his bed. I was appointed to spend the next five hours with him as he was screaming "Get those spiders away" at the top of his lungs. He pointed to some sores on his body and said, "That's where they bit me last night!" He sounded so believable that I started to look around for these big spiders. After hours of screaming at the top of his lungs, he finally decided to talk.

I found out that this guy drove himself to this state because of the bitterness and anger that he had toward a couple of people. I knew it was bitterness and anger that drove him to drink and do drugs for a number of reasons, one of which was because he would say a person's name and shout, "You watch, I'm going to kill him!" You see, anger and resentment hurts us. His former wife and friend sounded like they were doing just fine; he was the one in the hospital. Is there a better way than revenge?

I heard this true story from Richard Froth, a seminary president. When he was in Romania he sat down with some members of a church who told him about a young Protestant who went up to Moldova to begin a church. The people—the city fathers, the elders, the ruling people—didn't want him in town. They said if you come to this town and build anything, a church or anything, we will tear it down.

The young man felt God calling him to begin a work, and he went to Moldova and started by building a house for his family. He built the house, and he and his family moved in. The next morning, early in the morning they heard a knock. They went to the gate, opened it up and there stood eight men. They said, "We are here to tear down your house." The young pastor stepped back and said, "Do what you need to do."

They men proceeded to climb on the roof and they started tearing the roof off, one piece at a time. They worked all morning. About 11:30 the pastor said to his wife, "Honey, we need to fix some lunch." The wife agreed. "You probably should fix it for, oh, twelve people." She said, "What?" He said, "Yes, twelve people." "What for?" she asked. "Well, for the people up on the roof." She said, "What? They're our enemies. They hate us. They're tearing down our house." He said, "But Jesus said we are to love our enemies and to do good to those who hate us. They have been working hard. I'm sure their hungry." So she made them lunch, and the pastor invited them into the house. The weary men came down from the roof, entered the house and started to eat. They said, "Why are you doing this?" He said, "Because we are followers of Jesus. Jesus said to love your enemies; you're our enemies, at least you feel like you are. We don't know why you're doing this, but you think you're doing something that is good and right. We don't understand that, but we love you anyway and we forgive you for doing this." After lunch they thanked the woman for the food, climbed back on the roof and started putting the roof back on, one piece at a time. And when the young pastor and his wife opened a church in that village, those eight men were the first eight converts.

The kingdom of God is a different kind of place. It is different than the kingdom of this world and is made up of people who know how to love others. If we are going to learn to love one another like this, loving our enemies, we must practice forgiveness.

LIVING IT LOCALLY

As a gifted pastor at Kairos Hollywood in Los Angeles, Audrey Blumber, a bivocational minister, finds time to help the congregation embody reconciliation and engage in life-giving spirituality. Every congregation has conflict, but not every congregation seeks to resolve conflict in healthy ways. As a conflict mediator Audrey is well aware that Jesus calls us to resolve conflict. She not only facilitates conflict resolution but helps train others to do the same. When she and the other equippers are having a difficult time coming to unity in resolving issues, she will ask probing or challenging questions that help people to share their heart with utmost honesty. As a team builder she encourages the team of equippers to regularly confess any wrong and seek forgiveness. In this way the equippers lead the congregation by example.

In addition to being a mediator, Audrey and her husband, Eric, provide premarital and marriage counseling for those who are engaged, close to getting engaged or married. She regularly takes prayer walks through the streets of East Hollywood, praying for healing, restoration, reconciliation, hope and freedom for her neighbors.

And maybe one of the most important acts of service that she engages in is soul listening. She makes herself available to listen to anyone who wants to talk. There are no rules. People can just share their heart with her, ask questions and pray with her. Audrey has found that listening is one of the most important acts of love she does. She recognizes that what is deep in people's heart and soul needs to be heard by a caring human being and that many times it is in the context of listening that people finally hear their own voices and God's voice.

Discerning If You Are a Pastor

- Do you have a heart for those hurting in the congregation?
- Do you find yourself seeking ways for your community to be more like a family?
- Do you feel that the other leaders are too outward oriented and are not paying enough attention to the internal needs of the church?
- Do you find yourself walking with people through their pain, helping them to pursue wholeness and holiness in the context of community?
- Are you a peacemaker in the congregation, seeking to help the congregation embody forgiveness and reconciliation?
- Do you find yourself equipping others to do these same things?

15

Teachers
Light Givers

The Bible is there to enable God's people to be equipped to do God's work in God's world, not to give them an excuse to sit back smugly, knowing they possess all God's truth.

N. T. WRIGHT

When Jesus had finished saying these things, the crowds were amazed at his teaching, because he taught as one who had authority, and not as their teachers of the law.

MATTHEW 7:28-29

On a recent trip to the Sundance Film Festival, I had the opportunity to see a number of amazing films, including *Higher Ground*. As I watched this film I identified with the main character, Corinne. Though I came to faith later in life, I shared some of the same struggles she experienced in my first experiences with Christian community.

In the film Corinne grew up going to church and raised her hand to "get saved" at a young age, but her faith soon faded into the background. After getting pregnant and then married just out of high school, Corinne and her husband, Ethan, had a dramatic conversion to Christ and became involved with a fundamentalist group. The film goes beyond the typical one-dimensional portrait of unlovable Christians, showing a genuine faith within this fundamentalist church. This Christian community was lovable, sincere, intelligent and caring. But the movie is not without its haunting moments; while the group loved God and immersed themselves in the Scriptures, they shut out theological dialogue, including the role of women in ministry.

Sometimes, when Corinne would speak during the open sharing time, she would be interrupted for transgressing the line between "sharing a testimony" and "preaching." After twenty years in this community, it became too suffocating for Corinne. Despite her deep yearning for God, she decided to leave. Corinne had suffered enough from the effects of the leader's particular approach to interpreting Scripture. The film ends with her standing in the doorway of the church, looking out and then looking in, unsure of which way to go.

During the question-and-answer session, Vera Farmiga, the director of the film as well as the actress who played Corinne, was asked if Corinne was ridding herself of the faith or not. Vera answered, "She is not ridding herself of the faith, *she is ridding herself from an impoverished faith.*"

As I have pondered that response, I have come to realize how important it is for the community of faith to have gifted teachers. While all of the equippers communicate privately and publicly, teachers help the community interpret the text with a hermeneutic of love.

TEACHERS AS LIGHT GIVERS

Gifted teachers, whom I call *light givers*, shed light on the text and help us understand it in a life-giving and liberating way.[1] Teachers help the congregation to actively inhabit the sacred text by *immersing ourselves in Scripture* and *dwelling faithfully in God's story.* Teachers understand the importance of the Word of God in transforming lives. They help God's people remember that the Bible is a voice to be heard, not just a book to read. A good teacher does not approach Scripture with a wooden literalism but as the voice of God, pulling us into transformative dialogue with him. Teachers help the community understand that interpreting Scripture is both an art and a science. They seek to help the congregation develop a hermeneutical approach that allows us to be "a community capable of hearing the story of God we find in the scripture and living in a manner that is faithful to that story."[2]

Table 15.1. Teachers

Equipper	Focal Concern	*Telos* (Destinations) Marks
Teacher (light giver)	Inhabiting the sacred text	Immersing ourselves in Scripture and dwelling faithfully in God's story

IMMERSING OURSELVES IN SCRIPTURE

The first *telos* of teachers is to help the congregation be *immersed in Scripture*. There are of course many ways to do this. The Navigators teach five primary ways of learning Scripture, using the fingers on a hand.[3] The pinky finger is for hearing, the ring finger for reading, the middle finger for studying, the forefinger for memorizing, and the thumb, the strongest digit, represents meditating. We would do well to immerse ourselves in these ways. Other methods include *lectio divina*, singing Scripture and using the lectionary.[4] All of these are great ways to immerse ourselves in Scripture, and the more we do these communally the better. Here are a few lesser known but rewarding ways to immerse ourselves in Scripture.

The first month after I became a Christ follower, I was a resident assistant in a college dorm, praying that God would give me an opportunity to share my faith with the guys on my hall sometime during the school year. This desire led to a fascinating year. I would often find conversations with the residents turning toward questions about the Bible and God. When answering someone's questions about the Bible, the dorm room would spontaneously fill up with other residents eager for answers to spiritual questions. At times like this I realized the power of studying the Scripture with those who considered themselves outside of the kingdom of God. Because I wanted to be able to help them understand God's story better, I was motivated to understand, know and memorize the Scripture. Studying with those who didn't believe opened my eyes to the importance of being immersed in Scripture communally. They asked questions of the text that I had never thought of, helping me see the text from different angles and gaining fresh insights I would have never developed on my own.

In addition to studying Scripture with students, some of whom became Christ followers, I also studied with those at the psychiatric hospital where I worked, most of whom were depressed and suicidal. Seeing the power of Scripture to bring healing to their lives, demonstrated that God's Word is indeed living and active.

Reading Scripture with the oppressed can show us the power of the Word to liberate the imagination. Reading with the poor demonstrates the power of the Word to give hope. Bob Ekblad explores this idea in *Reading the Bible with the Damned*. His richest reading of Scripture has come with "outsiders." The chapter titles of Ekblad's book are revealing: "Encountering God in Exodus and at Today's Margins," "Reading Paul with Undocumented Immigrants" and "Reading the Gospels with Tax Collectors and Sinners."[5] I would contend that if more people read the Bible with "the damned," more of us would be reminded of the power of God's Word to transform lives, even our own. Whether through spiritual disciplines or reading Scripture with the marginalized, the teacher finds creative ways to immerse the community in Scripture so they can live faithfully in God's story.

DWELL FAITHFULLY IN GOD'S STORY

Besides helping the congregation immerse themselves in Scripture, a second *telos* of teachers is helping people to *dwell faithfully in God's story*. To stay true to the God of the story, we not only need to interpret Scripture with a lens of love but we have to reclaim Scripture as narrative. N. T. Wright likens Scripture to a five-act play. He says:

> Suppose there exists a Shakespeare play whose fifth act had been lost. The first four acts provide, let us suppose, such a wealth of characterization, such a crescendo of excitement within the plot, that it is generally agreed that the play ought to be staged. Nevertheless, it is felt inappropriate actually to write a fifth act once and for all: it would freeze the play into one form, and commit Shakespeare as it were to being prospectively responsible for work not in fact his own. Better, it might be felt, to give the key parts to highly trained, sensitive and experienced Shakespearian actors, who would immerse themselves in the first four acts, and in the language and

culture of Shakespeare and his time, *and who would then be told to work out a fifth act for themselves.*[6]

Wright proposes that in this fifth act, the actors would improvise, using both innovation and consistency: innovating as they move the story forward, all the while being consistent to the subplots and themes that the author has already developed. The actors are not called to merely imitate an earlier act. Rather, the authority of the first four acts inform the way they live out the fifth act, bringing the various threads of the story together in a way that is faithful to the author.

It's as if we've been given the first four acts (Creation, Fall, Israel, Jesus) and the last piece of the fifth act (New Creation) in the Scriptures. Now, as people who live in this real-life drama, we are called to know these acts so well that we can improvise our lives in ways that are faithful to the God of the story.

But we are not left to do this on our own. In *Theology for the Community of God*, Stanley Grenz reminds us of the key role of the Holy Spirit. He says that it is "ultimately not the book itself we are affirming" but the Spirit who speaks to us through the sacred text.[7] He explains that the Bible, "the Book," points to God as the One who has authority, and how inspiration and illumination are best emphasized as one act of the Holy Spirit. So as we engage the interrelated sources of Scripture, heritage and culture, we strive to hear what the Spirit has to say to us as we are on mission in the world. Without the duality of inspiration and illumination of the Spirit in the early church, we wouldn't have the New Testament.

If we are going to interpret Scripture in a life-giving and liberating way, we must recognize the faithfulness of the Spirit from creation until new creation. As we listen to the Spirit by immersing ourselves in the story of Scripture—the events of the past (e.g., the liberation of the Israelites from Egypt and the life, death and resurrection of Jesus) and the events in the future (the new heavens and new earth)—we can faithfully join God in his mission of renewing all things.

It is true that we sometimes make the Bible say what *we* want it to say. Any of us can misunderstand Scripture and use it improperly, and many have. We often find Jesus rescuing the Bible from the hands of the religious leaders—the scribes, the Sadducees and the Pharisees—who sometimes used it to oppress others. Jesus used the Scriptures to subvert the religious leaders' interpretation of Scripture in order to liberate the people and set them free to reach their divine potential. Jesus used a hermeneutic of love to inaugurate a kingdom built by love.

For teachers within the missional church, equipping the community in the art and science of reading the text is an especially difficult job. Missional teachers need to develop a missional hermeneutic, an eye for reading the text so that the people of God will be equipped to do God's work in God's world. Unfortunately, since missiology and ecclesiology have been estranged, the practice of a missional hermeneutic is still in an embryonic state. In this young field, George Hunsberger has identified four new approaches to missional hermeneutics.

The missional direction of the story. "The *framework* for biblical interpretation is the story it tells of the mission of God and the formation of a community sent to participate in it."[8] Chris Wright and others are developing this approach. The idea is that the *missio Dei* (the mission of God) provides the key for interpreting and understanding the Scriptures. Wright proposes a shift from "the biblical basis for mission" to "the missional bases of the Bible." We used to simply look at Scripture for the verses and stories that call us to mission. But now we also understand that Scripture is "a product of mission in action."[9]

The missional purpose of the writings. "The *aim* of interpretation is to fulfill the equipping purpose of the writings."[10] Darrell Guder and others are developing this approach. Guder wants congregations to recognize that God blesses us so that we might be a blessing to others. So the question we take to the text is not so much What can I get out of this? but rather "How does God's Word call, shape, transform, and send me . . . and us?"[11] Guder seeks the continual conversion of the church, understanding that all who do not live fully under the reign of God, all of us, need continued conversion. He also speaks of moving from a "theology of mission" to a "missional theology."[12]

The missional location of the readers. "The *approach* required for a faithful reading of the Bible is from the missional location of the Christian community."[13] Michael Barram recognizes the many insidious ways our culture shapes us. Our cultural fixations are with "bottom lines, quick fixes, and technological innovation," which can lead to our biblical interpretation becoming "formulaic, emphasizing method and technique over open-ended curiosity and introspection." This runs the risk "that our efforts will mirror our interests and proclivities rather than God's."[14] Barram suggests we protect ourselves from this proclivity by examining our own perspectives and presuppositions through critical questioning.[15] Does our reading emphasize the triumph of Christ's resurrection to the exclusion of the kenotic, cruciform character of his ministry? Does our reading of the text reflect a tendency to separate evangelism and justice? In what ways does the text challenge us to rethink our often cozy relationships with power and privilege? Does the text help clarify the call of gospel discipleship in a world of conspicuous consumption, devastating famine, rampant disease, incessant war and vast economic inequities?[16]

The missional engagement with cultures. "The gospel functions as the interpretive *matrix* within which the received biblical tradition is brought into critical conversation with a particular human context."[17] Jim Brownson is interested in how the New Testament authors appropriate the Old Testament into their local context while on mission. This might instruct us how we too might do it. He looks at the response of the church between the gospel and culture, believing the gospel is the inner guiding system that shaped Paul's approach to how he used the Old Testament in his missional contexts.

Each of these approaches to a missional hermeneutic brings a valuable contribution to a developing tapestry of missional theology, and provides interpretive tools that the light giver can teach the congregation so that people might live faithfully to the story of God and the God of the story.

LIVING IT LOCALLY

John Chandler, a bivocational church planter, lives in a city whose motto is "Keep Austin Weird."[18] Yes, that would be the sexy city of Austin, Texas. John's gift mix is teacher-prophet, and while teaching is his primary gift, the needs of the congregation and season of the church plant could move his prophetic gift to the forefront. When people visit the Austin Mustard Seed website (which he designed), they realize that

John is a gifted teacher. Moving from the site's beliefs section to the values section (both of which are found under "About"), you see the freshness in the words he uses as well as his holistic approach.

It just so happens that the first of the three core values for Austin Mustard Seed is "Story." As a community they approach Scripture as the history of God's work among humanity, recognizing that this story is still being written, much like N. T. Wright's fifth-act metaphor. When they engage in Scripture together, the core question they ask is, How can we continue to partner with God in the writing of this story going forward?

Twice a month at their weekly gatherings, they read Scripture together as a regular practice. Then they engage in dialogue based on what he has taught. Dialogue is preferred over monologue, because dialogue engages those who are learning. In addition, one Sunday a month they explore various spiritual disciplines for the purpose of recognizing the Spirit's direction day to day. Practices like *lectio divina* help them to hear God's voice and enriches their reading of Scripture, as their souls are more fertile to the call and transformation that come from it. Finally, one Sunday a month, rather than gather as a community, they go out to the community. Because they believe that God's story is one that is working toward redemption and repair, physically taking part in that work engages them in the story in a way that mere reading cannot.

Discerning If You Are a Teacher

- Do you have a hunger to devour and understand the Scriptures?
- Do you feel frustrated that others don't have the same hunger?
- Do you find yourself helping others to inhabit the sacred text?
- Do you demonstrate a passion to help the community understand Scripture in order to live faithfully to God and his mission?
- Do you help equip others to do these things as well?

PART FOUR

Embodying a Missional Culture

16

The Cultural Web and
the Neighborhood Church

It is surely a fact of inexhaustible significance that what the Lord left behind Him was not a book, nor a creed, nor a system of thought, nor a rule of life, but a visible community.

LESSLIE NEWBIGIN

His intent was that now, through the church, the manifold wisdom of God should be made known to the rulers and authorities in the heavenly realms, according to his eternal purpose that he accomplished in Christ Jesus our Lord.

THE APOSTLE PAUL, EPHESIANS 3:10-11

How do we create a missional culture that helps shape mature disciples who live *in* the world without being *of* the world, for the sake *of* their neighborhood?

While each neighborhood church is called to be a sign, foretaste and instrument of God's kingdom, she is to do so in light of *who* she is and *where* she is ministering. You have heard of original sin. When it comes to models or approaches to being the church, too many people have fallen for the "unoriginal sin."[1] There is a reason why, out of the trillions of snowflakes that have fallen, no two have been found to be identical and no two fingerprints are alike. God loves diversity. "God does not mass-produce his church."[2]

Every church is a unique expression of God's kingdom. The congregation's specific calling will be shaped as she considers her gifts, talents, passions and resources, in light of her context and theological understanding. A church uniquely expresses herself as she matches her deep hunger with the needs of the neighborhood.

THE CULTURAL WEB AND THE LOCAL CHURCH

With this in mind, let's look at how the six aspects of culture that I outlined in chapter two can be applied to a specific neighborhood church. To illustrate how the cultural web interacts with the culture of the congregation, I've put the different elements of culture on the cross, reminding us that the church is not just a social organization but has divine roots, and that the foundation of the church is Christ. The dove

Figure 16.1. The cultural web

in figure 16.1 reminds us that the church is holy as well as human. The same Holy Spirit who birthed the church at Pentecost is leading the church today. As we start to look at practical ways to create a missional culture we must remember the unique nature of the church. We must also remember that God has a part and we have a part in creating a missional culture. We can't do God's part, and he won't do ours.

As you look at figure 16.1, you can see that

language and *artifacts* are central to developing a missional culture, for they typically shape the other parts of the cultural web. The other four elements of culture—*narrative, rituals, institution* and *ethics*—give meaning to language and artifacts.

If the equippers and the leadership community hope to join God on his mission in the neighborhood, it is essential for them to have a clear understanding of their cultural web. Each element of the cultural web answers vital questions that the equippers and community need to address. Each element helps to create the DNA of the congregation. Let's first examine figure 16.1, which gives us the various elements of the cultural web, and then consider four crucial questions.

Language and *artifacts* are central to creating culture and are integral to the other four elements depicted on the cross—narrative, rituals, institution and ethics. Four questions will help us understand and shape the culture of the congregation we serve.

- Narrative—*What is God's calling for our church?*
- Rituals—*What are our core practices?*
- Institution—*How will we fulfill our calling?*
- Ethics—*What does it mean for us to be faithful and fruitful?*

Narrative. The communal calling of a church is shaped by her approach to theology, the significant stories that shape the community and the primary teachings of the community (doctrines). The church's calling is not something we invent; it is something we discover. The narrative of our missional calling is discerned by asking, *What is God's calling for our church?* This involves who God is calling us to be and what God is calling us to do. Some find it helpful to have a clear and concise slogan to capture the calling of the church in a succinct way. Imago Dei in Richmond, Virginia, articulates their calling this way: "Reflect One, Restore Many, Renew All." Notice how this statement is weighty but easy to remember. Trinity Grace church in New York City has embraced "Joining God in the renewal of all things." Notice the clarity, conciseness and depth of their statement. This particular *artifact* gives us a clue to Trinity Grace's approach to theology and ministry. First, they clearly understand that

God has a mission in the world, and we are invited to join him on his mission. Second, God's mission is not private, concerned *only* with people's souls, but holistic. It is cosmic, communal and personal.

While having a slogan reminds the community of her purpose, her calling goes beyond learning slogans. A community must understand her basic philosophical and theological assumptions, and how they shape her understanding of God's story.

For example, a basic assumption I have is that conversion is necessary for every man and woman who does not live under the reign of God. It is not enough for people to give mental assent to a certain set of facts without a concern for personal and global transformation. While there is a moment when people move from death to life, having placed their faith in the person and work of Christ, an undue emphasis on this event alone coupled with an anemic understanding of the gospel can stunt the process of genuine transformation. The good news is an invitation to "switch stories" and join God in the renewal of all things, which includes our own redemption. God gives us a new identity and new life in Christ so we might be a blessing to the world. That is what grace is all about. It is by grace through faith that we are forgiven and made new. And it is by grace through faith that we are enabled to live out our missional calling in the world for the sake of the world in the way of Christ.

When it comes to discerning truth and reality, I am convinced that truth is discerned communally through Scripture as narrative, through the focal images of community, cross and new creation.[3] Reason, tradition and experience help us understand Scripture and enable us to see and live in God's reality.

Each faith community needs to develop areas of conviction about the substance of their faith (doctrines), which become primary teaching points in the community, which in turn shape the community's calling in the world. As the community articulates these, they create artifacts that shape the culture. To create a missional culture, we need to examine our primary convictions and ask ourselves if they reflect a missional theology.

Rituals. Our missional practices are discerned through our rituals. In order to do this the church asks, *What are our core practices?* Identifying core practices moves us beyond *espousing* values to *living* values. If we hope to see transformation in our communities, we need to engage in thick practices, which are embodied practices that reshape our desires and form us into the kind of people we want to become (see chap. 17). Thick practices shape our identities and move us toward a particular vision of human flourishing.

When developing communal core practices, it is important to consider both the *environment* that practice creates along with the *telos* of each practice. I have placed rituals on the left side of the cross and ethics on the right (see fig. 16.1) because our rituals—in particular, our liturgies (thick practices)—shape who we become, our ethics. Core practices correlate with the kind of people we hope to become. Each equipper's focal concern and *telos* paint a vivid picture of what it means to be mature in Christ, and provide a solid and holistic matrix in which to think about core practices. The fruit of the Spirit and the seven virtues over against the seven deadly sins also offer solid pictures of human flourishing.[4] Identifying a set of *core* practices is not designed to limit the church to those specific practices; other practices should be encouraged as well. The core practices simply indicate those that the community considers most vital.

Institution. The institution describes our missional method. We discern this by asking, *How will we fulfill our calling?* This is a vital question because how we approach leadership and how we structure the church shape the culture of the congregation in hidden but powerful ways. Let's go back to the definition of an institution borrowed from Miroslav Volf (chap. 2). An institution is the stable structures of social interaction that develops when at least two people do the same thing together repeatedly. Each church needs to have a *clear approach* to fulfilling her mission—a method, a particular way to live out her calling so that there might be unity and movement. How a church fulfills her calling flows from understanding her marks, for the means ought to correlate with the ends.

I appreciate the strategy that a church in West Los Angeles has developed (see fig. 16.2). This church seeks to fulfill her calling by transitioning missional spaces into discipleship communities, and then connecting geographical clusters of discipleship communities into worship gatherings. So they encourage people to be involved in three spaces.

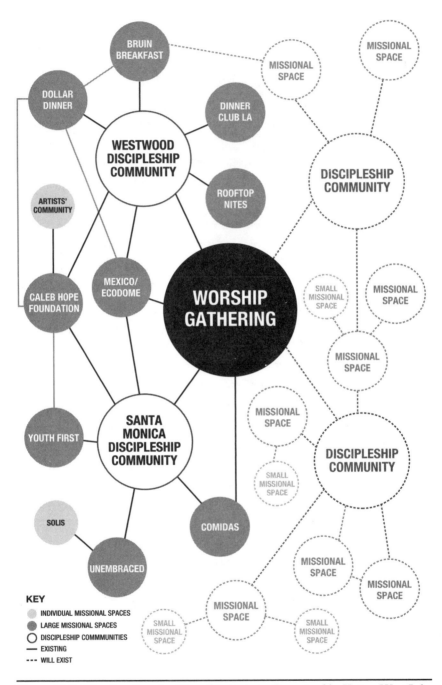

Figure 16.2. West Los Angeles Church's strategy. Conceived by Kairos West LA. Designed by Debbie Kim. Used by permission.

Missional spaces develop around where people work, live, relax or serve, and can be adopted by individuals, a few people or an entire discipleship community. A missional space typically has more unbelievers than believers, and these spaces have some regularity and rhythm about them. They could be gatherings that are started by a discipleship community. For example, the Westwood Discipleship Community hosts a dollar dinner for students at UCLA every other week. The dinner is a great place to meet new people and meet a social need. Missional spaces could also be places where a couple of people from the same discipleship community become active participants in something happening in the neighborhood, such as a neighborhood council. Missional spaces could involve a service to the neighborhood that involves people without faith. Missional spaces are where Christians are connecting meaningfully with non-Christians on a regular basis.

Discipleship communities, or what has become popularly known as missional communities, are mid-sized groups (15-50 people) expressing their "sentness" together in specific missional spaces and developing a communal rhythm of life which forms them to become more like Jesus, incarnating the good news in their neighborhood.

Worship gatherings are weekly times for discipleship communities to meet together to worship God, and to be shaped for and sent on mission. Every church has a liturgy, but in order to create a missional culture in the congregation, it is important for the weekly gatherings to intertwine worship and mission together. Missional liturgies do more than meet felt needs or tell a story, they reshape people to inhabit God's story in their everyday life. A solid missional liturgy incorporates thick practices within the service, which the congregation practices throughout the week within a communal rhythm of life. In this way the congregation is encouraged to move toward her God-given *telos*.

Ethics. Our ethics help us discern our missional marks: *What does it mean for us to be faithful and fruitful?* What are the marks of the church? Too often the prevalent response that people give for success is centered on butts (how many people come to a service), bucks (the church's annual budget) and buildings (the size of the church plant), or as some put it in the United Kingdom, success is defined by people, pounds and pews. Too often success is dictated by the business culture around: the bottom line. I'm thankful that many are recognizing the importance of redefining *success*, recognizing that quantity alone makes for a shallow and thin definition of success.

Henri Nouwen makes the case for us moving from talking about success to talking about being fruitful. He says,

> There is a great difference between successfulness and fruitfulness. Success comes from strength, control, and respectability. A successful person has the energy to create something, to keep control over its development, and to make it available to large quantities. Success brings many rewards and often fame. Fruits, however, come from weakness and vulnerability. And fruits are unique. A child is the fruit conceived in vulnerability, community is the fruit born through shared brokenness, and intimacy is the fruit that grows through touching one another's wounds. Let's remind one another that what brings us true joy is not successfulness but fruitfulness.[5]

So what are some marks of the church? What does it mean to be faithful and fruitful? The following are five pictures to help get your creative juices flowing.

First, there are the classic marks of the church. Whether one is Protestant, Catholic or Orthodox, most consider the four creedal marks of the church important: the one, holy, catholic and apostolic church. Some theologians view these traits as dynamic rather than static. For example, missiologist Charles Van Engen suggests that the marks are better read as adverbs rather than adjectives, capturing the dynamic character of the church on mission. Thus the missional ministry of the church is unifying, sanctifying, reconciling and proclaiming. In addition he makes the case that the four marks ought to be placed in reverse order as a reminder of the church's missional stance. So the missional church is called to be a "proclaiming, reconciling, sanctifying and unifying" community.[6]

Stanley Hauerwas gives us another picture of a mature church. He describes the role of the church as cultivating a people who "can risk being peaceful in a violent world, risk being kind in a competitive society, risk being faithful in an age of cynicism, risk being gentle among those who admire the tough, risk love when it may not be returned, because we have the confidence that in Christ we have been reborn into a new reality."[7]

A third picture comes from Stephen Fowl and Gregory Jones, who describe followers of the Way as people

> who see and do things differently. They are the kind of people who serve rather than dominate, who forgive and seek reconciliation rather than bear grudges and persist in alienating others, who feed the hungry and visit those in prison without any fanfare or expectations of return. They are the kind of people who speak out against injustice, who are more concerned about other's welfare than their own, the kind of people willing to risk their lives so that others may live.[8]

Glen Stassen in *Authentic Transformation* gives us a good picture of Jesus' incarnated life, as the kind of marks of Christian community.

1. Not judging, but forgiving, healing, and breaking down the barriers that marginalize or exclude.

2. Delivering justice: not hording money greedily, but giving alms, forgiving debts, breaking bread together in the common meal, feeding the hungry, announcing good news to the poor, sharing goods, investing money in God's reign and God's delivering justice.

3. Evangelism, preaching the gospel and calling for repentance and discipleship: not timidly seeking honor in society and respect in one's family.

4. Nonviolent transforming initiatives: not returning evil for evil but taking initiatives of peacemaking.

5. Love of enemy: not vague words and sentiments of love, but "the deed of love . . . : table fellowship, emergency aid, release of debt, healing."

6. Mutual servanthood: not patriarchal domination but community with mutual and egalitarian servanthood.

7. Prayer.[9]

And finally I contend that the five focal concerns, further defined by the *telos* toward which each equipper is seeking to move the congregation, would make some great missional marks for the church.

Table 16.1. Equippers

Equipper	Focal Concern	*Telos* (Destinations) Marks
Apostle (dream awakener)	Living out our calling	Creating a discipleship ethos and calling people to participate in advancing God's kingdom
Prophet (heart revealer)	Pursuing God's shalom	Calling the church to God's new social order and standing with the poor and oppressed
Evangelist (story teller)	Incarnating the good news	Proclaiming the good news by being witnesses and being redemptive agents
Pastor (soul healer)	Seeking wholeness and holiness	Cultivating life-giving spirituality within community and embodying reconciliation
Teacher (light giver)	Inhabiting the sacred text	Immersing ourselves in Scripture and dwelling faithfully in God's story

Vision. Once the congregation and equippers have identified their cultural web—their calling, core practices, method and marks—they can seek to discern their vision. People use the word *vision* many ways. When I speak of vision, I'm not talking about a twenty-year dream or a slick vision statement that people memorize but that has no practical relevance for day-to-day living. The vision of a church is a living dynamic expression of faith. It paints a vivid picture of where God is taking the congregation in the next six months to a year. We live in a time of rapid, discontinuous change, so we need adaptable leaders and dynamic visions. The vision of the congregation spells out the primary thing the congregation is trusting God to do in the coming year.

It is helpful for the vision to be clear enough to know whether and when the congregation has reached their destination. The vision should be specific about the next hill the congregation needs to take.

LIVING THE VISION

For the majority of my ministry life I, like Will Mancini,[10] have sensed the significance of having a vision that is both qualitative and quantitative in nature. The qualitative part expresses *why* the vision is important, while the quantitative part is specific and concrete: it is the faith goal.

For example, let's say that the next hill for the congregation is seeing more people in missional spaces become part of discipleship communities. How might the church articulate this vision? First you have the qualitative part: Who has your back? Check out our discipleship communities, where we look after each other's best interest and seek to be like Christ. Then you have the quantitative part of the vision: We hope to multiply our discipleship communities from three to six this year.

Notice that the qualitative part relates to the fact that discipleship communities are places where people can find authentic community and grow to become more like Jesus. That is the part that needs to be emphasized when sharing the vision and the whole reason for the quantitative part of the vision.

Before looking at specific ways to live out this vision, it is important to consider how we measure faithfulness and fruitfulness. Too often the only measure people prize is the bottom line. In other words, did we reach our vision? But there are so many more dynamics at play. We need a fuller and more vibrant way of measuring fruitfulness. Joseph Myers, author of *Organic Community*, gives us some wise advice: "We must understand what we are measuring. We are talking about measuring life—community, relationships, health. We are not talking about measuring inanimate entities. Reducing living organisms to a census count demeans the way we were created."[11]

FAITH GOALS AND WORK GOALS

So how do we measure our faithfulness and fruitfulness as we are seeking to move forward in our vision? First, it is important to remember that God plays a part and we play a part. We can't do God's part, and God won't do ours. Our part is to plant and water; God's part is to cause the growth (1 Cor 3:6). In other words, growth is not in our control. This is why it is important to distinguish between faith goals and work goals. Faith goals typically relate to the quantitative part of our vision. They are goals we are unable to do on our own. They require the intervention of God and the decisions of people. If each discipleship community had the faith goal of multiplying their group by the following year, what might their work goal look like?

If they desire to see missional spaces transformed into discipleship communities, then they would need to examine their current missional spaces to see if they are connecting to enough people in a meaningful way. Discipleship communities (missional communities) will either have one common missional space—a particular neighborhood or people group—or they will be a community of missionaries who support one another in their missional spaces. In this particular case, let's say the discipleship community has multiple missional spaces. Just as Jesus sent people out two by two, if a discipleship community decides to be a community of missionaries that support one another, it is important that at least two people own that particular missional space. It is helpful for discipleship communities to identify up front their approach to missional spaces; this way people will understand the nature of the discipleship community before getting involved.

Then, each discipleship community should discern what their work goals might be to multiply their group. One of the work goals might include regular times of group prayer, specifically praying for people of peace (people open to the gospel who are interested in you and want to be around the community of faith; see Lk 9–10). Other work goals may include enlarging their missional spaces to include more people and developing formal pathways for people to move from missional spaces to discipleship communities.

The Westwood Discipleship Community collectively hosts a dollar dinner every other week to meaningfully connect with UCLA students. That is their missional space. The dollar dinners meet social needs. Some people who come to the dollar dinner may be people of peace (receptive to the discipleship community and to the gospel) who may not be bringing their friends because they are still testing the waters. Praying for these people and their connections would be a wise work goal, a way to water the soil. Another work goal might be to find ways of creating formal paths from the missional space to the discipleship community. One formal pathway, depending on the readiness of the people, might be to invite anyone in the missional space to be a part of a six-week study on basic topics, such as "What is a Christian?" or "Who is Jesus?" The point is to develop formal paths by which people can move from missional spaces toward the discipleship community. These short studies and the response to them could help the discipleship community discern people's readiness to become part of the discipleship community. It is also possible to slowly transform an entire missional space into a discipleship community by introducing a couple of thick practices to the group as a kind of experiment in following Christ, and then assessing people's response along the way.

Too often churches will say, "Unless you believe what we believe and behave like we behave, you cannot belong." In my estimation, when we give people a place to belong, and encourage them to engage in thick practices (behaving), they will discover that they are starting to believe. Think of Cornelius, who with his family was devout and God-fearing: "He gave generously to those in need and prayed to God regularly" (Acts 10:2). Cornelius engaged in thick practices before he ever came to believe. I've often found this to be the case in regard to how people come to faith today: they engage in a thick practice of serving the neighborhood with the faith community, or studying Scripture, or praying, or any host of practices before they have faith and self-identify as a Christian.

The point being, if a discipleship community has the *faith* goal of multiplying itself within the year, they need to work out in detail some quarterly *work* goals that match their faith goal. What kind of planting and watering needs to happen if this faith goal is going to come about? What does faithfulness on our part look like? Then the group must pray and wait on God for the fruit, seeking to be sensitive to the Spirit, always learning and growing and listening.

If the group develops quarterly faith goals and corresponding work goals, the community can assess their faithfulness by whether or not they have kept to their work goals. If they were able to stay faithful to their work goals, doing their part, they can celebrate God's work in their life, whether or not the faith goal came to fruition, because the faith goal is not under their control.

Understanding the difference between faith and work goals is imperative for a congregation. It is also important for a community to grow in discernment in what these goals ought to be. Examining how we have kept or not kept our work goals is one way to measure our faithfulness.

But how do we measure our fruitfulness? Is there a way to measure our faithfulness and fruitfulness that goes beyond the bottom line approach? Joseph Myers gives us some good advice here as well. He reminds us that measurement is not neutral, saying, "We measure that which we perceive to be important. That which we measure will become important and will guide our process. That which we do not measure will become less important." So "measurement has dynamic power over the journey and the results. It is not neutral. The measurement is the message. Our way of measuring is not a neutral tool that simply tells us what there is to see. No, our way of measuring influences that facts in a way that has a profound effect on our perception of reality."[12]

What does Myers propose to be a better way to measure life? He suggests that story is the measurement of community. Someone has said, "Life is not measured by the numbers of breaths we take, but by the number of moments that take our breath away."[13] Because the journey is as important as the destination, story becomes a more holistic way of measuring faithfulness and fruitfulness. But is it an adequate tool to measure what is happening?

As the discipleship community is involved in missional spaces, meaningfully connecting with people and sharing the good news as the Spirit prompts them, stories will be told, and the community will be shaped by these stories. If there is no planting or watering, the story line will indicate a need for more missional stories.

> Shared stories may not fit neat and tidy into a chart or on the back of the Sunday bulletin, but we grow to trust them as a powerful way to measure whether what we are hoping for is taking place. Shared stories are the easiest way to ensure what is important is taken into account. Story helps us measure the life of our communities.[14]

EQUIPPERS CULTIVATING A MISSIONAL CULTURE

If equippers are going to create a missional culture, they need to be able to create a thriving, liberating, welcoming, healing and learning environment in the congregation. In order to do this equippers must understand the power of rituals, especially "thick" practices (liturgies), which have the ability to reshape our desires and redirect our hearts toward God, his kingdom and mission. Helping the congregation develop and engage in a communal rhythm of life (multiple practices and liturgies) will go a long way in creating a missional culture.

17

Cultivating Missional Environments

If the church is to be effective in advocating and achieving a new social order in the nation, it must itself be a new social order.

LESSLIE NEWBIGIN

Therefore I urge you to imitate me. For this reason I am sending you Timothy, my son whom I love, who is faithful in the Lord. He will remind you of my way of life in Christ Jesus, which agrees with what I teach everywhere in every church.

THE APOSTLE PAUL, 1 CORINTHIANS 4:16-17
(NIV 1984, EMPHASIS ADDED)

The prescription for spiritual transformation has often been too individualistically oriented. We are encouraged to engage in spiritual disciplines so that we might have the power to do what we can't do by will power alone. But what happens when people don't have the "will power" to engage spiritual disciples on a consistent basis? Our character is left untended. "In a wild world like ours, your character, left untended, will become a stale room, an obnoxious child, a vacant lot filled with thorns, weeds, broken bottles, raggedy grocery bags, and dog droppings. Your deepest channels will silt in, and you will feel yourself shallowing. You'll become a presence neither you nor others will enjoy, and you and they will spend more and more time and energy trying to be anywhere else."[1] So what are we to do?

As Christians, we eagerly await God's redemption of all things, including ourselves. We were made in the image of God, but through the Fall that image has been shattered. We all need to experience restoration in order to more fully share in God's image and be capable of a greater sense of love, joy, peace and wisdom.

When Paul writes of the five equippers, he says, "Christ himself gave the apostles, the prophets, the evangelists, the pastors and teachers, to equip his people . . . until we all reach unity in the faith and in the knowledge of the Son of God and become mature, *attaining to the whole measure of the fullness of Christ*" (Eph 4:11-13, emphasis added). We are to grow until we become like Christ, and the equippers are to help us grow into that maturity. One of the ways they do this is by helping the congregation (ideally the mid-sized communities or the basic group the congregation is seeking to multiply) to adapt a communal rhythm of life together.

If we want to experience transformation, we need to be a part of a community which develops a rhythm of life together that allows us learn the unforced rhythms of grace. I love how Eugene Peterson puts it in *The Message:*

> Are you tired? Worn out? Burned out on religion? Come to me. Get away with me and you'll recover your life. I'll show you how to take real rest. Walk with me and work with me—watch how I do it. *Learn the unforced rhythms of grace.* I won't lay anything heavy or ill-fitting on you. Keep company with me and you'll learn to live freely and lightly. (Mt 11:28-30, emphasis added)

The unforced rhythms of grace, which include thick practices (liturgies), form us into the kind of people we want to become. Why is it important for communities to develop a rhythm of life, a collection of thick spiritual practices?

THE SIGNIFICANCE OF THICK PRACTICES

In *Desiring the Kingdom* James K. A. Smith makes the case that *if* education is formational rather than informational, then we need to move from people-as-thinkers and people-as-believers *to* people-as-lovers as our primary understanding of human beings. Because humans are intentional creatures whose conscious and unconscious desires and loves are always aimed at some vision of the good life, some articulation of the kingdom, we need to engage thick practices that grab our hearts through our imagination in order to reshape our desires for the kingdom of God.

His proposal is that we are what we *love* more than what we *think* or what we *believe*. And our ultimate love is what we worship. Thus, if we want to experience transformation, we need to recognize that we are liturgical animals who are primarily formed by our desires and loves through our imaginations, which are fueled by stories, images and narratives.

DEVELOPING A COMMUNAL RHYTHM OF LIFE

Thus, if equippers are going to create a missional culture, they need to help the discipleship communities develop communal rhythms of life that reshape our aims, loves and desires toward Christ. A communal rhythm of life is a collection of thick, bodily practices that engage our senses, grab our hearts, form our identities and reshape our desires. These practices cultivate particular environments in the congregation, thereby transforming us. Marjorie Thompson explains:

> The caterpillar must yield up the life it knows and submit to the mystery of interior transformation. It emerges from the process transfigured, with wings that give it freedom to fly. A rule of life [or rhythm of life] gives us a way to enter into the life-long process of personal transformation. Its disciplines help us to shed the familiar but constricting old self and allow our new self in Christ to be formed—the true self that is naturally attracted to the light of God.[2]

Taking part in communal rhythms of life helps break us from our American individualism and shapes us toward Christ within the practices of the community. Table 17.1 is an overview of where we are going and how each equipper seeks to cultivate the particular environments introduced in chapter three through particular practices.

Table 17.1. Thick Practices and Creating Missional Environments

Equipper	Thick Practices (Liturgies)	Environments They Cultivate
Apostles (dream awakeners)	Sabbath Making disciples	Cultivate a *thriving environment* that calls people to join God in the redemption of all things by developing a strong discipleship ethos
Prophets (heart revealer)	Being present to God *(silence, solitude, fasting)* Breaking bread	Cultivate a *liberating environment* that dares people to embody a holistic gospel, helping people experience liberation from personal and social sins, by forming spirit-transforming communities
Evangelists (story tellers)	Hospitality Sharing God's story	Cultivate a *welcoming environment* that invites people to bless their neighbors and be redemptive agents in their vocation
Pastors (soul healers)	Confession Peacemaking	Cultivate a *healing environment* in which people learn to embody the ministry of reconciliation and cultivate a life-giving spirituality in God's new family
Teachers (light givers)	Sacred assemblies Future-oriented living	Cultivate a *learning environment* where people immerse themselves in God's narrative and engage in praxis and future-oriented living

As each equipper seeks to cultivate these various environments in the congregation, there is a sense of renewal within the church, and when renewal takes place within the church, there is a natural overflow into the world.

THRIVING ENVIRONMENT

The apostle, or dream awakener, cultivates a *thriving environment* through helping the congregation participate in the liturgy of *sabbath* and engage in the practice of *making disciples*. Because apostles tend to be highly active, they are tempted to neglect sabbath. One of the characteristics of the host culture of the United States is that worth is often determined by the ability to produce and achieve. This has a tendency to shape us into slaves of production.

In the first church I helped to plant, it was rare for me to take a day off. I was like a rat running in the wheel with no rest. The problem is that when we enter the rat race, we often become rats in the process. I had little patience, which—according to 1 Corinthians 13—means I had little love. I thought patience was for underachievers. Being an Achiever (a 3 on the Enneagram), one of my basic desires is to feel valuable and worthwhile, whereas my basic fear is of being worthless. The corresponding weakness is that I can try to find my value and worth through achievement. Sabbath becomes (for me and for any who are gifted as apostles) a needed concrete practice that can act as a counterforce to the dominant culture.

In *Working the Angles*, Eugene Peterson gives a beautiful description of biblical sabbath. He says sabbath is "uncluttered time and space to distance ourselves from the frenzy of our own activities *so we can see what God has been and is doing.*"[3] The dream awakener's role is not "to make things happen" but joining God where God is already at work. Sabbath might feel counterintuitive to cultivating a thriving environment, but this practice is vital because it helps people live into their sacred potential, recognizing what God is already doing around them in their life, their neighborhood and vocation, inviting them to step into it. As the apostle helps the congregation practice sabbath, the community is more likely to see what God is doing in and around them, and thus discover and live out their calling in life.[4] Making disciples involves helping people live out their primary calling to follow Christ through their gifts and vocation.

LIBERATING ENVIRONMENT

The prophet or heart revealer cultivates a *liberating environment* by helping the congregation practice communing with God, *being present to God* through prayerful solitude, silence and fasting, and through the practice of the *breaking of bread*.

Connecting with the liberating God creates a liberating environment. As people connect with the God of the exodus (who hears the cries of his people), the God of the cross (who dies that we might live), the God of the resurrection (who gives hope for liberation from all sin) and the God of Pentecost (who pours out his Spirit to all), they experience freedom.

Henri Nouwen wonderfully describes the practices of silence, solitude and fasting. Within a world of words, silence allows us to hear the voice of God and ultimately gives us a liberating word for others. Solitude, as Nouwen says, is "the place of purification and transformation, the place of the great struggle and the great encounter."[5] Solitude is the place where we stand alone, naked before a holy God, and learn to accept his grace and love, which set us free. Finally, fasting allows us to enter into the sufferings of Christ and walk closer with God. As Eddie Gibbs says, "The Church in the West has got to learn to suffer. We love Easter, but we don't like Good Friday."[6] Fasting gives a needed break to our digestive organs and sharpens our spiritual senses. As we engage in the three practices of silence, solitude and fasting, we can overcome a noisy, overwhelming, frenzied life and connect with the heart of God. Here we find love and liberation for all, responding to the suffering and captivity in the world.

Breaking bread and receiving Communion together allows us to remember Christ's death and live as people of the resurrection. When we gather together at the Lord's Table as a community, we become a foretaste of God's future community, together with the triune God and all God's people. This new community around the Eucharist keeps us from separating Communion and justice, for we are all equal before God. As Paul instructs us in the book of Corinthians, "Whoever, therefore, eats the bread or drinks the cup of the Lord in an unworthy manner [dividing the community] will be answerable for the body and blood of the Lord" (1 Cor 11:27 NRSV). The Eastern Orthodox Church considers the Eucharist central and foundational and catholic (universal), which is why John Zizioulas says, "A eucharist which discriminates between races, sexes, ages, professions, social classes etc. violates not certain ethical principles but its eschatological nature. For that reason such a eucharist is not a 'bad'—i.e. morally deficient—eucharist but no eucharist at all. It cannot be said to be the body of the One who sums up all into Himself."[7]

As the prophet helps the community engage in silence, solitude and fasting, as well as understand the significance and divine power present at the Eucharist, they help to cultivate a liberating environment. And as a liberating environment shapes the community, it in turn seeks, by the power of the Spirit, to bring liberation to the world.

WELCOMING ENVIRONMENT

Evangelists or story tellers help to cultivate a *welcoming environment* by equipping the community to practice *hospitality* as a way of life and *share God's story* with others in the right spirit at the proper time.

During one of my first visits to Honduras I was invited to stay at a pastor's house in the city. I still remember his words to me, a complete stranger at the time, as I was entering his house: "My house is your home." And all throughout my stay with him and his family, this is what I felt. There wasn't pressure to have to talk with them constantly, and they didn't feel pressure to entertain me. They had simply created a space for me that was so free that I felt as if I were home.

The practice of hospitality creates a space of mutual exchange between guest and host. It is interesting that the Greek word for hospitality in the New Testament can be translated as both "host" and "guest." For hospitality is remembering we are fellow travelers in life, each of us sharing in the same broken humanity, each of us with stories to share and gifts to bear. We can practice hospitality at home, in our vocations, with the stranger and in the congregation, especially to the newcomer. Paul tells us to "welcome one another as Christ has welcomed you" (Rom 15:7 ESV).

As we take time to truly welcome people as they are, where they are, they often want to know *why* we are so welcoming. They want to hear a bit about our story, and because our story is so intertwined with God's story, it may be the "proper time" (1 Tim 2:6) to share God's story with them, always in a gracious way.

Sharing God's story does not entail using a prepackaged approach with the hopes of getting people to pray a prayer. God doesn't call us to be salespeople but journalists, announcing to those in our path that God's kingdom is at hand. It is about embodying the good news to the point that people want to switch their narrative and live under the rule of Christ and his kingdom.

As we learn to truly welcome and embrace all who God brings our way, we create a welcoming environment, which allows host and guest to give and receive, to share important things with each other, to give people space to be who they are, and to give God room to do his work.

HEALING ENVIRONMENT

The pastor or soul healer helps to cultivate a *healing environment* by modeling the thick practices of *confession* and *peacemaking*.

In *Telling Secrets* Frederick Buechner gives us solid reasons why we all need to engage in the practice of confession.

> I have come to believe that by and large the human family all has the same secrets, which are both very telling and very important to tell. They are telling in the sense that they tell what is perhaps the central paradox of our condition—that what we hunger for perhaps more than anything else is to be known in our full humanness, and yet that is often just what we also fear more than anything else.[8]

We confess so we may be known in the midst of our fear to be fully known. We confess to repent and move toward wholeness and holiness. We confess to find forgiveness and that we might experience reconciliation. Confession helps us to take off our masks, understand our false selves and move toward deeper community. We may not like to admit failure, yet healing and wholeness come as we confess our true selves to others.

Confession is not just sharing the garbage in our lives. Confession is a practice between two or three trusted allies who share their victories and defeats, their joys and pains, their ups and downs, their highs and lows. When we engage in the practice of confession, it signifies that we believe we have some trusted allies in the world, people we know are for us. When we help cultivate safe places where people can be real with one another, we cultivate a healing environment. When we move from a programming approach to being the church, to helping mid-sized missional groups develop a shared rhythm of life, we make space for this healing practice to take place. Too often ministry and busyness become a way to avoid facing our true selves. When there is all work and no play, there is no family atmosphere.

Besides confession, pastors help people engage in peacemaking, which is perhaps one of the most vital rhythms of life that a community can adopt. Peacemaking is a thick practice that helps us move toward the *telos* of embodying reconciliation, which is a learned skill. Gregory Jones puts it this way:

We should begin . . . identifying forgiveness as a craft. The craft of forgiveness is a lifelong learning process that people are initiated into as apprentices to those who excel at the craft. Those who excel have a moral authority as teachers, and apprentices must recognize a gap between their present competencies and genuine excellence.[9]

The soul healer has learned the craft of forgiveness and equips others to practice forgiveness and reconciliation.

Peacemaking is learning to live with each other as forgiven and forgiving people, resolving conflict in God-honoring ways. Jean Vanier reminds us that

communities need tensions if they are to grow and deepen. Tensions come from conflicts. . . . There is nothing more prejudicial to community life than to mask tensions and pretend they do not exist, or to hide them behind a polite façade and flee from reality and dialogue. A tension or difficulty can signal the approach of a new grace of God. But it has to be looked at wisely and humanly.[10]

Conflict is normal—but unresolved conflict creates a toxic atmosphere, which is why soul healers must model the craft of peacemaking. Soul healers equip the congregation with the practices of confession, prayer for each other during conflict, humility, reflection on our own forgiveness in Christ, and going to the person of conflict first. If we desire to see shalom in the world, we must first embody peacemaking within our congregation.

As the pastor helps the congregation adopt the rhythms of confession and peacemaking, he or she will help to create a healing environment, inviting others in to experience God's restoration.

LEARNING ENVIRONMENT

The teacher or light giver seeks to cultivate a *learning environment* by encouraging the community to actively participate in *sacred assemblies* and *future-oriented living*.

Sacred assemblies include the weekly gatherings (chap. 16) and the equipper guilds (chap. 18), but they also involve creating more intensive training times, gatherings and retreats.

The light giver takes time to assess the community and looks for opportunities in the coming year to gather people together to learn, both as a congregation and in the greater church. In Los Angeles we host an annual citywide gathering around a missional theme, such as discipleship or missional living. In these city gatherings we have fourteen leaders from fourteen churches share for fourteen minutes each on the theme. The gatherings encourage us to think imaginatively about the future of the church with others in a participatory and open-source way.[11]

We also participate in regional and national gatherings with the Ecclesia Network, which gives us the opportunity to connect with other missional churches.[12] Built into these times is space for meaningful *relational* connections, which helps create a missional movement. There are *equipping* times where we learn practical missional theology from seasoned leaders, as well as a time of *resourcing:* connecting people to various resources in areas of theology, spiritual formation, community building, missional living and social justice.

In addition to encouraging people to participate in sacred assemblies, the light giver helps people engage in future-oriented living. The apostle Paul's hope was in God's future—he continued on his mission, despite the enormous amount of suffering he endured, because he had an unwavering hope that God the Father, Son and Spirit would bring the world toward its intended purpose through the church. And as the teacher helps the congregation put her hope in God and lets God's future shape the mission of the church, the community of faith will be able to endure hardship, setbacks and disappointments.

As mentioned previously, N. T. Wright imagines Scripture as a five-act play. We have the first four acts and the last scene of the fifth act—God's future—but are now called to immerse ourselves in God's story so well that we get to know the God of that story and faithfully live for him in the context in which we find ourselves—the fifth act.

If we understand the last scene of the final act—God's intended purpose for all of creation—and *let the future shape the church's mission*, then we will have a good chance of being faithful to God. So what does future-oriented living look like?

Through the prophets and John the Seer, we see the renewal of all creation. John doesn't say that God will make all new things, but that he is "making everything new" (Rev 21:5). So as we freshly grasp what God has promised in the final scene of the fifth act, and allow that to shape our calling, we can join God in writing a new future for the world by anticipating his future in the present. If God's future is the elimination of hunger and thirst, how are our economic practices at this moment anticipating the reality of abundance? If God's future is the elimination of weapons of war and having people live peacefully with each other, how should we treat our enemies at this moment? If God's future is renewed creation with clean air, fresh water and natural beauty, are we living sustainable lives in the present? Future-oriented living forces us to answer these questions in concrete ways.

HOW WE SPEND OUR DAYS

Annie Dillard profoundly said, "How we spend our days is of course how we spend our lives."[13] So as mid-sized communities discern a communal rhythm of life together, the daily, weekly, monthly or annually thick practices they engage in, they cultivate a thriving, liberating, welcoming, healing and learning environment, which in turn shapes the community. For we create culture and culture recreates us.

IDENTIFYING EQUIPPERS AND UNDERSTANDING THEIR WORK

If we are going to create a missional culture in the congregations we serve, if we are going to cultivate these various environments, we need to cultivate an equipper ethos. What does that look like? How do we spot and develop equippers? What is some of the specific work of equippers in the congregation, in discipleship communities (missional communities) and missional spaces? What are ways to cultivate the growth of the equippers? What does it look like to commission equippers in the congregation?

18

Cultivating an Equipping Ethos

The more I considered Christianity, the more I found that while it has established a rule and order, the chief aim of that order was to give room for good things to run wild.

G. K. CHESTERTON

Keep watch over yourselves and all the flock of which the Holy Spirit has made you overseers. *Be shepherds of the church of God, which he bought with his own blood.*

ACTS 20:28 (EMPHASIS ADDED)

What would the church look like if everyone in the church used their God-given gifts and talents to equip the rest of the church in such a way that the entire church became more like Jesus? And if the whole church looked more like Jesus, how much more would our neighborhoods and cities look more like heaven?

One idea that has helped to shape how I think about cultivating an equipping ethos in the congregation comes from the pen of G. K. Chesterton. In his classic book *Orthodoxy*, he writes, "The more I considered Christianity, the more I found that while it has established a rule and order, the chief aim of that order was to give room for good things to run wild."[1] Until the congregations we serve recognize that all believers are priests who have the Holy Spirit and the ability to equip others, the church will never reach her sacred potential in Christ.

In *The Permanent Revolution*, Alan Hirsch and Tim Catchim help us to understand that we must have a three-dimensional reading of Ephesians 4. We should understand the fivefold gifting as *calling* (everyone may have a gifting), *ministry* (everyone ministers through at least one of the five ministry paths) and *leadership* (not everyone will be an equipper, equipping others).[2] In other words, some may be recognized as apostles, but the whole community is to be apostolic. "Some will be called to be evangelists, but the whole community is to be evangelistic."[3]

I think about this three-dimensional reading of Ephesians 4 through a sports analogy. Imagine players and coaches on a continuum.

| -- |
Players   **Coaches**

Figure 18.1. Player-coach continuum

We are all players. But we are also all coaches in the sense that we encourage and equip our fellow teammates. But over time, some people, due to their sense of calling, character, influence, experience, gifting and the work of the Holy Spirit, start to spend more time coaching or equipping other players. And these people are recognized or commissioned as equippers (elders).

I remember the first church that I helped restart. I adopted a group of twenty-four people who didn't seem to have much of a heart for those outside the kingdom. I took to heart what Albert Schweitzer said, "Example is not the main thing in influencing others, it's the only thing," and I sought to connect with as many non-Christians as I could. After five years I looked out at our congregation one Sunday morning and realized that out of the one hundred people sitting in front of me, God had allowed me to be present when about half of them came to faith. At that point, in light of the needs of the congregation, I realized that I needed to devote more time to equipping others to do what I had been doing. So I moved more toward the coaching part of the continuum. This doesn't mean I stopped being a player; I just needed to spend more time coaching. And as I devoted more time to coaching, the church started to grow in ways beyond our imagination. We started to experience the power of multiplication instead of just addition.

To build an equipping ethos, we need to understand this three-dimensional reading of Ephesians 4, where the five equippers are a community of priests ministering to other priests. There is the *leadership* matrix—the equippers, the *ministry* matrix and *calling*. All are living apostolic, prophetic, evangelistic, pastoral and teacher kind of lives. Lesslie Newbigin reminds us that

> it is the whole Church which is called to be—in Christ—a royal priesthood, and that this priesthood is to be exercised in the daily life and work of Christians in the secular business of the world. But this will not happen unless there is a ministerial priesthood, which serves, nourishes, sustains and guides this priestly work. The priestly people need a ministering priesthood to sustain and nourish it.[4]

The equippers must also remember that the church exists for the sake of the world. Thus is it important to ask how the various equippers function in the neighborhood as the church scatters. As Ray Bakke says in *A Theology as Big as the City*, "Personally, I am committed to the vision of a local church and its pastors with two basic functions: pastor to the faithful and chaplain to the whole community."[5] Some deep thought needs to be given to what the neighborhood might look like if the roles of the apostle, prophet, evangelist, pastor and teacher were activated in the neighborhood for the sake of the whole community.

EQUIPPERS AS COACHES AND AIR TRAFFIC CONTROLLERS

When equippers understand that the chief aim of a church is to "make room for good things to run wild," they will also need to operate as overseers, helping to bring a sense of synergy to the congregation on mission. As people feel empowered by the Holy Spirit and start to live out their sacred potential, ministry will happen—lots of it. Consequently, one of the roles of the equipping community is to help bring a sense of synergy to what is happening, like an air traffic controller, while at the same time allowing the wind of the Spirit to blow freely. For structure should always submit to Spirit. Being an air traffic controller (administrator) is also a gift of the Spirit.

Besides creating an ethos where good things can run wild and bringing a sense of synergy to the whole, the equippers, along with the rest of the leadership community, discerns the annual vision of the church. And then, like good coaches, they help the congregation move toward the goal. When the whole church understands the primary thing that the Holy Spirit wants to do over the next twelve months and moves in beat with the Spirit, it brings a sense of unity and momentum to the congregation.

This is where polycentric leadership comes into play. It is important to remember that leadership is not limited to the *recognized* equippers—leadership is unlimited in the Holy Spirit. So while the church ought to appreciate and respect the role of *formal* leadership and move toward a concrete (annual) vision, the church also ought to make space where "good things run wild." Thus there is an appreciation of the role of the Spirit in the "informal leadership" or the not-yet-recognized leadership of the church. In this way Christ and the Spirit are honored in the church.

A CLEAR PICTURE OF THE EQUIPPERS AND MULTIPLICATION STRATEGY

Two other elements are vital in developing an equipping ethos in the congregation. First, the leadership community must have a clear picture of the nature and ministry of each of the five equippers.[6] The church needs to have a good understanding of the part of the cultural web (institution) which asks the question, *How will we fulfill our calling?* In particular she needs to ask, *What is the church multiplying at the most basic level?*

Second, it is important for each minister (all members) in the congregation to understand the cultural web and annual vision of the congregation. In particular, in terms of missional methods or basic strategy, each person should understand what I call the *basic building block* of the congregation, or what the church is multiplying at a basic level. Every church is called to make more and better disciples. When we do this well, we do it together, because disciple making is primarily a communal ministry. So each congregation, if it is going to multiply disciples, needs to understand the basic building block of the community, the bread and butter of the congregation, the ministry that they are multiplying.

For some churches the basic building block is the small group, a group of ten to fifteen people. For others it is the mid-sized group, twenty to fifty people. This is the missional community or what I call discipleship communities. Others are multiplying congregations of 100 to 150. While each church is unique in its method of ministry and context, it is important for every church to understand what it is seeking to multiply. It's also important that discipleship is taking place at every sociological level.

DISCIPLESHIP IN EVERY SOCIOLOGICAL SPACE

Writing in *The Search to Belong,* Joseph Myers, with the help of anthropologist Edward T. Hall, identifies four kinds of spaces that we live in. Each congregation would be wise to think through how they pursue making disciples in each of these spaces.

Public space is about sharing a common experience in larger space, like fans at a basketball game, where strangers who *belong* to the same team connect with a "high five" after a score. This can happen at a larger public worship service, or if the church is not large, at a city, regional or national gathering of some type. This space becomes missional if it reshapes people to inhabit God's story in their everyday life.

Social space is where people select a community—people with whom they want to go deeper—to belong to. In the congregational setting this space is more like a mid-sized group of twenty to fifty people. Biblically this space is what the New Testament calls *oikos,* which is a Greek term typically translated "house" or "household." It refers to the basic building block of ancient society, the household, and its close network of relationships, the extended family. Mike Breen and Alex Absalom make a theological, sociological, historical and practical case for mid-sized communities to be the prime building block of the church.[7]

Personal space is where we connect through private relationships. Personal space includes the eight to twelve people whom we feel close to, whom we spend a lot of time with, like Jesus and the Twelve. This is a key area for discipleship to take place in a deeper way.

Intimate space is where we share experiences, feelings and thoughts. Intimate relationships are those in which another person knows the "naked truth" about us, and yet the two of us are "not ashamed." This is like the space Jesus had with the three: Peter, James and John.

A strong discipleship and equipping culture develops when a church seeks to make disciples in each of these spaces, which is why I am a fan of the neighborhood congregation that connects occasionally with the citywide church. One church that does this well is Trinity Grace Church in New York City. They encourage discipleship in each of these spaces. They have missional communities as their basic building block and neighborhood parishes for their weekly gathering. About every six weeks they have a citywide gathering, which, in addition to their neighborhood congregation, creates a sense of momentum and movement in the public space.

Ever since I came to Christ in college, I have been a part of mid-sized missional communities. The bread and butter of the first church I helped to restart at Virginia Tech in 1989 were home groups, which were mid-sized communities that grew through discipleship and mission. These mid-sized communities are also the basic building block of our churches in Los Angeles. While in the early days I didn't have the sociological evidence for the importance of these mid-sized groups or all of the theological reasoning, both intuitively and practically I have always sensed the power they have had. Thus, I am a personal fan of making mid-sized communities the basic building block of the church. As Mike Breen is fond of saying, they are small enough to *care* and big enough to *dare* (be mission focused). This is the group that adopts missional spaces. The mid-sized community can adopt a common missional space like a neighborhood or people group, or it can be a collection of missionaries that help and encourage one another in their missional spaces.

The next level of multiplication is the congregation. I define a congregation as three to five mid-sized groups, which means a congregation includes 100 to 250 people. In my experience, it is helpful for each congregation to have five equippers, which is why we seek to recognize equippers at this stage. The definition and the size of a congregation are clearly more descriptive of what we are doing, not prescriptive. Each congregation will need to work through the details herself, in light of her context, team, tradition and theological understanding.

Once the congregation understands the basic group she is seeking to multiply, it is important to understand how to spot, develop and commission equippers in the congregation. I trust that as I talk about this in my context, you will find ways to practice it in yours.

SPOTTING EQUIPPERS

I decided to start an experimental "leaderless" discipleship community with the framework of the five equippers in my mind. I brought with me the five focal concerns and the ten destinations of the equippers (see table 16.1). By this time in my ministry I had a clear picture of each equipper in mind. I wanted to start this group with people I had met in Los Angeles. We started as a small group of five people. For the first five or six months, being a new group, it was important for us to get to know each other better. So we would have a meal, and then one person would share his or her story with us for the next two hours. The group members were vulnerable, sharing personal wounds and personal highlights, their spiritual highs and lows and the things they were proud of or that brought shame. These times were so powerful and community-forming that our group grew every week. As I was listening to people's story, I was thinking about the gifts, passion, personality and experiences that made them who they were. I started to think about the leadership matrix, the ministry matrix and calling dimensions of the equippers, and was getting a sense of people's primary ministry or gifting.

Because each week new people came to the group (it was an open group where anyone could invite anyone), it took us six months of meeting weekly to get through everyone's story. At this point the group had grown to around twenty people. This phase of building community is something that the pastor loves, but each equipper can benefit from it.

Now that the group had been together for six months and grown to around twenty regularly involved people, some hungered to study the Scriptures. So the discipleship community decided to take the next couple of months to work through one of the Gospels. During this time I was seeking to spot the budding "teachers" in the group. I was looking for the people who came alive and had an uncanny ability to help the community understand the Word.

It is important to note that at the onset of the group, I told them that I would not lead the group. I would help, but would not lead. With no designated leader, group members sometimes weren't sure about the schedule and what we were doing. Eventually someone from the group would send an email to the rest of us announcing when and where we were meeting. This happened spontaneously.

Eventually the group decided it was important to make quarterly plans. My friend asked me, "Who should we invite to make plans?" I said, "Why don't we invite anyone who wants to come?" The group agreed, and so we started having a quarterly planning meeting. At this time I wanted to introduce the communal-rhythm-of-life idea in light of the framework of the equippers. As we started to experiment with this, it became obvious who the budding teachers, prophets, evangelist, apostles and pastors were. Spending time with people, doing ministry together, seeing people's passions and seeing how people were interacting in the group served as the best way to spot potential equippers. There are three simple questions I ask: What is the person good at? What do others believe the person is good at? In what areas does he or she bear fruit?

Some people were clearly passionate about the poor and oppressed, and would not allow the community to go on without actively standing with the disadvantaged. Others had a deep passion for the Word, and when they shared from Scripture the entire group paid attention. Some sought to create a family atmosphere for the group. Others had a passion for multiplication. Essentially, what I found in my experiment was that God had clearly given various people different passions. With a clear picture of each kind of equipper, spotting them was not difficult. And as budding equippers started to live out their calling, the group continued to grow and ended up multiplying another group.

Another way to identify people on the equipping ministry matrix is that people gifted in one area tend to judge others not similarly gifted. For example, the budding evangelist would criticize those in the group who didn't have a similar heart for those outside of the kingdom. What budding evangelists need to know is that God wants to use them to bring that heart to the rest of the group. The process of identification can take place with the other equippers as well.

DEVELOPING EQUIPPERS

Not only is spotting equippers best done in the *basic building block* of the church, this is a good space for the developing equippers as well. We are less familiar than we should be with the nature and function of the five equippers because we have lost the art of apprenticeship in our local congregations. We need to expand the craft of equipping from the classroom to the living room, and from the sanctuary to the streets. Equipping needs to move beyond reading books and writing reports to practicing the craft under the guidance of a mentor.

My friend Pavi Thomas believes that the medical field gives us some practical insights into how we can better engage the craft of equipping. He sat down with four of his relatives who are in the medical field—a surgeon, gynecologist, cardiologist and pediatrician—and had a long conversation about their training experience. After reflecting on the conversation, he identified five fundamental elements that shaped their training.

1. They received strong theoretical foundations.

2. Integration of theory and practice—nothing was learned only theoretically.

3. Mentoring—they were always under the oversight and care of experienced specialist.

4. Experience—everything they were trained to do required broad and repetitive experience.

5. Specialization—they were trained to specialize, since the overall body of knowledge is vast.[8]

Spiritual training has, or should have, a similar process.

EQUIPPER GUILDS

The renaissance was a rebirth of creativity. During the renaissance there were guilds for merchants, artists and crafts. A person had to work through three phases to become top-notch in their field—apprentice, journeyman and master. In rebirthing the equippers, a community of faith can establish equipper guilds.[9] Apostles can create apostolic guilds; prophets, prophetic guilds; evangelists, evangelistic guilds; pastors, pastoral guilds; and teachers, teacher guilds.

This is a key role for those who have already been recognized as equippers in a church. They would work with each of the discipleship communities (mid-sized group) within the congregation, inviting *budding* apostles, prophets, evangelists, pastors and teachers to participate. Here the craft of equipping is learned and refined.

The equipper guild is a place where budding equippers are encouraged and enabled through the process of self-discovery. The guild is first and foremost a place of encouragement and support for apprentices. Thus an important skill for those leading equipper guilds is being able to ask the right questions and listening well. The guild should also be a place where apprentices can share victories and defeats, the pain and the joy of equipping. It should be a place of mutual peer encouragement, sharing of best practices and the development of relationships.

In addition to being a place of mutual encouragement and support, these should be spaces for people to grow personally and in ministry skills. Equippers leading the guild could use the equipper candidate reference form (see appendix 2) as a tool for an initial assessment in the areas of theology, character, equipping skills and missional living. This will give both equipper and apprentice a sense of direction for personal growth. Based on this assessment, the current ministry needs of the apprentice and the role of the equipper (see appendix 1), the equipper and apprentice will develop a specific equipping project together, which meets the needs of the congregation and develops the apprentice.

Finally, within the equipping guilds the apprentices would be encouraged to find historical and contemporary mentors in their equipping role. Historical mentors are equippers who have already passed on to be with the Lord but still have much to teach us (e.g., Lesslie Newbigin). Contemporary mentors are people living out the equipping role that you want to emulate.

It is important that each budding equipper has some experienced mentors, peer mentors (both within the congregation and outside of the congregation) as well as someone he or she is mentoring. Often our best learning takes place as we teach others what we are learning.

LEADERSHIP COMMUNITIES

Along with equipping guilds, a church can have leadership communities for all who are leading and apprenticing different ministries in the congregation. Together they can develop an approach to being the church that develops upcoming equippers on a regular and meaningful basis.

COMMISSIONING EQUIPPERS

As you discern ways to spot and develop equippers, you will see that the Holy Spirit has been developing character, knowledge, skills and fruit in the lives of these budding equippers. Thus, it is helpful to develop a process by which you formally commission the equippers in the congregation. An equipper's readiness is primarily determined by examining the fruit of his or her life and ministry. As Jesus said, we will know them by their fruit.

As a discipleship community (mid-sized group) multiplies and a new congregation starts, it is likely that the Holy Spirit will have cultivated equippers to the point that they could be appointed as elders (or equippers) in the congregation.

When it comes to officially recognizing equippers in the congregation, it is important that they be people of the Word, people of virtue, people who have developed equipping skills through the Spirit, and people who live missional lives for the sake of the world. Therefore, I have developed an equipper candidate reference form (see appendix 2). Each candidate gives the form to three to five people close to them (including his or her spouse, if married). This reference enables others to evaluate the candidate's theology, character, equipping skills and missional life.

While all are ministers, the Scriptures illustrate that it is helpful to officially recognize specific equippers (elders) through the laying on of hands. Equippers are servants who understand they are ministers to other ministers, helping each disciple fulfill his or her ministry in the church and in the world for the sake of the world.

Equipper candidates with good referrals then go through an interview process with current equippers. Here they are queried about their character, missional lifestyle, theology, skills, the potential equipping role and understanding of the various associations of the church (see appendix 3). Upon a successful interview the candidate is presented to the congregation. The current equippers inform the congregation that it seems good to them and the Holy Spirit that this person is qualified to be an equipper in the congregation. We give people two weeks to share with any current equipper why this candidate may not be qualified. If there is no objection, then at a designated date the equipper is formally recognized before the congregation.

If the candidate is not yet ready to be an equipper, due to lack of character, skills, theological training or missional living, the process becomes a learning experience. The person now knows areas in which he or she needs to grow in character and equipping abilities. The equippers and candidate can then discern specific ways the candidate needs to develop and grow, and develop a plan accordingly.

During the commissioning ceremony we share Scripture related to missional leadership; we discuss the process that each candidate has gone through; we talk about the specific equipper role the person will play in the congregation; and we have a liturgy of commissioning the equipper. Within the liturgy of commissioning, we ask the candidate to make, with God's help, certain commitments to God and the congregation. And we ask the congregation to make some commitments to the equipper. Then each of the current equippers lay hands on the equipper and pray for him or her, dedicating the person and ministry to God, and sending him or her off to serve. We often follow this commissioning ceremony with Communion.

CULTIVATING A MISSIONAL CULTURE

Not only do Spirit-filled leaders cultivate a missional culture, but our very approach to leadership helps create a missional culture. But there aren't many examples of how polycentric leadership works. For example, how does decision making work in the context of shared leadership? Are there any good resources for those leading as a community among the community? These are a few of the questions we will tackle in the final chapter.

19

Polycentric Leadership at Work

Studies of self-organizing, emergent systems have shown similar traits running through them, whether they are in computing, biology, or economics. In every area of life it seems there are historically top-down organizations that are having to adapt and evolve; that have realized that the only way that they can survive is to transform themselves from . . . monolithic, flabby, grey institutions that do not and cannot respond to realities on the ground, into conjunctive, devolved, bottom-up, adaptable networks that are trim, agile, and flexible enough to face and meet the ever-changing challenges of the fast-moving post-Enlightenment world.

KESTER BREWIN

Go to the ant, you sluggard;
consider its ways and be wise!
It has no commander,
no overseer or ruler,
yet it stores its provisions in summer
and gathers its food at harvest.

PROVERBS 6:6-8

Transformation. We all long for transformation. We just hate change.

Life as a caterpillar isn't so bad, is it? After all, if we decide to enter into that dark mysterious cocoon, we might die! We don't want to die. We prefer life. But what kind of life have we settled for?

We dream of living up to our sacred potential. We want to spread our wings and let the breath of God lift us. Flying beats crawling around, any day. When we fly, it changes everything. It changes what we see. It changes how we feel. Our minds think differently. Our imaginations are awakened to what could be.

But flying requires death. Death to preserving the status quo. Death to real and imagined fears. Death to *our* power. Death to *our* ability to control. Death to *our* status and reputation. Death to *our* idea of success. The threat of death seems too high a price to pay. Let's just stick to crawling. This is the world I know and am comfortable with.

Make no mistake about it. Leading as a community within the community requires death. It requires a willingness to live in the dark for a period of time. It will take living through stages of development that are mysterious and seem impractical. It will take a willingness to feel awkward and underproductive. It will take faith.

One of my life verses, which I stashed in my heart early in my life of faith, comes from the mouth of Jesus. "If anyone would come after me, he must deny himself and take up his cross [daily] and follow me. For whoever wants to save his life will lose it, but whoever loses his life for me and for the gospel will save it" (Mk 8:34-35 NIV 1984).[1] Paul said, "I die every day" (1 Cor 15:31). Because the apostle Paul took this teaching of Jesus to heart, he bore much fruit in his life. With Christ, death means new life. This teaching is transformative, which is why it is included in all four Gospels. In John we hear Jesus saying, "Very truly I tell you, unless a kernel of wheat falls to the ground and dies, it remains only a single seed. But if it dies, it produces many seeds. Anyone who loves their life will lose it, while anyone who hates their life in this world will keep it for eternal life" (12:24-25).

The discovery of how seeds work introduced what is known as the agricultural revolution. Prior to this, people simply ate seeds for sustenance. The idea of putting a seed into the ground and throwing dirt over it seemed ridiculous. It seemed insane. To bury seed is to dispose of food for the day. Consequently you'd go hungry. But what looks like death is actually the secret to life.

LESSONS FROM ST. PAUL

If we want to see the spontaneous expansion of the church, we need to learn important lessons on how to approach leadership from the premier church planter, the apostle Paul. For *how we approach leadership* creates culture. Roland Allen, an Anglican bishop who spent much of his life living, ministering and writing in China, England and Africa, is a good resource in helping us understand Paul's methods.

As a missionary desiring to join God's mission, Allen sought to understand why many missionary societies were failing. So he studied the life and ministry of the apostle Paul to understand why he was so fruitful. In his book *Missionary Methods: St. Paul's or Ours?* which is a classic for church planters, Allen examined the conditions and circumstances in Paul's day, the way Paul preached the gospel, how he trained new believers, and his method of dealing with discipline and unity. In the concluding section of his book, Allen summarized Paul's practice, saying, "The principles which seem to underlie all the Apostle's practice were two: (1) that he was a preacher of Gospel, not of law, and (2) that he must retire from his converts to give place for Christ. The spirit in which he was able to do this was the spirit of faith."[2]

Allen's own experience on the mission field verified these foundational elements in *the spontaneous expansion of the church*, which happened to be the title of a subsequent book, in which he responded to some of his critics. These foundational elements can be remembered with two words: *cross* and *wind*. These two words have deep implications in how we approach missional leadership, and in turn create a missional culture.

THE CROSS AND THE WIND

The cross, which was ever before Paul, is a *symbol* of the gospel. The cross represents the way Jesus lived. The cross represents his death. And the empty cross his resurrection. Missional leadership, for the apostle Paul, meant helping those he brought to faith grow in their understanding and relationship to Christ in the context of community. He sought by his example to share the mind and life of Christ. Paul did not preach himself, he preached Christ. Paul was not the *king* of the communities of faith he started, he was their servant, for Jesus' sake (2 Cor 4:5). Paul "believed that Christ was able and willing to keep that which he had committed to Him. He believed that He would perfect His church, and He would establish, strengthen, settle his converts. He believed, and acted as if he believed."[3]

The wind, the mighty rushing wind that birthed the church, is the power and source of the spontaneous expansion of the church. The Acts of the Apostles is actually the Acts of the Holy Spirit, for the apostles were just trying to keep in step with the Spirit. Allen writes, "Spontaneous activity is a movement of the Spirit in the individual and in the Church, and we cannot control the Spirit."[4] When studying the apostle Paul, Allen recognized that for Paul the cross and the wind were the foundational elements to the missional church. In chapter sixteen I said the cross and dove (wind) are central and must always remain so. We aren't building and expanding a business, we are partnering with God to build the church for the sake of his kingdom. A friend of mine tweeted in regard to the church, "When a body becomes a business . . . that's prostitution." Often business principles teach us to be in control. But Paul understood that he planted and Apollos watered, and that God causes the growth—not us (1 Cor 3:6).

The significant lesson Roland Allen repeats throughout his writings is Paul's unwavering belief in the Holy Spirit's work in other people's lives. He notes how Paul "practiced retirement" (released control and literally moved on to another city within two years or so) to allow the Spirit to work freely among the new believers. Allen brings to our attention that the Paul planted churches and taught the new believers how to rely on the Spirit apart from Paul's direct involvement. Allen observes,

> It is not enough that those with whom we have to do should see our activities and recognize that they are inspired by a good spirit; it is not enough that they should imitate our activities; it is not enough that they should help us in them; there is no satisfaction until they are actuated by the Holy Spirit and express the Holy Spirit in their own activities.[5]

For the apostle Paul the cross and the wind are the key elements to missional leadership. Central to developing a missional culture is for leaders to cede control to and to model and teach reliance on the Holy Spirit. Allen, speaking of the apostle Paul says,

> He believed in the Holy Ghost, not merely vaguely as a spiritual Power, but as a Person indwelling his converts. He believed therefore in his converts. He could trust them. He did not trust them because he believed in their natural virtue or intellectual sufficiency. If he had believed in that, his faith must have been sorely shaken. But he believed in the Holy Ghost in them.[6]

GETTING PRACTICAL WITH POLYCENTRIC LEADERSHIP

One of the ways we can teach reliance on the Holy Spirit to our fellow priests is by moving from dependence on a solo pastor or senior pastor to dependence on the Spirit through polycentric leadership. Polycentric leadership is not merely about a team of equippers equipping the congregation for ministry, though that is an important step. It's ultimately about recognizing the leading of the Holy Spirit in the congregation, and understanding that Christ himself is the Head. It is recognizing that leadership can come from the youngest Spirit-filled person in the congregation as much as it comes from the equippers. Polycentric leadership is keeping in step with the Spirit, which is different from flat leadership. Flat leadership often falls flat. But with polycentric leadership, leader-follower relations are not necessarily determined by formal leadership but by the Spirit. And the recognized equippers seek to demonstrate how leadership rotates.

A practical suggestion I give to people who desire to engage in polycentric leadership is that they write out the role of the senior or lead pastor, and find the best way to share that role among the equippers, whether there be three or five. For example, often the lead pastor takes charge of teaching—deciding what is going to be taught and who is going to teach. What I suggest is that the equippers look at the upcoming year together and develop the teaching calendar based on the following steps.

First, I encourage people to use the Christian calendar from Advent to Pentecost for half the year, and then teach what is most needed for ordinary time (the rest of the year). Second, besides teaching from the various parts of the Bible and each of the different genres, which the lectionary helps us do, I encourage them to give space to teaching on the focal concerns and *telos* of each of the equippers. So one series (four to eight weeks) of teaching is more apostolic, another series would be pastoral and so on. In this way the congregation grows to the full stature of Christ. So, when it comes to the evangelist series, the evangelist takes charge of what is taught and who teaches. The evangelist leads and the others follow. When it comes to the pastoral series, the pastor leads and the other equippers follow. In this way people learn how to lead in the way of Christ, and leaders learn how to be followers as well, since being a follower is central to all of our lives as Christ followers.

When leadership is shared among the equippers, it provides a positive model of polycentric leadership to the entire congregation. In this way they are like a flock of geese flying, where one goose takes the lead, doing most of the work for a while, and then moves to the side so another goose can take the lead and share the load. Polycentric leadership gives opportunity to demonstrate reliance on the Holy Spirit as well as give leaders needed rest.

Polycentric leadership does not necessarily mean that each equipper spends the same amount of time teaching the congregation in weekly gatherings. Some are more gifted and skilled to communicate in that setting than others. I have found that having two or three primary communicators is ideal. More than that feels overwhelming. So the equippers should see who is best in this role.

Brutal honesty comes into play here. When approaching polycentric leadership, there are a number of important factors to keep in mind. As a community of leaders the relational nature of God should shape the equippers' approach to leadership. The Trinity is interdependent, communal, relational, participatory, self-surrendering and self-giving. This is how the equippers should lead. In addition, it is important for the equippers to have mutual respect for one another, appreciating the gifting and experience of each person, giving weight to each. Appreciation for each other occurs as the team has a history of relating to each other. Trust takes time to build.

DECISION MAKING AND POLYCENTRIC LEADERSHIP

What about making decisions? What approach should be taken? I encourage the entire leadership community to analyze their cultural web together, with input from the whole congregation. In this way the congregation owns the mission of the church. Having developed a common cultural web solves a lot of decision-making issues. The missional methods will reveal the basic building blocks of the church, what the church is seeking to multiply. And if the church is seeking to multiply a mid-sized community, the equippers give a framework for that community, appoint leaders and let them go about the business of multiplying themselves. In other words, once a basic framework is established, decision making should be decentralized as much as possible, giving decision-making authority to those who have responsibility for a given ministry, with the understanding that everyone should work interdependently.

I encourage the framework for the basic building block to include the focal concerns and *telos* of the five equippers. In this way the community grows holistically, and this community becomes the place to spot and develop more equippers. To include this as part of the framework, each community should discern their rhythm of life. At least *one thick practice* should correlate with the focal concern of each equipper. While some equippers will help lead these mid-sized groups, a group doesn't need a recognized equipper to function. Equippers are there to serve each community, primarily through the various equipping guilds, the occasional leadership community gatherings and special training times that are open to the entire community. The rhythm of life can vary from group to group, depending on the nature and need of the group and in light of the core practices of the congregation. When each group has adopted a communal rhythm of life, discipleship starts to take place in all of life, not just during the gathering times.

One way to help people move from missional spaces to discipleship communities (mid-sized groups) is by helping people in the missional spaces to adopt one or two of the thick practices of the discipleship community, assuming they are ready. In this way discipleship is participatory, active and embodied. Discipleship takes the path of belonging, behaving and then believing. Faith comes as people encounter the story of God in the body of Christ. And as they are wooed by the Holy Spirit to "change stories," they engage in thick practices that create thriving, liberating, welcoming, healing and learning environments in the congregation. These, in turn, shape the community to be more like Christ.

It is best to keep decision making as decentralized as possible. Decisions that affect the whole body ought to be more centralized, while decisions within a ministry should be decentralized. This takes advantage of polycentric leadership and gives authority to those who have responsibility.

I encourage the equippers to discern the annual vision (with the input of the congregation). In discerning the annual vision, it is important for the equippers to understand what is happening in the congregation and the neighborhood, and engage in adaptive leadership. Each equipper should be fully present when discerning the annual vision, and they should seek the sense of the Spirit.

It is natural for each equipper to have different concerns—indeed, this is what keeps polycentric leadership diverse. However, what often happens is that the apostle and evangelist will feel that the church needs to expand. But the pastor believes that the community needs to grow deeper. The prophet, on the other hand, is concerned that the church ought to be more fully engaged with the poor and oppressed. And the teacher feels the congregation doesn't know the story of God well enough. Obviously, because of their gifting, they each feel the need to pull the congregation in a slightly different direction (see fig. 19.1).

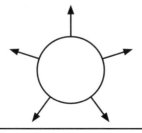

Figure 19.1. Equippers' different focal concerns

While this can create tension, as the equippers listen to the Spirit through one another, they can gain a sense of the Spirit. One resource I recommend teams work through is Patrick Lencioni's *The Five Dysfunctions of a Team.*[7]

LESSONS FROM THE QUAKERS

We have much to learn from the Quakers when it comes to discerning the leading of the Spirit in decision making. The Quakers, or Society of Friends, demonstrate a deep trust in the Holy Spirit at work in the entire body. I was talking with C. Wess Daniels, who pastors a Quaker congregation near Portland, Oregon, about how they approach decision making. He said, we have "a meeting for worship for business." In other words, for Quakers, business is another expression of worship. For some congregations these meetings are monthly. The congregation Wess serves holds them quarterly. These meetings could be impromptu if needed. How do these meetings operate?

There is a fundamental belief that unity comes by communally listening to God's Spirit through one another. The meeting's clerk presents the business at hand. Then comes a time of worship. The worship typically starts with silence, which could last five or ten minutes, though the time is not fixed. The people simply listen to the Spirit. The clerk, who is a "weighty person," not someone in the pastoral role, brings business items to the table. Those who feel guided to say something speak. When people speak, they are encouraged to speak the words they sense the Spirit is calling them to speak, not their own words.

To make this concrete, let's say the church is seeking to discern whether a person is ready to be an equipper. Twelve members speak in the affirmative, and one person is hesitant. The goal is to listen to the Spirit through the various people. Sometimes the clerk may call for silence again. But when the clerk discerns that a "sense of the meeting has taken place," he or she says, "Friends, do we have approval?" And all who approve say so.

Again, the goal of the meeting is not necessarily unanimity but getting a sense of the Spirit, a "sense of the meeting." If most people lean one way but a "weighty person" (one who has wisdom, character and a strong reputation for discerning the Spirit) speaks another way, it could block or delay the decision. But the person's position would have to be a matter of conscience, not just preference.

I asked Wess what he considered to be the strengths and weaknesses of this approach to decision making. He said, "A weakness would be it can take a long time to make some decisions, so if you are trying to get something through quickly, it is difficult. The biggest strengths are that it is participatory, involving the entire congregation, and therefore there is high ownership in regard to the decision. Another huge strength is that we regularly practice listening to God's Spirit together, and anytime you can do that, it is good."

Richard Wood, former dean of Yale Divinity School and a Quaker, writes,

> The search for the sense of the Meeting is time-consuming, and many people who are used to voting procedures think it highly inefficient. However, after many years of working with it in a variety of different Quaker institutions, I believe that the time from *idea* to *action* may be about the same in both systems, and that a truly shared sense of the Meeting facilitates collective action. What is shorter in voting systems, where the majority rules, is the time from *idea* to *decision*; but if the decision does not reflect a consensus, the time from decision to action can be long indeed.[8]

Quaker congregations in Wess's region tend to range from 50 to 150 people, close to the size of what I call a congregation (three to five mid-sized groups). So this could be a practice that congregations engage. Wess told me about the regional Meeting he just attended where one item of business was to consider the nomination of a person to be a superintendent for the region. There were three to four hundred people present at the meeting, and over twenty people shared something from the Spirit. In the end the sense of the meeting was that the new superintendent should be approved. If three to four hundred people can come to the sense of the Spirit in regard to the appointment of a regional leader, then certainly five equippers can come to the sense of the Spirit when making decisions for the local congregation. A community of leaders is more likely to hear the Spirit better than one person. This

Quaker practice demonstrates and teaches the entire community of faith to depend on the Holy Spirit.

LESSONS FROM ANTS AND CITIES

God has given us many ways to learn; he speaks to us many ways. He speaks through his Word, his Spirit and creation itself. No wonder Solomon says,

> Go to the ant, you sluggard;
>   consider its ways and be wise!
> It has no commander,
>   no overseer or ruler,
> yet it stores its provisions in summer
>   and gathers its food at harvest. (Prov 6:6-8)

While this was written thousand of years ago, scientists from a variety of disciplines, including life sciences, social sciences and hard sciences, are studying and sharing information regarding living systems, complex adaptive systems, in a scientific movement called emergence. Emergence occurs when simple components self-organize into wonderfully rich functioning systems, without any top-down control. Scientists first examined ants and slime molds. And the more scientists looked, the more they found new ways of behaving and organizing. They found it in the brain, in the development of cities, in cell structures, in termite colonies and in immune systems.

Kurt Fredrickson writes, "This new systems understanding sees the world more as decentralized than centralized, more networked than hierarchical, more organic than fixed. It is not random and disorganized; it is rather organized through an understanding of complexity and emergence. This new understanding offers new possibilities for ecclesial organization."[9] I share these thoughts about ants, the brain and cities to encourage us to learn more about emergence, because these discoveries in God's creation will shed light on ways for the church to organize in such a way that every single part of the body lives up to its sacred potential.

In his book *Emergence*, Steven Johnson talks about the connected lives of ants, brains, cities and software. When it comes to ants, scientists have confirmed that no one ant tells the other ants what to do. They have discovered that the queen ant is not command central but rather a giant womb the other ants seek to protect. But there are tasks to be done, food to gather, garbage to dump and the dead to bury. How do ants know what to do without a leader? When first observing an ant colony, it appears chaotic, with ants running around and climbing over each other. But for them it is an essential act of community. Ants take direction from a small set of signals, or pheromones (a secreted or excreted chemical factor that triggers a social response), released by other ants. When an ant identifies food, it leaves behind a pheromone trail that other ants pick up and follow to the food source. Ants respond to the frequency of ant encounters and the gradient of pheromone trails rather than messages from individual ants. In addition to being able to discern the different tasks from the various scents, they can also discern if more help is needed for a particular job.

We learn from ants the

> principle of low-level interaction and feedback. The colony works only because of the high number of interactions between ants. A stationary ant could not make an informed decision about which task to undertake because it would be out of the information loop, just as a "super ant" moving at ten times the speed of any other would be unable to lay trails, as well as leave them. Without the low-level, walking-pace interactions the community could not self-organize, could not emerge. Quite simply: no low-level feedback, no community.[10]

We see the same kind of thing happening in the brain and the development of cites. Why do thriving neighborhoods spontaneously develop without the help of City Hall? Emergence, interactions between individuals, defines and shapes various kinds of communities around the city—from artist communities to hipster communities. No central office makes sure enough food is delivered to the city, but food is easily found. No governmental office ensures that each city has enough plumbers, but the pipes get fixed.

> This is because of the individuals on the ground reacting and responding to one another—seeing opportunities and gaps in the market, seizing

new technological advances and putting them to use—all of these people and transactions interconnected through a dense web of *horizontal* connections, not needing to route everything up through to some queen ant controller or mayor before being given permission to act.[11]

It's not that nothing helpful happens top down. Regulation is sometimes needed when people start taking advantage of the system or fail to participate. The point is that complex solutions emerge in the absence of any central form of leadership; the complex whole is created, rather, by individual agents—ants, neurons, people in cities—when they "pay attention to their immediate neighbors rather than wait for orders from above. They think locally and act locally, but their collective action produces global behavior."[12]

Is it possible that the body of Christ can work similarly to so much of God's creation? If the church is going to wake up and move forward with great energy, could it be we need to look to the ant, yield to the Spirit and give up on trying to control things? When Roland Allen talks about the spontaneous expansion of the church, he says, "I mean something which we cannot control. The great things of God are beyond our control. Therein lies a vast hope. Spontaneous expansion could fill the continents with the knowledge of Christ: our control cannot reach as far as that."[13]

BRING ON THE WIND

Polycentric leadership is not a new concept for the church. It is as old as Scripture. *Diverse* leadership, the five equippers, is not new. It is at least as old as the book of Ephesians. Embodying a diverse and polycentric leadership approach in the local church feels new to many because it is rare for a church today to practice genuine shared leadership with a community equippers (apostles, prophets, evangelists, pastors and teachers).

While the reasons for this are many, if the church is going to cultivate a fruitful missional ethos, she needs a variety of gifted leaders working together as a community to stimulate the entire body to join God in the renewal of all things. For this to happen we need to remember two words—*cross* and *wind*. In 1968 Ignatius, an Eastern Orthodox patriarch, gave an address at the Assembly of the World Council of Churches. In that address he spoke of the Holy Spirit in a way that is hard to forget.

> Without the Holy Spirit God is far away.
> Christ stays in the past,
> The Gospel is simply an organization,
> Authority is a matter of propaganda,
> The Liturgy no more than an evolution,
> Christian loving a slave morality.
> But *in the Holy Spirit*
> The cosmos is resurrected and grows with the
>   birth pangs of the kingdom.
> The Risen Christ is there,
> The Gospel is the power of life,
> The Church shows forth the life of the Trinity,
> Authority is a liberating science,
> Mission is a Pentecost,
> The Liturgy is both renewal and anticipation,
> Human action is deified.[14]

If we are going to develop mature disciples and mature communities of faith, we must recognize the power of culture to transform lives. The culture of our congregations shape us in hidden and powerful ways, thus Spirit-filled equippers need to understand the various elements of the cultural web and seek to cultivate thriving, liberating, welcoming, healing and learning environments in the congregation. Not only Spirit-led leaders but our very *approach to leadership* creates culture in profound ways, which is why Christ gave the church apostles, prophets, evangelists, pastors and teachers to equip the entire church so that every part of the body is awakened to live out their calling together, and in this way we become more like the Head of the body—Christ.

I trust you have been encouraged to cultivate a missional culture in the congregation you serve, so that we might see God bring more of heaven to each of our neighborhoods. As you contemplate what God would have you do as a result of reading this book, please join me in one of my favorite prayers.

Father,

> We yearn to be the church you want us to become,
> Shape us into something beautiful.
> We recognize that you are the Potter and we are the clay,
> Please continue to mold us into the image of Christ.

> We want to join in what you are already doing in the world.
> In our worship and life together, in our ministry and service to others,
> we want to give people a glimpse of your intentions for the whole world.

> Help us to welcome the outcasts, love our enemies,
> and form a Community that is visibly different from the culture around us
> as a sign of what you are doing in the world.

> Help us experience your love and grace,
> grow in our relationship with Jesus,
> and experience the power of your Spirit
> as we offer your good news to others.

In Jesus' name we pray, Amen.[15]

Equippers and Their Roles

EQUIPPERS AS CULTURAL ARCHITECTS

Cultural architects are people who help shape the culture of the congregation in theological and practical ways. They help the community to dialectically dance between identifying with and challenging the host culture, and thus the ethos developed in the congregation enables people to live faithful lives to God in the context in which they find themselves.

THE CRAFT OF EQUIPPING

Equipping is both a repairing and preparing ministry. Equipping needs to take place in multiple environments: the classroom and the living room, the sanctuary as well as the streets. Equipping others involves helping people gain a strong theoretical foundation, integrating theory and practice as well as mentoring and experience.

THE VALUE OF EVERY MEMBER

Peter says all followers of Christ are priests (1 Pet 2:9), and Markus Barth reminds us that, "The whole church is the clergy appointed by God for a ministry to and for the world."[1] Each person in the body of Christ is a disciple uniquely made by God with particular gifts, personalities, passions, talents and experiences. Equippers are servants who understand that they are ministers to other ministers, helping each disciple fulfill his or her ministry in the church and in the world for the sake of the world.

EQUIPPER ROLES, GIFTS, THE BODY AND MULTIPLICATION

While we are all ministers, it is helpful to *officially recognize*, through the laying on of hands, congregational equippers in our community to oversee a particular area of congregational life. Those who are recognized equip the congregation and oversee a particular area of ministry in the church.

While each equipper is a gift to the body in a primary way, he or she may be a gift to the body in a secondary way as well. Each equipper is called to live a holistic life in which he or she is being shaped and formed not only by the other recognized equippers but the congregation as a whole.

EQUIPPERS, MISSION AND MULTIPLICATION

Following the pattern of the New Testament, newly recognized equippers of the congregation are selected by the current congregational equippers and brought before the congregation for approval. Each equipper is proactive in training apprentices so that there might be five equippers for every 100 to 250 people. Equippers will also seek to cultivate a team who will help them fulfill their particular ministry. If someone is appointed as a congregational equipper and feels the need to step down due to time constraints or other issues, then the equipping team would seek to find a replacement.

Table A1.1. Apostles: Dream Awakeners

Mission What is the primary mission?[2]	Apostles help to create a discipleship ethos and call people to participate in advancing God's kingdom by awakening people and communities to discover and live out their calling in life.
Heart How do they reflect the heart of God?	Dream awakeners have a deep desire to see God's kingdom become more tangible in the world through the church, and they do whatever it takes to see this come about.
Focus What are the issues that deeply concern them?	Their deep concerns are the health and faith of the church, the future direction of the church, the atmosphere and attitude of the community, identity in Christ, organizational dynamics, individual and communal callings, working with other faith communities, lifecycles of ministries, forward movement with the big picture in mind.
Ministry What are the primary ways that they embody this gift in the church?	They help people live into the cultural web, according to their calling. They engage in systems thinking and systems renewal, creating an atmosphere where good things can run wild in a synergetic way. They develop and help focus resources for the mission, and monitor and cultivate discipleship in all four social spaces. They cultivate the multiplication of leaders, missional communities, ministries and churches and explore ways to network with other churches. They train apprentices and build teams to help with these ministries.
Weakness What is their primary blind spot?	Apostles may find their value in achievement instead of God, and thus could value the mission at the expense of the individual.
Effect What is their effect within the body?	Apostles cultivate a thriving environment where they awaken people to join God in the renewal all things through discipleship and multiplication of leaders, missional communities, ministries, churches and movements of churches.

Table A1.2. Prophets: Heart Revealers

Mission What is the primary mission?	Prophets help people pursue God's shalom by calling the church to live in God's new social order and stand with the poor and the oppressed.
Heart How do they reflect the heart of God?	Heart revealers have a deep desire for people to experience the divine romance and have an intimate walk with the Spirit. They are the conscience of the church.
Focus What are the issues that deeply concern them?	Their deep concerns are social justice, prayer, developing God-centered contrast communities, true worship, holiness, practicing God's presence, listening to God's Spirit, spiritual practices, Spirit-formed people, global consciousness and downward mobility.
Ministry What are the primary ways that they embody this gift in the church?	Heart revealers help people, missional communities and the congregation develop a communal rhythm of life. They equip people to live Spirit-filled lives and practice the presence of God through silence, solitude and fasting. They cultivate the prayer life of the congregation and creatively speak truth to power and equip others to do the same. They give spontaneous words of encouragement, comfort and exhortation and help people move from a politics of exploitation and oppression to one of justice and compassion. They encourage the congregation to live more simple, sustainable lives, and find ways to stand with the poor and oppressed in concrete ways locally and globally. They train apprentices and build a team of people who help them with these ministries.
Weakness What is their primary blind spot?	Prophets potentially mistake their words for God's words and undervalue contextualization.
Effect What is their effect within the body?	Prophets cultivate a liberating environment that dares people to embody a holistic gospel by forming Spirit-imbibed contrast communities for the glory of God and the good of the world.

Table A1.3. Evangelists: Story Tellers

Mission What is the primary mission?	Evangelists help the congregation incarnate the good news by being witnesses and redemptive agents, redeeming every aspect of society.
Heart How do they reflect the heart of God?	Story tellers have a deep passion for reconciliation. They love all people and desire to see what was lost at the Fall be mended: people's relationship with God, with each other, with their own self and all of creation.
Focus What are the issues that deeply concern them?	They are concerned for the missional church; missional living; philosophy; culture; redeeming lives, culture, vocations, social systems and creation; short- and long-term missions; being a faithful church in a pluralistic world; sharing faith respectfully, intelligently, lovingly and contextually; crosscultural living; apologetics; hospitality; and blessing the neighborhood.

Ministry What are the primary ways that they embody this gift in the church?	Story tellers live missionally and equip others to engage in missional living as a way of life. They help people to meaningfully connect to missional spaces which connect Christians with non-Christians. They teach people how to live and share their story and God's story. They view the congregational life through the eyes of those outside of the faith and find practical ways for missional communities to meet and serve their neighbors and neighborhood. They help connect the congregation to what is happening in the neighborhood. They train apprentices and build a team of people who help them with these ministries.
Weakness What is their primary blind spot?	Evangelists may engage in overcontextualization by identifying too closely with culture and not valuing the development of a contrast community.
Effect What is their effect within the body?	Evangelists cultivate a welcoming environment and an outward focus toward the world for the sake of the world helping people to be and share the good news contextually.

Table A1.4. Pastors: Soul Healers

Mission What is the primary mission?	Pastors help the congregation pursue wholeness and holiness within community through cultivating a life-giving spirituality and helping them embody reconciliation.
Heart How do they reflect the heart of God?	They have a deep desire for people to experience the life-giving fellowship of authentic community as modeled by our triune God.
Focus What are the issues that deeply concern them?	Their concerns are identity in Christ, conflict resolution, self-awareness, emotionally healthy living, healing of past wounds, living in brokenness and vulnerability, receiving the gift of limits, embracing grieving and loss, loving well, spiritual friendships, spiritual direction, family life, peacemaking, soul mapping, counseling, coaching, living confessional lives, sharing victories and failures, and helping the congregation join in the Table fellowship of the Trinity.
Ministry What are the primary ways that they embody this gift in the church?	Soul healers cultivate a life-giving spiritually within community so that the congregation can sustain herself in mission.
Weakness What is their primary blind spot?	Pastors could value the individual over mission, pitting the two against each other in such a way as to create a false dichotomy between community building and mission.
Effect What is their effect within the body?	Pastors cultivate a healing environment in which people learn to enter into a life-giving spirituality within God's new family, understanding their new identity in Christ.

Table A1.5. Teachers: Light Givers

Mission What is the primary mission?	Teachers help the congregation to inhabit the sacred text by encouraging the community to immerse herself in Scripture and live faithfully in God's story.
Heart How do they reflect the heart of God?	Light givers desire that God's people would be nourished by Scripture so they might better understand the ways of God and build their lives on the solid rock of his Word.
Focus What are the issues that deeply concern them?	They are concerned about theology, ethics, practical theology, hermeneutics, philosophy, the Torah, the Prophets, the Writings, the Gospels, the early church, narrative theology, systematic theology, creeds, truth and error, wisdom, word studies, languages, memorization and meditation of Scripture, current theological trends and hot-button issues.
Ministry What are the primary ways that they embody this gift in the church?	Light givers find multiple ways for the community to be shaped by the living Word. They create, gather and share resources for the congregation so that people might learn and practice God's Word. They teach, write books, write pamphlets on hot topics and involve people in active learning. They create hunger for the Word and help the congregation think and act in theologically sound ways. They help to develop the teaching calendar in a holistic way with the other equippers. They train apprentices and build a team of people who help them with these ministries.
Weakness What is their primary blind spot?	Teachers may put study above practice, and seek to master the text instead of allowing the text to master them.
Effect What is their effect within the body?	Teachers cultivate a learning environment where people immerse themselves in God's narrative and engage in praxis—enacted reflection—as well as future-oriented living.

APPENDIX 2

Equipper Candidate Reference Form

THE REQUEST

Because of your relationship with the congregational equipper candidate, you are being asked to fill out a reference on his or her behalf. This reference is a vital part of the selection process, so your honest evaluation is requested. It is our desire to recognize those whom God is working in and through, so that the congregation might move forward in fulfilling God's mission in the neighborhood.

THE EVALUATION

This evaluation is designed to help in the selection of and evaluation of an equipper candidate. While we are all ministers, the Scriptures illustrate that it is helpful to officially recognize, through the laying on of hands, specific equippers in a congregation to help oversee, cultivate and nurture various ministries in the congregation. Equippers are servants who understand they are ministers to other ministers, helping each disciple fulfill his or her ministry in the church and in the world for the sake of the world.

AREAS OF EVALUATION

Because of the nature of the equipper role, it is important that equippers are people of the Word, people of virtue, people who have developed equipping skills through the Spirit and people who live missional lives for the sake of the world. Therefore, this evaluation will ask you to evaluate the candidate's theology, character, equipping skills and missional life.

This evaluation is guided by the various lists of virtues found throughout the New Testament. These include the Pastoral Epistles (1 Tim 3:2-7; 2 Tim 3:10-11; Tit 1:6-9), the fruit of the Spirit (Gal 5:22-23), the fundamentals of faith, hope and love (1 Cor 13), and Peter's letters (1 Pet 5; 2 Pet 1). In addition, this evaluation is guided by other virtues and ways of life discovered in the life and teachings of Jesus (e.g., the Sermon on the Mount [Mt 5–7] and various parables), the Pentateuch, and in the biblical narrative as a whole. The Scriptures paint a picture of a mature disciple: a person who is able to equip others in the congregation through example and ministry.

EVALUATION KEY

Throughout this evaluation, please use the five-point scale in table A2.1 in evaluating the candidate. You may use whole numbers (e.g., 1, 2, 3) or half numbers (e.g., 3.5, 4.5). If it is an area that you have not observed, then indicate that with the letters UN, for unobserved. Space is provided throughout the evaluation for your written comments.

Table A2.1. Five-Point Scale

5—Exceptionally Mature	A way of life; consistently excels in this area
4—Commendable	A strength in this person's life
3—Competent	Acceptable, solid, capable
2—Growth Needed	Growth needed in this area
1—Poor	Major growth needed
UN –Unobserved	Haven't observed this area of their life

THEOLOGY

According to Jesus, we are not to live by bread alone but by every word that proceeds from the mouth of God. Scripture is God's word to us, a faithful guide to our lives when understood and applied well. As Miroslav Volf has said, "At the heart of every good theology lies not simply a plausible intellectual vision but more importantly a compelling account of a way of life, and that theology is therefore best done from within the pursuit of this way of life."[1]

The apostle Paul says, "Keep a close watch on how you live and on your teaching. Stay true to what is right for the sake of your own salvation and the salvation of those who hear you" (1 Tim 4:16 NLT). Please use table A2.2 to evaluate the candidate in these various areas dealing with theology and practice.

Table A2.2. Theological Evaluation

Area	Rating (1-5)	Description
Devotion		Regularly spends time with God through his Word in a way that he or she hears the voice of God and falls more in love with him.
Gospel		Has a holistic understanding of the good news, that it is good news for the poor and the poor in spirit, for the present and the future. Understands that the good news is focused on the life, death and resurrection of Jesus.
Kingdom		Understands, teaches and lives out the teachings of Jesus and the kingdom, that the kingdom is here and coming, that we are called to pray and participate in seeing God's kingdom become a greater reality on earth through his Spirit.
Narrative		Understands, teaches and abides by the basic narrative of creation, Fall, redemption and the renewal of all things.
Comprehensive		Understands, teaches and lives by the fact that God intends to redeem or restore "all things" in heaven and on earth, including our bodies and creation itself.
Interpretation		Takes into account the Scripture, the Holy Spirit, the local church, the current context, theological history, reason and experience when it comes to seeking understanding of the sacred text.
Creeds		Understands and abides by the Nicene and Apostles' creeds.
Encouragement		Is able to encourage others with Scripture.
Application		Is able to apply Scripture appropriately, with humility and grace in various situations.
Critical Openness		Allows people room to freely explore the truth under a vast umbrella of God's grace, not naively but with intelligence, wisdom and love. Realizes that critical openness allows us to fully listen to another's perspective without prejudging them or their viewpoint. Respects others when conversing over revelation and reality. Knows that understanding expands incrementally, which means it is continually evolving.

Comments. The following space is provided for you to add further information in regard to this candidate's theology, teaching and way of life.

CHARACTER

Christ's followers are called to increasingly become more Christlike. The apostle John says, "Whoever claims to live in him must live as Jesus did" (1 Jn 2:6). Being a Christian means following the way of Jesus, living like Jesus. While we all have room for improvement, equippers should be spiritual fit, moving toward becoming a fully mature human being.

Being mature entails having a different character. It is important to keep in mind that there is a big difference between a generous act and being a generous person, or a courageous act and being a courageous person. "Most people are capable of a generous act from time to time, by a supreme effort of will. But that is very different from having generosity built into the very fabric and tenor of life."[2] God wants to transform our lives in such a way that the basic way we live is patterned after the life of Christ. This is why Paul said a half dozen times that we should follow him as he follows Christ. Please use table A2.3 to evaluate the equipper candidate in these indispensable virtues.

Table A2.3. Character Evaluation

Area	Rating (1-5)	Description
Trustworthy and Trusting		Fulfills promises and obligations. Demonstrates a consistency in values, skills and actions. Authentic. Has learned to trust others as well.
Servant		Downwardly mobile. Does not lord it over others but serves others from the heart. Willing to do the lowly jobs and connect with those of no reputation. Is not self-willed or controlling. Others-centered. Builds God's kingdom, not own.
Lover		Has experienced the love of God to the point that he or she loves God fervently from the heart and loves people. Loves the unlovely; loves friends as well as enemies.
Peace Maker		Does not gossip or slander others. Realizes that conflict is natural, but unresolved conflict is not. Actively seeks to resolve conflict in healthy ways. At peace with everyone, as much as possible. Understands own forgiveness and forgives others.
Faith-Filled and Faithful		Maintains spiritual vitality through a rhythm of life involving spiritual practices. Confident of calling. Risk-taker. Demonstrates courage to actively move past fears. Trusts God to move mountains.
Humble		Demonstrates a healthy sense of self-forgetfulness. Rejoices with other people's successes. Cooperative, team player, seeks advice and responds well to authorities. Displays healthy interdependence. Doesn't feel the need to prove self. Actively learns from others.

Area	Rating (1-5)	Description
Hospitable		Friend to strangers. Welcomes people in his or her home or apartment. Goes out of the way to meet people he or she doesn't know at gatherings and in life.
Generous		Demonstrates a mindset of abundance, not of scarcity. Encourages a gift-oriented culture in the midst of a market economy.
Holy and Devout		Lives a morally pure life and seeks to please God in everything.
Joyful		Rejoices always and is thankful in everything. Radiates a contagious joy. Has a joy that gives them strength to persevere through all things.
Patient		Waits on God in the midst of a driven society that applauds productivity.
Self-Aware		Has a good sense of own strengths and weaknesses, gifts and calling. Emotionally intelligent. Reads social dynamics well. Has learned to listen to own self and process own experiences in healthy ways.

Comments. The following space is provided for you to add further information in regard to this candidate's character.

EQUIPPING SKILLS

We are all called to be ministers, but some are called to be equippers of other ministers. The craft of equipping is like any other craft: it is learned through apprenticeship and practice. Just as most basketball coaches started out as players, equippers seek to follow Christ in their life and in time realize they have passions and gifting in particular areas. In time they become mentors, coaches or equippers of others.

The apostle Paul identifies five equippers in Ephesians 4: apostles (dream awakeners), prophets (heart revealers), evangelists (story tellers), pastors (soul healers) and teachers (light givers). Each of these equips the body in various ways. Though each equipper has a different focus, every equipper needs to develop a set of skills in order to excel in their craft. A few of these skills are listed in table A2.4. Please evaluate the candidate in each area in the table.

Table A2.4. Skill Evaluation

Area	Rating (1-5)	Description
Catalyst		Casts vision. Able to communicate vision in such a way that others have a desire to use their gifts to contribute to what God is doing. An initiator, a passionate person who takes the lead in getting work done.
Cultural Architect		Helps to cultivate a culture in the congregation in which a particular ministry of Jesus is more fully lived out. Cultivates a thriving, liberating, welcoming, healing or learning culture.
Mentor		Demonstrates sincere interest in people. Responds with urgency and compassion to people's physical and emotional needs. Comforts, encourages and exhorts others wisely so they can move forward.
Listener		Engages in holistic listening through (1) asking good questions, (2) listening to the Spirit of God and (3) listening to what is happening with those they are serving.
Manager		Strives for excellence in everything. Delegates responsibilities to develop people according to their gifts and call. Creates synergy toward congregational goals and helps the congregation move forward.
Networker		Displays social intelligence and finds ways to network within the congregation as well as with other churches and movements in unity for the sake of the kingdom of God.
Resourceful		Not only is able to provide for self and close ones, but also finds multiple ways to resource others in terms of knowledge, networking and problem solving.
Team Builder		Involves people based on their God-given S.H.A.P.E. (Spiritual Gifts, Heart, Abilities, Personality, Experiences).[3] Engages in shared leadership. Language, posture and behavior inspire others to action as well as working together for a common vision.
Innovator		Creative and imaginative. Thinks outside the box. Considers fresh ideas to solve real problems.
Resilient		Remains hopeful and perseveres when convinced he or she is in God's will. Makes good use of support systems. Bounces back quickly from loss and discouragement. Evidences emotional stability.
Adaptive		Inspires faith and creativity within the congregation in a time of rapid and discontinuous change. Keeps an open mind and is willing to maintain a sense of flexibility while moving forward toward a horizon.
Discerner		Is able to look at circumstances and ask what God is doing. Then helps move the congregation or ministry to get the sense of the Spirit in how to respond to the issue at hand.

Comments. The following space is provided for you to add further information in regard to this candidate's equipper skills:

MISSIONAL LIVING

Jesus said, "You are the light of the world. . . . Let your light shine before others, that they may see your good deeds and glorify your Father in heaven" (Mt 5:14, 16). Karl Barth said, "A church which is not on mission is either not yet or no longer the church, or only a dead church—itself in need of renewal."[4] When we read Scripture, we learn that God's mission is to set all things right. He desires to redeem and restore the world to its intended purpose. The mission of God is the reason the church exists. Equippers help the congregation to join God in the renewal of all things.

Equippers live as cultural architects, helping to shape particular environments where life emerges in spontaneous ways. In this way they cultivate communities that are a sign—pointing people to something that is beyond their present horizon but can give guidance and hope now. These signs are instruments that God can use for his work of healing, liberating and blessing. They are a foretaste, a place where men and women can taste the joy and freedom that God intends for all.[5] Please use table A2.5 to evaluate the equipper candidate in the areas of missional living.

Table A2.5. Missional Evaluation

Area	Rating (1-5)	Description
Missio Dei		Understands that God is missional by nature and that the Father sent the Son and Spirit, and the triune God sent Christ's followers into the world for the sake of the world. Lives in light of this truth.
Missionary Consciousness		Understands that he or she is a missionary and is sent to be God's ambassador. Helps the congregation to live as missionaries in their context.
Incarnational		Understands the unique pulse, needs and character of the local neighborhood because he or she lives among the people. Helps the congregation join God's mission contextually.
Reconciler		Values helping people become reconciled with God, with others, with own self and with creation. Embodies the ministry of reconciliation and helps the congregation to be reconcilers as well.
Missional Space		Loves being in and creating missional spaces for self and for the congregation. Actively plants and waters seeds of faith; helps others to do the same as they trust God to do his work.
Missional Learner		Proactive in learning how to live more missionally as an individual as well as how to help the congregation live more missionally.
Bridge Builder		Helps those outside the community of faith find a sense of belonging in the congregation. Helps to break down walls and build bridges between Christians and non-Christians.
Missional Leader		A good example in living out God's mission in every realm of life. Helps the congregation to be a sign, foretaste and instrument of God's kingdom.

Comments. The following space is provided for you to add further information in regard to this candidate's missional life.

FINAL QUESTIONS

1. Is there anything you are aware of that would disqualify this person from serving as a congregational equipper? If so, what?

2. Would you recommend that this candidate become a congregational equipper? Please mark one of the following with an X.

   _____ I would highly recommend this candidate be a congregational equipper.

   _____ I would recommend that this candidate be a congregational equipper.

   _____ I have hesitations in recommending this candidate to be a congregational equipper.

   _____ I do not think that this candidate should be a congregational equipper.

3. Please give a short explanation to your answer to number two.

APPENDIX 3

Equipper Candidate Interview

CHARACTER AND VIRTUES[1]

1. *Faith*—How have you displayed faith in God in this past month?

2. *Discernment*—How do you discern God's will for your life and for congregational life?

3. *Presence*—How do you handle criticism? How do you minister without a private agenda?

4. *Patience*—How have you displayed patience this past month? Tell me about a time you had to forgive someone recently. Do you have any outstanding unresolved conflict with anyone that you are aware of?

5. *Resourcefulness*—What is your current financial status? Do you give at least 10 percent of your income to the local church? Why or why not? What is your understanding of wealth and generosity as it relates to Christ followers?

6. *Humility*—How have you demonstrated humility in the past three months?

7. *Love*—In what ways have you loved those who are hard to love the past three months?

8. *Integrity*—How are you doing in the area of moral and sexual purity?

MISSIONAL LIVING

1. In what ways do you live missionally?

2. Describe for me your current relationships with those who have no faith.

3. What missional spaces do you currently live in, and how do you live in them?

4. What does it mean for Kairos Hollywood to be a missional community?

5. When it comes to missional living, what are the strengths and weaknesses of your discipleship community?

6. What ways can you help Kairos Hollywood live more missionally?

THEOLOGY

1. How would you describe the good news?

2. What does it mean to join God in the renewal of all things?

3. What do you consider the three most controversial issues facing the church today, and where do you stand on these issues?

4. Describe for me your hermeneutical approach to the Scriptures.

5. Name the top five people who have shaped or are shaping your theological understanding.

SKILLS

1. *Self-understanding*—What do you consider to be your biggest strengths and weaknesses?

2. *Pulse of church*—What do you consider the three greatest strengths and weaknesses of Kairos Hollywood?

3. *Language*—How important is language when it comes to shaping a community?

4. *Learner*—In what ways do you educate yourself?

5. *Management*—What are the most important things to consider when building a ministry team?

6. *Performance*—What does a community need to effectively fulfill God's mission in the neighborhood?

7. *Conflict resolution*—Describe for me how you tend to resolve conflict.

8. *Missional cultivation*—In what ways have you cultivated a missional ethos within Kairos Hollywood?

EQUIPPER ORIENTATION (SPECIFIC TO THEIR PRIMARY EQUIPPING ROLE)

1. Describe the general role of an equipper.

2. How does each equipper relate to the others? Is there any hierarchy within the equipper team?

3. How does an equipper interact with the congregation as a whole?

4. In what ways will you seek to identify and cultivate other equippers?

5. Describe for me the primary mission of the _____ (add the relevant equipper to the blank here and below).

6. In what way does the _____ reflect the heart of God?

7. What are the issues that deeply concern the _____?

8. What are the primary ways these equippers embody this gift in the church?

9. In what ways have you embodied this gift in the church in this past year?

10. When working on an equipper team, what are the primary blind spots the _____ may bring to the table?

11. What kind of culture does the _____ develop in a congregation?

12. Describe for me your vision for the _____ role for this coming year.

CASE STUDY

[Develop a case study of a common issue the leaders of your church have faced. Write it out and ask the candidate how he or she would handle the problem and why.]

NETWORK ASSOCIATION

1. What is your understanding of Kairos Hollywood's relationship to Kairos Los Angeles?

2. Do you think it is important for Kairos Los Angeles to be an active member of the Ecclesia Network? Why or why not?

3. What theological statement does a church that is completely independent make to the world?

FINAL QUESTION

Are you consciously aware of any reason why you shouldn't be a congregational equipper? If so, what is it?

Notes

Introduction

[1]I'm borrowing some language here from James K. A. Smith, *Desiring the Kingdom: Worship, Worldview and Cultural Formation* (Grand Rapids: Baker Academic, 2009).

[2]Craig Van Gelder and Dwight J. Zscheile, *The Missional Church in Perspective: Mapping Trends and Shaping the Conversation* (Grand Rapids: Baker Academic, 2011). You can find my overview of the first half of the book at <http://t.co/Qt0M4hUI>.

[3]Saint Cyprian *The Unity of the Catholic Church* 6, http://orthodoxmetropolisportland .org/ecc_cyprian_unity_of_the_catholic_church.html.

[4]Lesslie Newbigin, *Signs of the Kingdom* (Grand Rapids: Eerdmans, 1980).

Chapter 1: What Is Missional Culture and Why Does It Matter?

[1]I heard this story from John Ortberg, but it appears to be used more broadly. One version of the story can be found online at <www.centralpc.org/sermons/2002/s020113.htm>.

[2]German missiologist Karl Hartenstein coined this phrase when summarizing a lecture of Karl Barth. Christopher Wright, *The Mission of God: Unlocking the Bible's Grand Narrative* (Downers Grove, Ill.: InterVarsity Press, 2006), p. 62.

[3]Jürgen Moltmann, *The Church in the Power of the Spirit: A Contribution to Messianic Ecclesiology* (Minneapolis: Augsburg Fortress, 1977), p. 64.

[4]Karl Barth, *Church Dogmatics* 4.3.2, *The Doctrine of Reconciliation* (Edinburgh: T & T Clark, 1962), p. 874.

[5]Lesslie Newbigin, *Lesslie Newbigin: Missionary Theologian: A Reader*, ed. Paul Weston (Grand Rapids: Eerdmans 2006), pp. 130-42.

[6]Neil Cole, *Ordinary Hero: Becoming a Disciple Who Makes a Difference* (Grand Rapids: Baker, 2008), p. 185.

[7]Stanley Hauerwas, *A Community of Character: Toward a Constructive Christian Social Ethic* (Notre Dame, Ind.: University of Notre Dame Press, 1981), p. 3.

[8]Kathryn Tanner, *Theories of Culture: A New Agenda for Theology* (Minneapolis: Fortress, 1997), p. ix.

[9]Marcus Borg, in Marcus Borg and N. T. Wright, *The Meaning of Jesus: Two Visions* (New York: HarperCollins, 2000), pp. 69-70.

[10]Andrea Sachs and Juliet Schor, "Junk Culture," *Time*, October 4, 2004, www.time .com/time/magazine/article/0,9171,995267,00.html.

[11]See Gerhard Lohfink, *Jesus and Community: The Social Dimension of the Christian Faith* (Philadelphia: Fortress Press, 1984).

[12]Timothy Keller, *Gospel in Life: Grace Changes Everything* (Grand Rapids: Zondervan, 2010), p. 126.

Chapter 2: How Culture Works

[1]Raymond Williams, *Keywords: A Vocabulary of Culture and Society* (Oxford: Oxford University Press, 1976), p. 76.

[2]This definition is shared by William Dryness, *The Earth Is God's* (Eugene, Ore.: Wipf & Stock, 2004); William Romanowski, *Eyes Wide Open* (Grand Rapids: Brazos, 2001); and Andy Crouch, *Culture Making* (Downers Grove, Ill.: InterVarsity Press, 2008).

[3]Crouch, *Culture Making*, p. 40.

[4]Tony Bennett, Lawrence Grossberg and Meaghan Morris, *New Keywords: A Revised Vocabulary of Culture and Society* (Malden, Mass.: Blackwell, 2005), pp. 64-65.

[5]Kathryn Tanner, *Theories of Culture: A New Agenda for Theology* (Minneapolis: Fortress, 1997), p. 3.

[6]Romanowski, *Eyes Wide Open*, p. 49.

[7]Philip D. Kenneson, *Life on the Vine: Cultivating the Fruit of the Spirit in Christian Community* (Downers Grove, Ill.: InterVarsity Press, 1999), p. 21.

[8]I get the term *cultural web* from Gerry Johnson, "Culture, Strategy and Change from the Creator of the Cultural Web," www.strategyexplorers.com/yourorganisation/culture-change.asp. While I appreciate his approach to understanding culture, I'm looking at culture from the viewpoint of the church, not a business, and thus have different elements and a different approach to the elements of culture.

[9]Stanley Hauerwas, *A Community of Character* (Notre Dame, Ind.: University of Notre Dame Press, 1981), p. 136.

[10]Ibid., p. 95.

[11]For example, I did a series of posts on a missional view of the doctrine of election, whereby I compared and contrasted Newbigin and Grudem's understanding of election. You can find that here: bit.ly/mBxeLN.

[12]Catherine Bell, *Ritual: Perspective and Dimensions* (New York: Oxford University Press, 1997).

[13]Ibid., p. 171.

[14]Ibid., p. 102.

[15]James K. A. Smith, *Desiring the Kingdom: Worship, Worldview, and Cultural Formation* (Grand Rapids: Baker Academic, 2009), p. 85.

[16]Dallas Willard, *The Great Omission: Reclaiming Jesus's Essential Teachings on Discipleship* (San Francisco: HarperCollins, 2006), p. 52.

[17]Smith, *Desiring the Kingdom*, p. 82.

[18]Ibid., p. 86.

[19]Miroslav Volf, *After Our Likeness: The Church as the Image of the Trinity* (Grand Rapids: Eerdmans, 1998), p. 234.

[20]Stanley J. Grenz, *The Moral Quest: Foundations of Christian Ethics* (Downers Grove, Ill.: InterVarsity Press, 1997), p. 261.

Chapter 3: What's Going on in the Culture of the Church You Serve?

[1]Tony Campolo, *Let Me Tell You a Story: Life Lessons from Unexpected Places and Unlikely People* (Nashville: Thomas Nelson, 2000), p. 69.

[2]Brian McLaren, *A Generous Orthodoxy* (Grand Rapids: Zondervan, 2004), p. 166.

[3]Richard Rohr, *Following the Mystics Through the Narrow Gate* (audio curriculum, Center for Action and Contemplation), available at http://store.cacradicalgrace.org/Merchant2/merchant.mvc?Screen=PROD&Product_Code=SP-C-34&Category_Code=&Store_Code=CFAAC.

[4]John Ortberg, *Everybody's Normal Till You Get to Know Them* (Grand Rapids: Zondervan, 2003), pp. 89-90.

[5]My friend A. J. Swoboda just finished a book titled *Messy: God Likes It That Way* (Grand Rapids: Kregel, 2012). It's a great resource to get a realistic picture of community and spiritual growth.

[6]Bishop Graham Cray said this at a Fresh Expressions Conference, Columbia Baptist Church, Falls Church, Virginia, December 2-3, 2010.

[7]Ibid.

[8]Cornelius Plantinga, *Not the Way It's Supposed to Be: A Breviary of Sin* (Grand Rapids: Eerdmans, 1995), p. 10.

[9]Campolo, *Let Me Tell You a Story*, p. 116.

Chapter 4: Polycentric Leadership and Missional Culture

[1]In 1 Corinthians 3:10 Paul calls himself a "wise builder" (in some translations a "master builder").

[2]Thomas Hoving, *Art for Dummies* (Foster City, Calif.: IDG Books, 1999), p. 3.

[3]Ibid., p. 6.

[4]Ibid.

[5]Markus Barth, *Ephesians: Translation and Commentary on Chapters 4-6* (New York: Doubleday, 1960), p. 437.

[6]Michael Frost and Alan Hirsch, *The Shaping of Things to Come: Innovation and Mission for the 21st Century Church* (Peabody, Mass.: Hendrickson, 2003), p. 169.

[7]Ibid.

[8]Ibid.

[9]Barth, *Ephesians*, p. 437.

[10]Suzanne W. Morse, "Five Building Blocks for Successful Leadership," in *The Community of the Future*, ed. Frances Hesselbein et al. (San Francisco: Jossey-Bass, 1998), p. 234.

[11]Edgar H. Schein, *Organizational Culture and Leadership* (San Francisco: Jossey-Bass, 2004), p. 11.

[12]Craig Van Gelder, *The Essence of the Church: A Community Created by the Spirit* (Grand Rapids: Baker, 2000), pp. 116-17.

Chapter 5: Facing Today's Challenges

[1]Eddie Gibbs, *LeadershipNext: Changing Leaders in a Changing Culture* (Downers Grove, Ill.: InterVarsity Press, 2005), p. 35.

[2]See the video at www.youtube.com/watch?v=JUs7iG1mNjI.

[3]Marshall McLuhan and Quentin Fiore, *The Medium Is the Massage: An Inventory of Effects* (New York: Bantam Books, 1967), p. 11.

[4]Ibid., p. 26.

[5]Some Christian works that argue we have become blind to effects of technology include Jacques Ellul, *The Technological Bluff* (Grand Rapids: Eerdmans, 1990); Marva Dawn, *Unfettered Hope* (Louisville: Westminster John Knox Press, 2003); Albert Borgmann, *Technology and the Character of Contemporary Life* (Grand Rapids: Brazos Press, 1984); Albert Borgmann, *Power Failure* (Grand Rapids: Brazos Press 2003); and Shane Hipps, *The Hidden Power of Electronic Culture* (Grand Rapids: Zondervan, 2005).

[6]Rex M. Miller, *The Millennium Matrix: Reclaiming the Past, Reframing the Future of the Church* (San Francisco: Jossey-Bass, 2004), p. 114.

[7]This chart is my own summary of information from chapter six from the chart in the middle of Miller's *Millennium Matrix*. Some of the word choices are mine. I have not included the Oral Age in this chart because it is less relevant in the Western context, and Miller did not talk about it in the chapter on leadership.

[8]Miller, *Millennium Matrix*, p. 124.

[9]James K. A. Smith, *Who's Afraid of Postmodernism? Taking Derrida, Lyotard, and Foucault to Church* (Grand Rapids: Baker Academic, 2006), p. 23.

[10]Jim Powell, *Derrida for Beginners* (New York: Writers & Readers, 1997), p. 7.

[11]Smith, *Who's Afraid of Postmodernism?* p. 54.

[12]Ibid., p. 51.

[13]Jacques Derrida, quoted in ibid.

[14]Michel Foucault, quoted in Smith, *Who's Afraid of Postmodernism?* p. 85.

[15]Ibid., pp. 81-107.

[16]Miroslav Volf, *After Our Likeness: The Church as the Image of the Trinity* (Grand Rapids: Eerdmans, 1998), p. 234.

[17]Ibid., p. 236.

[18]Kurt Fredrickson, "Fire in the Church: Organic Structures for the Missional Congregation," a paper written for MP800 Tutorial in Postmodern Culture, Fuller Seminary, Pasadena, California, 2007, p. 9.

[19]Mark Lau Branson, *Memories, Hopes and Conversations: Appreciative Inquiry and Congregational Change* (Herndon, Va.: Alban Institute, 2004), p. 36.

[20]Kester Brewin, *Signs of Emergence: A Vision for Church That Is Organic/Networked/ Decentralized/Bottom-up/Communal/Flexible {Always Evolving}* (Grand Rapids: Baker, 2007), p. 92.

[21]Ibid., pp. 97-117.

[22]Ibid., p. 116.

[23]See a helpful chart at this literary review of Brewin's *Signs of Emergence:* http:// jrwoodward.net/2007/12/signs-of-emergence-by-kester-brewin-a-literary-review.

[24]Andrew Davey, *Urban Christianity and Global Order: Theological Resources for an Urban Future* (Peabody, Mass.: Hendrickson, 2002), p. 5.

[25]Ibid., p. 7.

[26]Craig Van Gelder, "Understanding the Church in North America," in *Missional Church*, ed. Darrell Guder (Grand Rapids: Eerdmans, 1998), pp. 48-49.

[27]This report is based on over 54,000 interviews conducted between February and November 2008.

[28]"Catholics on the Move, Non-Religious on the Rise," ARIS 2008, http://commons .trincoll.edu/aris/2009/03/05/catholics_on_the_move_non-religious_on_the_rise.

[29]Gerard Kelly, *Retrofuture: Rediscovering Our Roots, Recharting Our Routes* (Downers Grove, Ill.: InterVarsity Press, 1999), p. 212.

[30]Stuart Murray, *Post-Christendom: Church and Mission in a Strange New World* (Milton Keynes, U.K.: Paternoster, 2004), p. 126.

[31]Stuart Murray, *Church After Christendom* (Milton Keynes, U.K.: Paternoster, 2004), p. 185.

[32]Leonard Hjalmarson, "Leading from the Margins," *NextReformation* blog, www .nextreformation.com/wp-admin/resources/Margins.pdf (accessed on June 13, 2011).

[33]Ibid.

[34]David Bosch, *Transforming Mission: Paradigm Shifts in Theology of Mission* (Maryknoll, N.Y.: Orbis, 1991), p. 21.

Chapter 6: Hearing the Story

[1]T. J. Gorringe, *A Theology of the Built Environment: Justice, Empowerment, Redemption* (New York: Cambridge University Press, 2002), p. 1.

[2]Eugene Peterson, *Reversed Thunder: The Revelation of John and the Praying Imagination* (New York: HarperCollins, 1988), p. 61.

[3]Ibid., p. 60.

[4]Elliot N. Dorff, "Jewish Models of Leadership," in *Traditions in Leadership: How Faith Traditions Shape the Way We Lead*, ed. Richard J. Mouw and Eric O. Jacobsen (Pasadena, Calif.: De Pree Leadership Center, 2006), p. 4.

[5]Gayle Erwin's sermon "The Last Supper" can be found at http://media.sermonindex .net/21/SID21783.mp3.

[6]James Fleming, "Exploring the World of Jesus," *BAR Magazine*, www.bib-arch.org /e-features/exploring-world-jesus.asp.

[7]Gayle Erwin, in his famous sermon "The Last Supper" (http://media.sermonindex .net/21/SID21783.mp3), gives the breakdown of where the disciples likely sat. There are a number of scholars who contest that John was the "one Jesus loved," but even if this is the case, we know that it wasn't Peter, who signaled to whoever might have been in this seat. I base my seating arrangement on Erwin's sermon and on William R. Cannon, "The Gospel of John," http://webcache.googleusercontent .com/search?q=cache:Dap2IwXUEagJ:www.religion-online.org/showchapter.asp% 3Ftitle%3D692%26C%3D927+peter+signals+across+the+table&cd=1&hl=en&ct= clnk&gl=us&client=firefox-a&source=www.google.com.

Chapter 7: Deepening Theological Roots

[1]Leonardo Boff, *Holy Trinity, Perfect Community* (Maryknoll, N.Y.: Orbis, 2000), p. 3.

[2]Ibid., p. 4.

[3]Miroslav Volf, *After Our Likeness: The Church as the Image of the Trinity* (Grand Rapids: Eerdmans, 1998), p. 11.

[4]Ibid., p. 17.

[5]In addition to *After Our Likeness*, Volf's major work on this topic, he has also co-edited with Michael Welker *God's Life in Trinity* (Minneapolis: Augsburg Fortress, 2006). Leonardo Boff's academic book is *Trinity and Society* (Maryknoll, N.Y.: Orbis, 1988). *Holy Trinity, Perfect Community* is Boff's more popular book.

[6]Leonardo Boff, *Trinity and Society* (Maryknoll, N.Y.: Orbis, 1988), pp. 77-78.

[7]Ibid., p. 154.

[8]Boff, *Holy Trinity, Perfect Community*, p. xii.

[9]Volf, *After Our Likeness*, p. 217.

[10]Boff, *Trinity and Society*, p. 138.

[11]Volf, *After Our Likeness*, p. 249.

[12]Boff, *Trinity and Society*, p. 139.

[13]Leonardo Boff, *Ecclesiogenesis: The Base Communities Reinvent the Church* (Maryknoll, N.Y.: Orbis, 1986), p. 46.

[14]Boff, *Holy Trinity, Perfect Community*, p. xvi.

[15]Michael Battle, "How Should We Live? The Christian Life," in *Essentials of Christian Theology*, ed. William C. Placher (Louisville: Westminster John Knox Press, 2003), p. 283.

[16]John Zizioulas, *Being as Communion: Studies in Personhood and the Church* (Crestwood, N.Y.: St. Vladimir's Seminary Press, 1985).

[17]Volf, *After His Likeness*, p. 104.

[18]Zizioulas, *Being as Communion*, p. 18.

[19]Walter Wink, *The Powers That Be: Theology for a New Millennium* (New York: Doubleday, 1998), p. 1.

[20]Veli-Matti Kärkkäinen, *Pneumatology: The Holy Spirit in Ecumenical, International, and Contextual Perspective* (Grand Rapids: Baker Academic, 2002), pp. 23-24.

Chapter 8: Embracing Emotional Health

[1]Dan B. Allender and Tremper Longman III, *The Cry of the Soul: How Our Emotions Reveal Our Deepest Questions About God* (Colorado Springs: NavPress, 1994), pp. 24-25.

[2]Henri Nouwen, *Can You Drink the Cup?* (Notre Dame, Ind.: Ave Maria Press, 1996), p. 57.

[3]Rosabeth Moss Kanter, quoted in Harvey Seifter and Peter Economy, *Leadership Ensemble: Lessons in Collaborative Management from the World-Famous Conductorless Orchestra* (New York: Times Books, 2001), p. 19.

Chapter 9: Relinquishing the Need to Control

[1]Leonardo Boff, *Church, Charism and Power: Liberation Theology and the Institutional Church*, trans. John W. Diercksmeier (New York: Crossroad, 1985), pp. 8, 125-26.

[2]"Leonardo Boff," *Wikipedia*, http://en.wikipedia.org/wiki/Leonardo_Boff.

[3]Ori Brafman and Rod A. Beckstrom, *The Starfish and the Spider: The Unstoppable Power of Leaderless Organizations* (New York: Penguin, 2006), p. 35.

[4]Ibid., p. 154.

[5]"Defining 'Quality of Living,'" Mercer, May 17, 2010, www.mercer.com/reference content.htm?idContent=1380465.

[6]Harvey Seifter and Peter Economy, *Leadership Ensemble: Lessons in Collaborative Management from the World-Famous Conductorless Orchestra* (New York: Times Books, 2001), p. xiv.

[7]Ibid., p. 3.

[8]Orpheus Chamber Orchestra home page, www.orpheusnyc.com.

[9]Seifter and Economy, *Leadership Ensemble*, p. 27.

[10]Ibid., p. 4.

[11]Ibid., pp. 16-17.

[12]Ibid., pp. 15-16.

[13]Philip Yancey, *Church: Why Bother?* (Grand Rapids: Zondervan, 1998), pp. 48-50.

[14]"Alcoholics Anonymous," *Wikipedia*, http://en.wikipedia.org/wiki/Alcoholics_ Anonymous#Organization_and_finances.

Chapter 10: Jesus the Archetypical Culture Creator

[1]John Howard Yoder, *The Royal Priesthood: Essays Ecumenical and Ecclesiological* (Scottdale, Penn.: Herald, 1998), p. 91.

[2]I heard this story from Dave Tomlison at "Emerging Church Conference (The Post-Evangelical)," San Diego, California, February 27, 2003.

[3]Allen O. Wesley Jr., *New Proclamation: Year A, 2008, Easter to Christ the King* (Minneapolis: Augsburg Fortress, 2007), p. 23.

[4]Megan McKenna, *Prophets: Words of Fire* (Maryknoll, N.Y.: Orbis, 2001), p. 15.

[5]Edwin K Broadhead, *Mark* (Sheffield, U.K.: Sheffield Academic Press, 2001), p. 91.

[6]Ched Myers, *Binding the Strong Man* (Maryknoll, N.Y.: Orbis, 1988), p. 290.

[7]Augustine *On Christian Teaching* 1.36, trans. R. P. H. Green (Oxford: Oxford University Press, 1997), p. 27.

[8]Alasdair MacIntyre, *After Virtue: A Study in Moral Theory*, 2nd ed. (Notre Dame, Ind.: University of Notre Dame Press, 1984).

[9]Alasdair MacIntyre, cited in Jonathan Wilson, *Why Church Matters: Worship, Ministry and Mission in Practice* (Grand ᴿapids: Brazos Press, 2006), p. 14.

Chapter 11: Apostles

[1]N. T. Wright, *For All God's Worth: True Worship and the Calling of the Church* (Grand Rapids: Eerdmans, 1997), pp. 23-24.

[2]Craig Van Gelder, *The Essence of the Church: A Community Created by the Spirit* (Grand Rapids: Baker, 2000), p. 37.

Chapter 12: Prophets

[1]Marcus Borg, in N. T. Wright and Marcus Borg, *The Meaning of Jesus: Two Visions* (New York: HarperCollins, 1999), p. 72.

[2]Gerhard Lohfink, *Jesus and Community: The Social Dimension of the Christian Faith* (Philadelphia: Fortress, 1984), p. 93.

[3]Shane Claiborne, *The Irresistible Revolution: Living as an Ordinary Radical* (Grand Rapids: Zondervan, 2006), p. 163.

[4]Bryant Myers, *Walking with the Poor: Principles and Practices of Transformational Development* (Maryknoll, N.Y.: Orbis, 1999), p. 115.

[5]Ibid., p. 155.

[6]Jayakumar Christian, *God of the Empty-Handed: Poverty, Power and the Kingdom of God* (Monrovia, Calif.: MARC Books, 1999), p. 1.

Chapter 13: Evangelists

[1]"Latest Population Estimates," *Los Angeles Almanac*, www.laalmanac.com.

[2]"I'm New," East Hollywood Neighborhood Council, www.easthollywood.net.

[3]This data is from a Percept Ministry Profile we had done for East Hollywood.

[4]"Medium Home Prices," *Los Angeles Almanac*, www.laalmanac.com/economy/ec37b .htm (accessed June 28, 2011).

[5]"About East Hollywood," East Hollywood Neighborhood Council, www.east hollywood.net/about.html.

[6]Ibid.

[7]Darrell L. Guder, *Be My Witnesses* (Grand Rapids: Eerdmans, 1985).

[8]Dietrich Bonhoeffer, *Letters and Papers from Prison* (New York: Touchstone, 1997), p. 282.

[9]James Choung, *True Story: A Christianity Worth Believing In* (Downers Grove, Ill.: InterVarsity Press, 2008), p. 195.

[10]Ibid., p. 205.

[11]Ibid., pp. 205-18.

[12]Andy Crouch, *Culture Making: Recovering Our Creative Calling* (Downers Grove, Ill.: InterVarsity Press, 2008), p. 37.

[13]Martin Luther King Jr., "What Is Your Life's Blueprint?" *Dr. Martin Luther King Jr.*, October 26, 1967, www.drmartinlutherkingjr.com/whatisyourlifes blueprint.htm.

Chapter 14: Pastors

[1]Rick McKinley, *Jesus in the Margins: Finding God in the Places We Ignore* (Sisters, Ore.: Multnomah, 2005), pp. 13-14.

[2]Ibid., p. 183.

[3]See A. J. Swoboda, *Messy: God Likes It That Way* (Grand Rapids: Kregel, 2012).

[4]David G. Benner, *Soulful Spirituality: Becoming Alive and Deeply Human* (Grand Rapids: Brazos, 2011), p. 21.

[5]Wil Hernandez, *Henri Nouwen: A Spirituality of Imperfection* (New York: Paulist, 2006), p. 27.

[6]Ibid., p. 32.

[7]Henri Nouwen, Donald P. McNeill and Douglas A. Morrison, *Compassion: A Reflection on the Christian Life* (New York: Doubleday, 1983), p. 61.

[8]To learn more about each of these various kinds of people, take some time to look at this series hosted by Wil Hernandez, based on his book *Henri Nouwen and Soul Care*: bit.ly/18Op6G.

[9]Henri Nouwen, *Reaching Out: The Three Movements of the Spiritual Life* (New York: Doubleday, 1975), p. 137.

[10]Hernandez, *Henri Nouwen*, p. 3.

[11]Ibid.

[12]Ibid., p. 2.

[13]Henri Nouwen, *With Burning Hearts: A Meditation on the Eucharistic Life* (Maryknoll, N.Y.: Orbis, 2003), p. 36.

[14]Lenore Terr, *Beyond Love and Work: Why Adults Need to Play* (New York: Touchstone, 1999).

[15]Stuart Brown and Christopher Vaughn, *Play: How It Shapes the Brain, Opens the Imagination and Invigorates the Soul* (New York: Penguin, 2009), pp. 17-18.

[16]Gregory L. Jones, *Embodying Forgiveness: A Theological Analysis* (Grand Rapids: Eerdmans, 1995), p. 164.

[17]For more on this story (or legend) see "The $50 Porsche," www.snopes.com/love/ revenge/porsche.asp.

Chapter 15: Teachers

[1]I discovered these important words in Harold Wells, *The Christic Center: Life-Giving and Liberating* (Maryknoll, N.Y.: Orbis, 2004).

[2]Stanley Hauerwas, *A Community of Character: Toward a Constructive Christian Social Ethic* (Notre Dame, Ind.: University of Notre Dame Press, 1981), p. 1.

[3]Navigators is an international, interdenominational ministry started in 1933 by Dawson Trotman.

[4]*Lectio divina* (literally "holy listening") is a particular way of reading and listening to Scripture individually or in a group. To learn more check out www.valyermo.com/ld-art.html.

[5]Bob Ekblad, *Reading the Bible with the Damned* (Louisville: Westminster John Knox Press, 2005), p. xiii.

[6]N. T. Wright, "How Can the Bible Be Authoritative?" Laing Lecture (1989) and Griffith Thomas Lecture (1989): www.ntwrightpage.com/Wright_Bible_Authoritative.htm.

[7]Stanley Grenz, *Theology for the Community of God* (Grand Rapids: Eerdmans, 1994), p. 403.

[8]George R. Hunsberger, "Proposals for a Missional Hermeneutic: Mapping the Conversation," Gospel and Our Culture Network, January 28, 2009, www.gocn.org/resources/articles/proposals-missional-hermeneutic-mapping-conversation.

[9]Christopher Wright, *The Mission of God: Unlocking the Bible's Grand Narrative* (Downers Grove, Ill.: InterVarsity Press, 2006), p. 49.

[10]Hunsberger, "Proposals for a Missional Hermeneutic."

[11]Darrell L. Guder, "Biblical Formation and Discipleship," in *Treasures in Clay Jars: Patterns in Missional Faithfulness*, ed. Lois Y. Barrett (Grand Rapids: Eerdmans, 2004), p. 70.

[12]Hunsberger, "Proposals for a Missional Hermeneutic."

[13]Ibid.

[14]Michael Barram, " 'Located' Questions for a Missional Hermeneutic," Gospel and Our Culture Network, November 1, 2006, www.gocn.org/resources/articles/located-questions-missional-hermeneutic.

[15]Ibid.

[16]Ibid.

[17]Hunsberger, "Proposals for a Missional Hermeneutic."

[18]This slogan was adopted by the Austin Independent Business Alliance to promote small businesses in Austin, Texas.

Chapter 16: The Cultural Web and the Neighborhood Church

[1]Will Mancini, *Church Unique: How Missional Leaders Cast Vision, Capture Culture, and Create Movement* (San Francisco: Jossey-Bass, 2008).

[2]Ibid., p. 6.

[3]See Richard Haynes, *The Moral Vision of the New Testament: Community, Cross, New Creation, A Contemporary Introduction to New Testament Ethics* (New York: Harper-Collins, 1996).

[4]The seven virtues and deadly sins are humility or pride, generosity or greed, moderation or gluttony, patience or anger, chastity or lust, love or envy, fortitude or slothfulness.

[5]Henri Nouwen, *Bread for the Journey: A Daybook of Wisdom and Faith* (New York: HarperOne, 1997), January 4 entry.

[6]Charles Van Engen, *God's Missionary People: Rethinking the Purpose of the Local Church* (Grand Rapids: Baker, 1991), p. 70.

[7]Stanley Hauerwas, *Against the Nations: War and Survival in a Liberal Society* (Notre Dame, Ind.: University of Notre Dame Press, 1992), p. 118.

[8]Stephen E. Fowl and L. Gregory Jones, *Reading in Communion: Scripture and Ethics in Christian Life* (Grand Rapids: Eerdmans, 1991), p. 78.

[9]Glen Stassen, D. M. Yeager and John Howard Yoder, *Authentic Transformation: A New Vision of Christ and Culture* (Nashville: Abingdon, 1996), pp. 164-67.

[10]If you want a dynamic and living understanding of vision, I recommend Will Mancini's *Church Unique*.

[11]Joseph Myers, *Organic Community: Creating a Place Where People Naturally Connect* (Grand Rapids: Baker, 2007), p. 77.

[12]Ibid., p. 75.

[13]Ibid., p. 78.

[14]Ibid., p. 80.

Chapter 17: Cultivating Missional Environments

[1]Brian McLaren, *Finding Our Way Again: The Return of the Ancient Practices* (Nashville: Thomas Nelson, 2008), pp. 11-12.

[2]Marjorie Thompson, *Soul Feast: An Invitation to the Christian Spiritual Life* (Louisville: Westminster John Knox Press, 1995), p. 147.

[3]Eugene Peterson, *Working the Angles: The Shape of Pastoral Integrity* (Grand Rapids: Eerdmans, 1987), pp. 72-73 (emphasis added).

[4]See JR Woodward, "Practicing Sabbath," JR Woodward (blog), August 12, 2006, http://jrwoodward.net/2006/08/practicing-sabbath.

[5]Henri Nouwen, *The Way of the Heart: Desert Spirituality and Contemporary Ministry* (New York: HarperCollins, 1981), p. 26.

[6]Eddie Gibbs, lecture at Fuller Theological Seminary, Pasadena, California, February 12, 2007.

[7]John Zizioulas, *Being as Communion: Studies in Personhood and the Church* (Crestwood, N.Y.: St. Vladimir's Seminary Press, 1985), p. 155.

[8]Frederick Buechner, *Telling Secrets* (New York: HarperCollins, 1991), pp. 2-3.

[9]L. Gregory Jones, *Embodying Forgiveness: A Theological Analysis* (Grand Rapids: Eerdmans, 1995), p. 226.

[10]Jean Vanier, *Community and Growth*, 2nd ed. (Mahwah, N.J.: Paulist Press, 1989), pp. 120-21.

[11]Learn more about the Unconferences at "LA: 2010—The Speakers," JR Woodward (blog), October 12, 2010, http://jrwoodward.net/2010/10/la-2010-the-speakers.

[12]You can learn more about the Ecclesia Network at www.ecclesianet.org.

[13]Annie Dillard, *The Writing Life* (New York: HarperCollins, 1990), p. 32.

Chapter 18: Cultivating an Equipping Ethos

[1]G. K. Chesterton, *Orthodoxy* (New York: Doubleday, 1959), p. 97.

[2]Alan Hirsch and Tim Catchim, *The Permanent Revolution: Apostolic Imagination and Practice for the 21st Century* (San Francisco: Jossey-Bass, 2012), pp. 21-23.

[3]Michael Frost and Alan Hirsch, *The Shaping of Things to Come* (Peabody, Mass.: Hendrickson, 2003), p. 170.

[4]Lesslie Newbigin, *The Gospel in a Pluralist Society* (Grand Rapids: Eerdmans, 1989), p. 235.

[5]Ray Bakke, *A Theology as Big as the City* (Downers Grove, Ill.: InterVarsity Press, 1997), pp. 80-81.

[6]When it comes to having a clear picture of the nature and ministry of each of the five equippers, tables A1.1-1.5 offer one-page descriptions of each equipper that you can refer to until your understanding of each equipper is crystal clear.

[7]If you are new to understanding the nature of missional communities, I encourage you to pick up Mike Breen and Alex Absalom's book *Launching Missional Communities*. Besides giving arguments for the missional power of mid-sized communities, they share nine steps to launching missional communities. I've reviewed this book at JR Woodward, "*Launching Missional Communities* by Mike Breen and Alex Absalom—A Review," JR Woodward (blog), April 6, 2001, http://jrwoodward.net/2011/04/launching-missional-communities-by-mike-breen-and-alex-absalom-a-review-part-2-of-2.

[8]Pavi Thomas, "The e4 Project," March 14, 2002, p. 8. Pavi shared his work on this with me.

[9]*Equipper guild* terminology was developed at Imago Dei in Richmond, Virginia.

Chapter 19: Polycentric Leadership at Work

[1]"Daily" is found in Lk 9:23-24.

[2]Roland Allen, *Missionary Methods: St. Paul's or Ours?* (Grand Rapids: Eerdmans, 1962), p. 148.

[3]Ibid., p. 149.

[4]Roland Allen, *The Spontaneous Expansion of the Church and the Causes Which Hinder It* (Eugene, Ore.: Wipf & Stock, 1997), p. 7.

[5]Roland Allen, *Mission Activities Considered in Relation to the Manifestation of the Spirit* (London: World Dominion Press, 1927), p. 30.

[6]Allen, *Missionary Methods*, p. 149.

[7]See an overview of Patrick Lencioni's *The Five Dysfunctions of a Team* at JR Woodward, "The Five Dysfunctions of a Team," JR Woodward (blog), May 21, 2008, http://jrwoodward.net/2008/05/the-five-dysfunctions-of-a-team.

[8]Richard J. Wood, "Christ Has Come to Teach His People Himself," in *Traditions in Leadership: How Faith Traditions Shape the Way We Lead*, ed. Richard Mouw and Eric O. Jacobsen (Pasadena, Calif.: De Pree Leadership Center, 2006), p. 214.

[9]Kurt Fredrickson, "Fire in the Church: Organic Structures for the Missional Congregation," course paper written for MP800 Tutorial in Postmodern Culture, Fuller Seminary, Pasadena, California, 2007, p. 10.

[10]Kester Brewin, *Signs of Emergence: A Vision for Church That Is Organic, Networked, Decentralized, Bottom-up, Communal, Flexible, Always Evolving* (Grand Rapids: Baker, 2007), p. 77.

[11]Ibid., p. 78.

[12]Steven Johnson, *Emergence: The Connected Lives of Ants, Brains, Cities, and Software* (New York: Scribner, 2001), p. 74.

[13]Allen, *Spontaneous Expansion of the Church*, p. 7.

[14]Patriarch Ignatius, cited in Michael Harper, "With or Without the Holy Spirit," Orthodox Research Institute, www.orthodoxresearchinstitute.org/articles/dogmatics/harper_holy_spirit.htm.

[15]This prayer is adapted from an unknown source.

Appendix 1: Equippers and Their Roles

[1]Markus Barth, *Ephesians: Translation and Commentary on Chapters 4–6* (New York: Doubleday, 1960), p. 437.

[2]Five of the questions in the equipper overview—mission, heart, focus, ministry and effect—were developed by Pavi Thomas and used by permission. The answers to the questions are mine. See Pavi Thomas, "The e4 Project," March 14, 2002, pp. 5-6.

Appendix 2: Equipper Candidate Reference Form

[1]Miroslav Volf, "Theology as a Way of Life," in *Practicing Theology: Beliefs and Practices in Christian Life*, ed. Miroslav Volf and Dorothy C. Bass (Grand Rapids: Eerdmans, 2002), p. 247.

[2]Graham Tomlin, *Spiritual Fitness: Christian Character in a Consumer Culture* (New York: Continuum International, 2006), p. 43.

[3]The S.H.A.P.E. acronym is from Rick Warren, *The Purpose-Driven Church* (Grand Rapids: Zondervan, 1995), pp. 371-73.

[4]Karl Barth, *Church Dogmatics* 4.3.2, *The Doctrine of Reconciliation* (Edinburgh: T & T Clark, 1962), p. 874.

[5]Lesslie Newbigin, in *Lesslie Newbigin: Missionary Theologian: A Reader*, ed. Paul Weston (Grand Rapids: Eerdmans, 2006), pp. 130-42.

Appendix 3: Equipper Candidate Interview

[1]Seven of these words come from David Fitch's blog: faith, discernment, presence, patience, resourcefulness, humility and love. The questions are mine. You can find great definitions for these words at David's blog: "The Seven Indispensable Virtues of a Missional Leader," *Reclaiming the Mission*, www.reclaimingthemission .com/the-seven-indispensable-virtues-of-a-missional-leader.